Berkeley's *Principles*: Expanded and Explained

Berkeley's Principles: Expanded and Explained includes the entire classical text of George Berkeley's *A Treatise Concerning the Principles of Human Knowledge* in bold font, a running commentary blended seamlessly into the text in regular font and analytic summaries of each section. The commentary is like a professor on hand to guide the reader through every line of the daunting prose and every move in the intricate argumentation. The unique design helps today's students learn how to read and engage with one of modern philosophy's most important and exciting classics.

Tyron Goldschmidt is Visiting Assistant Professor in the Department of Philosophy at Wake Forest University, USA. He is the editor of *The Puzzle of Existence: Why Is There Something Rather Than Nothing?* (2014) and the author of various articles in metaphysics, philosophy of religion and medieval philosophy.

Scott Stapleford is Associate Professor of Philosophy at St. Thomas University, Fredericton, New Brunswick, Canada. He is the author of *Kant's Transcendental Arguments: Disciplining Pure Reason* (2008) and various articles in epistemology and early modern philosophy.

D1522564

Forthcoming:

Hume's *Enquiry*: Expanded and Explained
Scott Stapleford and Tyron Goldschmidt

Locke's *Essay*: Expanded and Explained
Scott Stapleford and Tyron Goldschmidt

Berkeley's *Principles*
Expanded and Explained

Tyron Goldschmidt and
Scott Stapleford

Routledge
Taylor & Francis Group

NEW YORK AND LONDON

First published 2017
by Routledge
711 Third Avenue, New York, NY 10017

and by Routledge
2 Park Square, Milton Park, Abingdon, Oxon, OX14 4RN

Routledge is an imprint of the Taylor & Francis Group, an informa business

Library of Congress Cataloging-in-Publication Data
  Names: Berkeley, George, 1685-1753, author. | Goldschmidt, Tyron,
  1982- editor. | Stapleford, Scott, editor.
  Title: Berkeley's Principles : expanded and explained.
  Other titles: Treatise concerning the principles of human knowledge
  Description: New York : Routledge, 2016. | Includes index.
  Identifiers: LCCN 2016006636| ISBN 9781138934788 (hardback) |
  ISBN 9781138934795 (pbk.)
  Subjects: LCSH: Knowledge, Theory of.
  Classification: LCC B1331 .G65 2016 | DDC 121--dc23
  LC record available at http://lccn.loc.gov/2016006636

ISBN: 978-1-138-93478-8 (hbk)
ISBN: 978-1-138-93479-5 (pbk)
ISBN: 978-1-315-67773-6 (ebk)

Typeset in Goudy
by Sunrise Setting Ltd, Brixham, UK

To Stephanie and Michal—without which not

Contents

Introductory Note

What we're doing is criminal—so the purists will tell you. We're mucking about with the primary texts. We're gumming up the wording and ruining the grammar. It doesn't matter. That some scholars will bristle doesn't matter either. We are looking at Berkeley's *Principles* as philosophers, not poets. What matters are the arguments. And we are trying to make those arguments clear for students and specialists—and for ourselves. Berkeley's dated language is beautiful, but it should not be a hindrance to the analysis of his thoughts. This has been our guiding principle in producing this commentary.

The style of commentary is entirely new. We reproduce the entire text of George Berkeley's (1685–1753) *A Treatise Concerning the Principles of Human Knowledge* in bold font, weave explanations into the text in regular font and place synopses at the entrance. The ground rules for the in-text explanations— the 'expansions'—were simple: nothing could be dropped from the original or displaced, but anything could be added. If you were to remove our expansions and squeeze the bold text back together, you would have the original complete and unaltered.

The unique design makes for a more user-friendly commentary than any other. One thing we've noticed in teaching philosophy—Early Modern philosophy in particular—is that students often find it enormously difficult to connect an argument or interpretation directly with the primary text, even when they grasp the thought. We solve this problem by eliminating the gap between text and analysis altogether. The student is walked through the reasoning as she might be walked through a gallery by a curator: Her appreciation of the works—and her ability to criticize—will be honed through the process of instruction. She will learn to *read* a text that baffled her before.

The point of the expansions is to explicate and amplify Berkeley's reasoning, to bring out hidden assumptions and supply missing steps in the argumentation, to illustrate fine points with examples, to clarify the language, to put the arguments in historical context and connect them with the views of Berkeley's contemporaries, to import ideas from Berkeley's other works and blend them into the text unnoticed. All of this was to be done consistently with everything Berkeley says and so as to maximize the effectiveness of his arguments (even where we judge that they fail).

At the same time, we wanted the thing to be eminently readable. We didn't want a choppy analysis, but a smooth presentation that masks all the hard work. We wanted the reader to be able to *see* Berkeley's thought without seeing us. The requirement of historical accuracy thus ranked very high: We wanted the finished product to be such that, were Berkeley to read it, he would say, 'Yes, that's exactly what I meant'. This proved to be immensely challenging—far more difficult and time-consuming than standard commentary.

The aim was to create accurate interpretations of the arguments—*all* of the arguments. We couldn't just pick and choose passages to support one favourite interpretation over another, since we explain every single line of Berkeley. The fact that neither of us has any interpretative hobby horse we want to push, and the fact that we cling so closely to the text throughout, may increase the likelihood that our interpretations are accurate.

We anticipate that some scholars will scoff at our approach, since we don't bother to cross-reference our interpretations with the secondary literature or stop to refute competing interpretations. There is good reason for this: Scholarly controversy is frequently distracting, and the interpretations of specialists with their own agendas are often less faithful to the primary text than are the readings of commentators who take broader views and appraise particular passages in light of the whole. Though we don't cite the specialists, we hope to assist them: We offer fresh interpretations of *every* argument and of *every* move within every argument. There was no ignoring of difficult or inconvenient bits of text.

Lest we be accused of denigrating scholarship, it needs to be said: The importance of more traditional approaches to interpretation and analysis is very clear to us. We just don't think that a commentary is the right place for entering into polemics, or that polemics are all that count. That's not to say that we ignore the scholarly controversies altogether, however. We plant solutions to various interpretative and philosophical difficulties within the body of the text. That we are trying to answer objections from the literature—or dodge them, where appropriate—will be evident to specialists but invisible to students, whose focus should be on Berkeley. To take one obvious example, see our interpretation of Berkeley's 'master argument' in Section 24. Many others could be cited.

It should be clear that we are *not* translating Berkeley into modern English. Such an exercise might be useful in certain pedagogical settings, but translating is not our business. We are offering a full-scale, philosophical commentary designed to surpass any existing commentary in terms of comprehensiveness and closeness to the source. It could function as a handbook for undergraduates taking an historical survey, or as an accessible reference for professional philosophers—both equally well.

It wouldn't normally be necessary to make any disclaimers about one's own philosophical commitments in an historical commentary: It's just assumed that the commentator is not endorsing the views of the thinker in question.

Since we are writing in Berkeley's voice, however, it might be worth noting that we are *not* marketing his metaphysics as philosophically credible and we are *not* advocating his ethics, astronomy or theism. The *Principles* are teeming with insights, but they must be mined with care and evaluated along two distinct axes: plausibility in context and plausibility outright. We are arming the reader to make both sorts of evaluation for herself. Our own assessments are suppressed.

Some readers will notice that we use masculine pronouns in the expansions and that 'man' occurs more often than 'human' or 'person'. This was dictated by the special nature of the commentary: Having Berkeley write in gender-neutral language would have been awkward and anachronistic. (For the same reasons, we use examples like carriages and horses rather than rockets and robots.) To help offset this bias, we employ exclusively feminine pronouns in the bordering summaries. We hope that this is equitable.

Two editions of the *Principles* were published in Berkeley's lifetime: one in 1710, the other in 1734. We follow the 1734 edition, but wherever a useful idea from the first edition was omitted in the second, we try to incorporate it right into our expansions. We also restore the Preface, which Berkeley dropped, since his advice to the reader is good. We preserve the original punctuation as a rule, but occasionally modernize where the original would now be clumsy. Most modern editions strike a similar balance.

All interpretations are our own, but we have benefitted greatly by consulting several of the extant commentaries. We acknowledge our debt by citing them here:

References

Fogelin, R. J. *Berkeley and the Principles of Human Knowledge*. New York and London: Routledge (2001).

Kail, P. J. E. *Berkeley's A Treatise Concerning the Principles of Human Knowledge: An Introduction*. Cambridge: Cambridge University Press (2014).

Luce, A. A. *Berkeley's Immaterialism*. London: Thomas Nelson and Sons (1945).

Richmond, A. *Berkeley's Principles of Human Knowledge: A Reader's Guide*. London: Bloomsbury (2009).

The notes in Jonathan Dancy's edition of the *Principles* were also exceedingly helpful:

Dancy, J. *George Berkeley: A Treatise Concerning the Principles of Human Knowledge*. Oxford: Oxford University Press (1998).

We would like to thank Stephanie Allen for her scrupulous, eagle-eyed proofreading.

Analytic Table of Contents

A Treatise Concerning the Principles of Human Knowledge

Part I

Wherein the Chief and Main **Causes of** Philosophical **Errors and Difficulty in the *Sciences*,** together **with the Grounds** and Support these Errors provide for the false Doctrines **of *Scepticism, Atheism,* and *Irreligion,* are inquired into** and eliminated.

By George Berkeley, M.A. Fellow of Trinity College, Dublin

Second Edition of 1734

With Expansions and Explanations

By Tyron Goldschmidt and Scott Stapleford

Of the Principles of
Human Knowledge

The Preface

*Berkeley identifies the three main goals of the Principles: (1) to refute scepti-
cism (the view that knowledge of the external world is impossible); (2) to prove
the existence of God; and (3) to prove the immortality of the soul. He will in
fact spend much more time on (1) and (2) than on (3). Berkeley next alerts
us that some of what he says will strike us as surprising and strange if we don't
read his arguments carefully and in context. So he recommends that we read
the Principles patiently and through to the end before reaching any verdicts.*

The thoughts of several years are committed to print with the release of these
Principles. **What I here make public** in this manner **has, after a long,** careful
and scrupulous inquiry, seemed to me most **evidently true, and** exceedingly
useful (I would say, at the very least **not unuseful**), the sort of thing that ought
to be made **known, particularly to those** readers **who are** already **tainted
with** the doubts of **scepticism**—the extraordinary view that we have no firm
knowledge of the world around us. It may also prove valuable to those who
waver in their religious convictions, **or who want** to supplement their faith
with **a** strict **demonstration of the existence and immateriality of God, or of
the natural immortality of the soul. Whether it** really **be so or not,** whether
my thoughts relieve sceptics of their worries or deprive atheists of their hold
on the ignorant, **I am content if the reader should impartially examine** what
I say and decide for himself. I won't go to lengths in trying to persuade him,
**since I do not think my self any farther concerned for the success of what
I have written**—I do not insist any farther on the soundness of my arguments,
or the justness of my conclusions—**than as it is agreeable to *truth*:** My sole
concern is accuracy. **But to** promote **the end** of truth, and to ensure that **this**

project of mine **may not** give false impressions or **suffer** a hasty rejection, **I make it my request that the reader** show a little patience, **suspend his judgment,** and not jump to conclusions **till he has once, at least, read the whole** book **through with that degree of attention,** concentration **and** unbiased **thought which the subject matter shall seem to deserve.** For as there **are some** rather tricky **passages** to follow **that, taken by themselves** and not considered in light of the entire work, **are very liable** to misunderstanding, the reader must take care. (The novelty of my system made this inevitable, **nor could it be remedied** by adding further explanations.) Since I am thus susceptible **to gross misinterpretation, and** likely **to be charged with** endorsing the **most absurd consequences, which** my principles don't really have, I must implore the reader to bear with me. The ideas are difficult, to be sure. I hope, **nevertheless, that upon an entire perusal** of the book as a whole, the absurd consequences **will appear not to follow from them: so likewise,** there remains the possibility of misunderstanding even **though the whole book should be read over**—even if the reader pushes on, and doesn't stop every time he hits a tough passage. And **yet, if this** reading **be done transiently**—if the reader goes quickly, without thinking things through—**it is** still **very probable** that **my** meaning and the intended **sense** of what I say **may be** missed and that **mistaken** interpretations will prompt scholarly controversies; **but to a thinking** and careful **reader, I flatter my self** to believe that my words will be understood, and that **it will be throughout** the book **clear and obvious** what I am trying to convey. **As for** the apparent strangeness of my views, **the characters of novelty and singularity, which some of the following notions may seem to bear**—they are a bit surprising at first glance—**it is, I hope, needless** for me **to make any apology on that account.** Why should I apologize for stating the truth, even if the truth sounds strange? **He must surely be either** a **very weak** thinker, **or** else **very little acquainted with the sciences** (which introduce many strange notions), if he is amongst those **who shall reject a truth, that is** perfectly **capable of demonstration**—as my views are—**for no other reason but because it is newly known and contrary to the prejudices of mankind.** When Robert Hooke (1635–1703) announced his discovery of the cell, it was met by some with ridicule and disbelief (*Micrographia*, Observation 18). But there can be no doubt that these microstructures exist, however curious they may seem. **Thus much I thought fit to** state up front, to **premise** at the very outset, **in order to prevent, if possible, the** non-comprehending criticisms and the **hasty censures of a** very common **sort of men,** the ones **who are too apt to condemn an opinion before they rightly** and fully **comprehend it.** Perhaps this request for suspended judgement and fair consideration will help to minimize the irrelevant objections I am bound to receive.

Introduction

Philosophy is supposed to be the pursuit of wisdom and truth. So we'd expect phi-losophers to have more knowledge, certainty and intellectual contentment than ordinary people. But Berkeley has discovered quite the opposite: Most philoso-phers have become entangled in scepticism, whereas most ordinary people aren't troubled by scepticism at all. They're content to rely on common sense. Sceptical doubts only creep in when philosophers start asking questions. But philosophy doesn't go on to answer the questions it raises in any satisfying way. Instead, the more philosophy is pursued, the more deeply entwined in scepticism we become.

1. Philosophy being nothing else but the study of wisdom and truth, one would naturally expect philosophers to know things and to be wise. Given the aims of philosophy as a discipline, and the great pretension of philosophers, I think **it may with** good **reason be expected, that those who have spent** the **most time and pains in it,** studying and writing for long stretches over many years, **should enjoy a greater calm**ness **and serenity of mind** than non-philosophers, should have a better handle on most things and thus **a greater clearness and evidence of knowledge.** They should, in general, have much surer conviction, **and be** on the whole **less disturbed with doubts and difficulties than other men.** Yet the very opposite is the case; **so it is we see** those who do not study philosophy—**the illiterate bulk of mankind that** instead **walk the high-road of plain, common sense, and are governed by the dictates of** human **nature,** and the natural flow of events—**for the most part** resting **easy and** living their lives **undisturbed** by doubts. **To them nothing that's familiar** in their surround-ings **appears** very puzzling, **unaccountable or difficult to comprehend. They complain not of** unreliable eyes, untrustworthy ears or, in general, **any want of evidence in their senses,** which they trust implicitly. They believe what they see, **and are out of all danger of becoming sceptics,** who question those things which seem most clear and obvious to the common sort of man. **But no sooner do we depart from** our natural inclination to believe what we see—a healthy and artless custom of relying on **sense and instinct**—**to follow** instead **the light of a** supposedly **superior** philosophical **principle, to reason, meditate, and reflect on the nature of things, but** we run into grave difficulties. For once we so depart, straightaway **a thousand** puzzles and **scruples spring up in our minds, concerning those** very **things which before**hand struck us as perfectly ordinary and which **we seemed fully to comprehend.** When we start thinking philosophically, we suddenly become aware of many new grounds for doubt. **Prejudices and errors of sense** appear. Mistaken assumptions and various fallacies of argumentation **do from all parts discover** and reveal **themselves to our view; and** then, when we try to escape from our new position of uncertainty, **endeavouring to correct these** mistakes **by** using our powers of **reason**ing, **we are insensibly drawn into** so many more **uncouth** and twisted **paradoxes,** so many more intractable conceptual **difficulties, and** logical **inconsistences, which multiply and grow upon us** all the more **as we advance in** philosophical **speculation; till** we have considered these puzzles **at** great **length,** all to no avail. And then, **having wandered through many** abstract and **intricate mazes, we find our selves** unable to make any progress, and so we end up **just where we were** to begin with—relying once again on the senses, but without having satisfied our misgivings. So either we end up where we started, but now with doubts, **or** else, something **which is** far **worse, we sit down in a forlorn scepticism,** overwhelmed by these new doubts and not believing anything at all. This is where philosophy gets us, if we are to judge by its history.

Why does the pursuit of philosophy give rise to scepticism? One answer lays the blame on our intellectual capacities: Our minds were made for solving practical problems, for dealing with medium sized objects and performing run-of-the-mill tasks—for telling the difference between a rabbit and a fox, for figuring out the best way to plant a field, for conducting business or building a boat. They were not made for solving abstruse philosophical problems or contemplating the infinite. So it's no wonder that we fail. We should no more expect a human to solve a philosophical problem than we should expect a dog to play the piano. Dogs will do poorly at the piano because their paws are suited to walking and clawing—not to playing chords and doing scales. Similarly, we're going to do philosophy poorly, because our minds are attuned to the everyday, the finite and the concrete.

---

2. The cause of this sceptical impasse **is thought to be the obscurity of** the **things** we are trying to understand, since the objects of perception have hidden natures incapable of being seen; **or,** if not obscurity in the objects, then our ignorance is attributed to **the natural weakness and imperfection of our understandings,** which are very limited in ability and scope (see Sextus Empiricus, 2nd or 3rd century AD—*The Ten Modes,* for an early statement of the view). **It is said** that the root of our doubts and difficulties lies here—that **the** cognitive **faculties we have are** too **few** to tackle philosophical problems, **and** that **those** we do have are simply not up to the task. This explanation fits in with a general story about the origins of our cognitive powers: They have been **designed by nature** only **for the support and comfort of life, and** for conducting our daily business; they are just **not** calibrated **to penetrate into the inward essence and constitution of things** or to solve any philosophical puzzles arising from their contemplation. **Besides, the mind of man** is finite, and a **being** that is **finite** will inevitably go wrong when it considers that which exceeds it—especially, **when it treats of** such **things** as God and space, **which partake of infinity.** And so, **it is not** surprising at all or **to be wondered at** in the least, **if it** should turn out that our meagre minds **run into** all kinds of **absurdities and contradictions;** there are many open questions, many problems and uncertainties, which the mind of man will not get **out of** on its own. This is a predicament **which it is impossible** for us to escape; indeed, **it should never** have been supposed that an imperfect mind like ours could gain certain knowledge of the world, or **extricate itself** from metaphysical speculations about God and ultimate reality, **it being of the nature of infinite** things **not to be comprehended by that which is finite.**

There is a better explanation of our philosophical predicament: poor performance. It is not owing to any defects in our cognitive faculties that we are plagued by doubts and confusions. After all, God usually provides his creatures with what they need in order to acquire what they desire. And so it is likely that He has provided us with capacities suited to procuring the knowledge we seek. If we used our minds properly, we could overcome our doubts and attain to certain knowledge. Instead of blaming the Creator, we should blame ourselves: It is the misuse of the faculties that leads to uncertainty, error and ignorance.

---

3. But perhaps this is the wrong explanation of our perplexity: In chalking it up to the weakness of our minds and the mystery of infinity, **we may** have been **too** proud and **partial to our selves.** Anxious to point the finger at someone else, we were in fact reproaching God **in placing the fault originally in our** cognitive **faculties,** blaming the make-up of our minds for our inability to comprehend things, **and not** just admitting that our mistakes are grounded **rather in the wrong use we make of them.** A good instrument can be used poorly, after all. This opinion—that we fall into error only through the misuse of our faculties—has been defended ably by René Descartes (1596–1650—*Principles*, Part I, Sections 29–38; *Meditations* II). On this point, at least, we are agreed: If we used our minds properly, and reasoned well, then we would stand a better chance of gaining knowledge. **It is a hard thing,** I should think, **to suppose, that** good reasoning, consisting of **right deductions from true principles, should ever end in** paradox, or lead to absurd **consequences which cannot be maintained or made consistent.** In directing the blame at our creator rather than ourselves, we are being presumptuous and irreverent. **We should** rather **believe that God has dealt more bountifully** and kindly **with the sons of men, than to give them a strong desire for that knowledge** and understanding of things, **which He had** then unfairly **placed quite out of their reach** by giving them feeble **minds. This were not agreeable to the** usual generosity of God; it would be at odds with the **wonted, indulgent methods, of** Divine **Providence, which, whatever appetites** or desires **it may have implanted in the creatures, usually furnishes them with such means** and abilities **as, if rightly made use of, will not fail to satisfy them.** So if God has given us a desire for understanding, then he is also likely to have equipped us with minds capable of obtaining it, at least when employed skilfully. **Upon the whole, I am inclined to think that the far greater part, if not all, of those difficulties which have hitherto amused philosophers, and blocked up the way to knowledge, are entirely** avoidable. The real explanation of our perplexity and ignorance, in other words, is that they are **owing to** no one but **ourselves.** Rather than accusing God of stinginess, therefore, we should look to our own habits of reasoning and revise them in light of this rule: **That** a tool must be used correctly. Our complaints are wholly groundless, for **we have first raised a dust,** by using our minds improperly, **and then complain**ed, that **we cannot see.**

If our doubts and confusions do not stem from the nature of our minds or from the nature of the objects we investigate, they might instead be attributable to the improper use we make of our minds. There are at least two ways in which philosophers might be going wrong: They could be reasoning illogically from true starting points or reasoning logically from false starting points. Berkeley identifies false starting points as the problem: Philosophers begin their

investigations with mistaken assumptions. He hopes to eliminate doubt and confusion by discovering these mistaken assumptions and exposing them for what they are.

4. In what way, precisely, do we abuse our faculties? What tendency, or habit of mind, prevents us from acquiring knowledge? When you boil it right down, it comes to this: that we reason from false starting points. **My purpose therefore is to try, if I can, to discover what those** erroneous **principles are, which have introduced all that doubtfulness and uncertainty** into the minds of learned men, to identify the mistaken assumptions, which have injected all **those absurdities and contradictions into the several** schools and minor **sects of philosophy.** As I indicated in Section 2, the difficulties encountered by philosophers cause some to doubt the power of the human mind, at least **insomuch** as it deals with speculative questions concerning the nature of things. Thus we see **that the wisest of men have thought our ignorance incurable.** They regard bewilderment as a permanent state, **conceiving it to arise from the natural dullness and** inherent **limitations of our** minds—a symptom of weakness in the **faculties** or a flaw in their design (see Pierre Bayle, 1647–1706—*Historical and Critical Dictionary*, for a survey of sceptical arguments along these lines). My own hypothesis, however—proposed in Section 3—is that our hesitation and uncertainty in matters of speculation are owing to misuse and mismanagement of the faculties, rather than impotence. **And surely it is a work well** worth the effort anyhow, and **deserving of our pains, to make a strict** and careful **inquiry concerning the first principles of *human knowledge*—to** divide the true claims, on which it rests, from the false ones, which breed confusion. We want **to sift** through our beliefs, as a miner sifts through sand in order to separate the gold from the dirt. We must turn them over, as it were, **and examine them on all sides:** This is **especially** important in philosophy, **since there may be some grounds to suspect that** freeing philosophers of their old opinions would do some good: Solving **those** problems that now occupy their time would **let** philosophers turn their minds at last to concrete problems **and** perhaps make a real contribution to the world. That we can in fact end the major philosophical **difficulties** seems likely, for as I argued in the last section, the doubts and confusions, **which stay and embarrass the mind in its** faltering **search after truth, do not spring from any darkness and intricacy in the objects of** investigation, **or** arise from any **natural defect in the** mind or its powers of **understanding.** The problems, I repeat, stem not **so much** from our having been given shoddy intellectual equipment, **as from** our starting out with **false** assumptions. We accept **principles** as true **which have been** wrongly promoted and **insisted on** by philosophers, **and** which **might have been avoided**

altogether with a little more thought. If faulty assumptions are the problem, we should eliminate them. Real philosophical progress depends on it.

There is promise of succeeding where others have failed. Berkeley denies any arrogance or conceit on his part in trying to achieve what greater minds could not. He is not smarter than past philosophers. He modestly claims to be less smart. But it is precisely the weakness of his intellect that gives him an advantage. For he will have to think harder than great philosophers did about their basic assumptions and he will have to work patiently through ideas that they thought out quickly. A slower and more careful consideration of the issues might turn up errors that sharper minds overlooked.

5. How difficult and discouraging soever this attempt to identify the true principles of human knowledge **may seem,** and however challenging the task of uprooting those that are false, the effort must still be made. But perhaps you will accuse me of immodesty in undertaking to do what my predecessors could not. Indeed, **when I consider how many great and extraordinary men** have tried this already and failed, I should probably expect the same from myself: Their mental capacities certainly exceeded mine. When I think about those towering intellects who **have gone before me in the same designs**—all of them aiming to identify the most basic truths of nature—I feel intimidated, and deterred from my task. And **yet I am not without some hopes** that I may succeed where they have not. This hope, and my optimism, are founded **upon the consideration that the largest,** most sweeping **views are not always the clearest, and that he who is** as **short-sighted** as I am **will be obliged** by his visual impairment **to draw the object** he is looking at **nearer** to his eyes and consider it at short range**, and** that he **may, perhaps, by a close and narrow survey** of the thing—a careful and focused examination of all its properties— find that he is able to **discern that which had escaped far better eyes** and gone hitherto unnoticed. Weakness of mind can sometimes be an advantage, if it forces us to pay closer attention to what we are considering.

A commitment to abstract ideas is very widespread in philosophy and science, especially in logic and metaphysics. And this commitment is the chief source of trouble, for it breeds confusion, error and obscurity. What abstract ideas are,

how they cause difficulties and how science can get on without them are major themes of the book. For now, Berkeley just anticipates his conclusion that the theory of abstraction is false and obstructive.

6. In order to prepare the mind of the reader for the difficult arguments to come, I want to clear up one very common misunderstanding at the outset. The misunderstanding is based on a linguistic confusion to which philosophers are particularly susceptible. It leads them to posit the existence of something for which they have no justification whatever: abstract ideas. Anyone who has already fallen prey to this confusion and posited abstract ideas will have an **easier** time **conceiving** and comprehending **what follows,** if I settle the whole issue upfront and show that there are no such things. And given the links that obtain between words, ideas and thought, I feel **it is proper** anyway **to first premise somewhat, by way of introduction,** my views **concerning the nature and abuse of** ordinary **language** in general, and how misconceptions about language contribute to the puzzlement of philosophers. **But the unravelling** and development of my thoughts on **this matter** of language **leads me in some measure to anticipate my** plan here and put the overall **design** of my arguments against abstract ideas up for consideration already. I begin, therefore, **by taking notice of** the abstractionist view, and then laying out **what** its proponents have said in its favour, and what I have to say in response. This is absolutely crucial to my project, for the commitment to abstract ideas **seems to** me to **have had a chief part in rendering** philosophical **speculations** so bewildering and complicated, so **intricate and perplexed, and to have occasioned innumerable errors and** given rise to endless **difficulties in** philosophy and science—indeed, in **almost all parts of knowledge. And** this pernicious view—**that is** to say, **the opinion that the mind has a power of framing** *abstract ideas* or notions of things—is very widespread. **He who is not a perfect stranger to the writings and disputes of philosophers must** have noticed this himself and so he **needs to acknowledge that no small part of them are spent** arguing **about abstract ideas. These** fictitious entities are assumed in almost all of the sciences, but they **are in a more especial manner thought to be the object of those sciences which go by the name of 'logic' and 'metaphysics', and** to be their primary concern. Given the venerable history of logic and metaphysics, and the esteem in which they are commonly held, it follows that abstract ideas are the presumed subject matter **of all that which passes under the notion of** 'higher knowledge'. The study of abstract ideas will on this view be **the most** elevated and valuable—the most **abstracted and sublime**—of all branches of **learning.** We will make no advances in the 'noble sciences' of logic and metaphysics, therefore, until this false supposition has been invalidated. The impediment to progress posed by abstract ideas is present **in all** areas of philosophy **which** presuppose them—and this covers pretty much the whole field. For **one shall scarcely** ever **find any** philosophical **question handled in such a manner as does not** explicitly deal with abstract ideas, or at least implicitly **suppose their existence in the mind.** Indeed, philosophical discourses **and** debates presuppose not only that the mind contains abstract ideas, but **that it is well acquainted** and familiar **with them.** I shall make it my task in this introduction, therefore, to topple the theory of abstraction.

A first class of abstract ideas is considered: abstract ideas of single sensible qualities. No one believes that the qualities of things can exist on their own apart from other qualities and the things of which they are qualities: The colour pink cannot be detached from the pink thing, for instance, or from whatever shape that pink thing happens to have. But philosophers suppose that we can form ideas of such individual sensible qualities—a particular shade of colour, say, or a particular instance of motion—and consider them apart from the ideas of other qualities and things with which they are associated.

---

7. Let's start with some terminology: Those famous logicians, Antoine Arnauld (1612–1694) and Pierre Nicole (1625–1695) differentiate between a *thing*—'whatever is conceived as subsisting by itself and as the subject of everything conceived about it'—and a *quality* or *mode*—'that which, conceived as in the thing and not able to subsist without it, determines it to be in a certain way' (*Logic*, Part I, Chapter 2). Adopting these terms, we may draw a verbal distinction between a *thing*—say, a flower—and its *modes*—its particular shape, colour and state of motion or rest. No one would take issue with this division, since it is limited to *words*. But, just as surely, no one would suppose that the pink colour of a carnation, for instance, could take leave of the flower and ramble about on its own: **It is agreed on all hands,** I should say, **that the qualities or modes of things do never really exist each of them apart by it self** in isolation **and** actually **separated from all the others, but are mixed, as it were,** combined **and blended together,** so to speak, so that **several of** them appear joined **in the same object.** This much is uncontroversial. **But** beyond this **we are told** by Arnauld and Nicole (*Logic*, Part I, Chapter 5), and by many other philosophers besides, that **the mind**—which, they say, has the power of **being able to consider each quality singly** on its own, **or abstracted from those other qualities with which it is united** in the object imagined, or perceived—**does by that means,** through this process of abstraction, form or **frame to it self** an idea of a single quality or sensible feature. Philosophers call the thoughts or perceptions produced in this way **'abstract ideas',** since the mind has supposedly detached just one idea and separated or 'abstracted' it from all of the other ideas that appeared along with it when they were combined in the complex object of sensation or imagination. **For example,** when you watch a bird flying overhead, **there is perceived by sight an object** that is **extended, coloured, and moved; this mixed or compound idea** of a bird flying overhead, **the mind** supposedly breaks apart, **resolving** it **into its simple, constituent parts** (its distinctive shape, its reddish colour, its curved trajectory and so on). Performing a sort of *mental surgery*, if you will, the mind slices the poor creature up, splitting it into the various simple ideas that compose it, **and viewing each** idea **by it self, exclusive of** surrounding ideas and detached from **the rest, does** somehow **frame the abstract ideas of** a particular spatial **extension,** a particular patch of **colour, and** a particular **motion. Not that it is possible,** according to these philosophers, **for** a particular patch of **colour or** a particular **motion to exist without extension.** Not even a philosopher would go so far as to assert that a patch of red or an arching motion could exist on its own in nature without having any shape or occupying any space: **but** they do assert something equally surprising. They **only** want to deny **that** colour can *exist* apart from extension, but they are happy to assert that **the mind can frame to it self**—can form **by** this process of *abstraction*—**the idea of** a particular patch of **colour exclusive of extension.** They imagine themselves capable of conceiving a patch of red with no shape, **and** the idea **of an** arching **motion exclusive,** or free, **of both colour and extension.** This is the first sort of abstraction that philosophers recognize, and the first class of abstract ideas.

A second class of abstract ideas is identified: general abstract ideas of simple qualities. Philosophers have supposed the mind to be capable of isolating what is common to many instances of a sensible quality and creating in the process an idea of that quality in general. For example, they imagine that we can frame an abstract idea of colour in general by discovering what is common to all the ideas of specific colours—particular patches of red, yellow, blue, etc.—that we have seen.

---

8. Compounding their mistake, philosophers also insist on a second sort of abstraction and a second class of abstract ideas. **Again,** we are told that **the mind** can frame abstract ideas of individual colour patches, individual shapes and individual motions. These are abstract ideas of the first kind, formed through the process of abstraction just depicted. But there is more: The mind may notice that all particular colours have something in common, that all

particular shapes have something in common, and that all particular motions do too. Together they form a second class of abstract ideas created by a second kind of abstraction. These are alleged to be ideas of more general signification. Consider shapes and sizes: The mind first perceives particular extensions— individual shapes, each of a definite size. Then, **having observed** these, it discovers **that in the particular extensions perceived by our senses there is something common and alike in all** of them. They are all *extensions*, obviously enough, **and** are alike in at least that respect. The mind also discovers **some other things** which are **peculiar** to each bit of extension, and which makes each one of them different from all the rest. They differ insofar **as** one piece has **this** particular shape **or that** particular size, whereas another is bigger or smaller, rounder or longer, and that sort of thing. A well-fed housecat has a very boxy **figure or** shape, and a large **magnitude,** for example, while a hungry alley cat has an angular figure and a small magnitude. These are the sorts of discrepancies **which distinguish them one from another.** The mind discerns the common features, while duly noting the differences. That done, **it** may complete the process of abstraction. It **considers apart or singles out by it self that which is common** to all the shapes and sizes it perceives, **making thereof a most abstract idea of extension, which is** supposedly distinct from the idea of any particular extension. The product of this process is the idea **neither** of a **line,** nor a **surface, nor** a **solid, nor has** it **any figure or magnitude,** neither great nor small, **but is** rather **an idea entirely** divorced and **prescinded from all these** specific sizes and shapes. **So likewise** with colour: According to the same process, **the mind, by leaving out of the particular colours perceived by sense, that** element **which distinguishes them one from another**—the red of the bird, the blue of the sky, the white of a cloud—**and retaining** in memory **that** feature **only which is common to all** of them **makes an idea of colour in the abstract which is neither red, nor blue, nor white, nor any other deter-minate colour. And in like manner, by considering motion abstractedly**— distinct **not only from the body** that is **moved, but likewise from the figure it describes, and all the particular directions and velocities** in which it is, or ever could be moved—**the abstract idea of motion is framed;** the mind distils this general idea of motion out of every moving thing perceived. It is meant to be an idea over and above the individual motions which suggested it, but **which equally** represents and **corresponds to all particular motions whatso-ever that may be** imagined or **perceived by** the **senses:** Or so the story goes.

A third class of abstract ideas is identified: general abstract ideas of objects or compounds. These are combinations of ideas thought of as belonging to every individual of a certain type. The mind notices that individual people, for instance, all have certain properties in common: Every person has some *colour, some shape, some history and so on. Leaving out the individuating properties—the particular colour, shape, circumstances of time and place, etc., that make an individual the person she is—and focusing on those qualities that all humans share—the having of some colour, some shape, some history—the mind forms the abstract idea 'human'. This is not the idea of any particular human, but of 'human nature' in general. The process can be repeated at higher levels: The mind notices that humans, monkeys, birds and fish, etc., all have certain properties in common—body, life, sense perception, spontaneous motion, etc. By the same act of leaving out and retaining, the mind forms the general abstract idea 'animal'.*

9. And these same philosophers tell us that just **as the mind** supposedly **frames to it self** both (1) specific and (2) general **abstract ideas of qualities or modes,** it can also frame general abstract ideas of another sort. More precisely, as the mind can frame (1) abstract ideas of individual sensible features—single sensible qualities such as a patch of red, a darting motion or an angular figure—and (2) abstract ideas of qualities in general—colour, motion, shape—**so does it** manage to frame (3) abstract general ideas of bodies. What I mean is that, **by the same precision**—the same act of cutting away **or mental separation**—the mind can, with some effort, **attain** (3) **abstract ideas of the more compounded beings** we see around us (such as horses, carriages and men). These are ideas **which,** having been mentally detached from complex beings, **include** within themselves **several coexistent** sensible **qualities** combined into one. They are thus ideas of *bodies* or *objects* rather than of *qualities*. **For example, the mind having observed that** the individual men, **Peter, James, and John, resemble each other, in certain common agreements** or points **of** similarity with respect to **shape and other qualities, leaves out of the complex or compounded idea it has of Peter, James, and any other particular man, that** set of features **which is peculiar** or unique **to each** individual (features such as Peter's broad shoulders or James' blue eyes), **retaining** in the abstract idea allegedly formed by this means **only what is** shared by or **common to all** of the particular men from which the idea has been taken; **and so on this theory the mind makes an abstract idea wherein all the particulars**—all the individual existing things—**equally partake.** To put it another way, the mind makes an abstract idea of 'man' that applies equally to all men. In this process the mind is **abstracting entirely from and cutting off all those circumstances and differences,** all those distinctive features, **which might determine** or tie **it**—the abstract idea—**to any particular** man or individual **existence. And after this manner** just described, **it is said** that **we come by the abstract idea of 'man' or, if you please,** to make it more general, the idea of **humanity or human nature; wherein it is true,** that **there is included** more than simply 'rational animal' or some other such pithy definition. The idea must also contain some reference to **colour, because there is no man but has some colour**—clearly every human partakes of colour in *some* fashion, since people are not invisible—**but then it, the idea, can be neither white, nor black, nor any particular colour; because there is no one particular colour wherein all men partake**, no single colour that all men share. And we have just said that the abstract idea of 'man' applies equally to all men, regardless of colour. **So likewise there is included** in the abstract idea of 'man' some sort of **stature, but then it is neither tall stature nor low stature, nor yet middle stature,** since the idea must apply to all men; **but** this means that the stature contained in the idea will have to be **something abstracted** or distinct **from all these** particular statures. **And so** the same reasoning applies to all **of the rest** of the sensible features contained in the abstract idea of 'man'. **Moreover, there being a great variety of other** living **creatures that partake in some parts, but not all, of the complex idea of 'man',** creatures sharing some features, though not others—consider a monkey—**the mind** must disregard those features possessed by men but not possessed by other animals, **leaving out,** in other words, **those parts which are peculiar to men, and retaining those** features **only which are common to all the living creatures.** And so, it **frames** in this way a new idea, **the idea of 'animal', which abstracts** or takes away several features **not only from all particular men, but also** from **all birds, beasts, fishes, and insects,** since the abstract idea of 'animal' contains only what is common and applies to all of them. **The constituent parts of the abstract idea of animal are body, life, sense, and** self-propulsion or **spontaneous motion,** since these are the essential features of animals. **By 'body'**—as it occurs in the abstract idea of 'animal'—**is meant body without any particular shape or figure, there being no one shape or figure common to all animals,** since some animals are round, some thin, some big and some small. And it is an idea **without** any reference to **covering, either of hair or feathers, or scales, etc., nor yet naked** like the elephant, which has no covering: **hair, feathers, scales, and nakedness being the distinguishing properties of particular animals, and for that reason left out of the *abstract idea.*** Such features must be left out, since the abstract idea 'animal' should pertain to all animals, and no animal has hair, feathers, scales and nakedness simultaneously. **Upon the same account** and for the very same reasons, **the spontaneous motion** contained in the idea of 'animal' **must be neither walking, nor flying, nor creeping,** yet comprehend them all the same; **it is nevertheless a motion, but what that motion is, it is not easy to conceive.** In fact, I find that I cannot conceive of motion in an animal that is not some particular motion such as walking, flying or creeping. What motion is there beyond *motions*?

Berkeley finds himself incapable of forming abstract ideas in any of the above-mentioned ways. If we reflect honestly on our own ideas, we'll see that we can't either. There are related imaginative tasks that clearly can be performed. Berkeley can imagine the detachable features or parts of things as so detached. He can imagine the head of a dandelion detached from its stem, for instance. This kind of 'abstraction' is quite innocent. But he cannot single out in the imagination features or parts that are actually inseparable. He cannot consider yellow, say, apart from shape. Most people will find themselves in the same position, unable to abstract in the philosophical sense. Creating abstract ideas is said to cost more effort than most people make.

10. Whether my readers or any **other** philosophers **have this wonderful**—I would say 'magical'—**faculty of *abstracting their ideas*, they best can tell.** Honest reflection in your own case will inform you; I highly doubt that you do. As **for my self, I find indeed** that **I have** no such power, but only **a faculty of imagining, or representing to myself the ideas of those particular things I have perceived**—such as hands, horses and men—**and** making representations of other things by **variously compounding and dividing them. I can** in this way rearrange my ideas so as to **imagine a man with two heads or the upper parts of a man joined to the body of a horse**, producing by this means the idea of a centaur. **I can consider the hand, the eye**, or **the nose, each** individually **by it self** and **abstracted, or separated, from the rest of the body. But then** I cannot consider anything abstracted in the more philosophical sense, which involves conceiving it apart from any particular ideas; **whatever hand or eye I imagine, it must have some particular shape and** some definite **colour. Likewise the idea of man that I frame to my self** cannot be general, as the philosophers suppose is possible. It **must be either of a white, or a black, or a tawny, a straight, or a crooked, a tall, or a low, or a middle-sized man. I cannot by any** mental contortion or **effort of thought conceive the abstract idea** of a hand, an eye, a man—anything at all—apart from particular instances possessing specific sensible qualities. The process of abstraction as **above described** exceeds my cognitive abilities. **And**, as I observed in the last section, **it is equally impossible for me to form the abstract idea of motion distinct from the** idea of an individual **body moving, and which is neither swift nor slow, curvilinear** (having a curved trajectory) **nor rectilinear** (having a straight trajectory)**; and the like may** similarly **be said of all other abstract general ideas whatsoever. To be plain, I'm** quite ready to **own** that I **my self am able to abstract in one sense, as** happens **when I consider some particular parts or** detachable **qualities** of a thing alone and **separated from** its **other** parts and qualities. My imagination allows me to remove the head of a dandelion from its stem, for instance, or the wings of a bird from its body. I can consider the nose or beard of a man apart from his face, the top of a pastry apart from the bottom. Though the nose and beard are actually connected **with** other features of the face, I can picture them parting ways: the nose could be detached; the beard could be slapped on a cow.

This is an easy matter of mentally separating adjacent parts: Parts appearing *alongside each other* in a perception can be conceived apart as well. For qualities it's much the same: That peculiar shade of yellow seen in the dandelion's head can be imagined without the flower, detached from the green of its stem. I can divorce it from its shape as well. But I cannot for anything conceive yellow without extension. Qualities accidently conjoined in an object may well be conceived apart. In this rather uninteresting sense of 'abstract', I can certainly abstract parts and qualities. But they are always parts or qualities **which, though they are** in fact **united** with other parts and qualities **in some object, yet it is** in principle **possible** that **they may** each **really exist without them. But I deny that I can** achieve any other sort of **abstract**ion. I cannot consider **one** quality separate **from another,** if they are fused in the object, **or** perfectly mixed. I cannot **conceive separately, those** parts or **qualities which it is impossible should exist so separated. N**or can I form the general notion of 'man' by ignoring all the differences between Peter, James and John and extracting a common essence, for a common essence is not the sort of thing **that** could exist on its own. Indeed, **I cannot frame any general notion**s at all **by abstracting** common features **from particulars, in the manner aforesaid** in Section 9. **Which two last** senses of 'abstraction'—separating qualities that are fused, or drawing general notions from particulars—**are the proper** meanings and the standard **acceptations of** the word **'abstraction'.** These are the senses philosophers have in mind when they speak of 'abstraction', and no others. Tacking the upper parts of a man onto the body of a horse, by contrast, or imagining that my cow is yellow—such operations are called 'abstraction' only by courtesy. **And there are grounds to think** that **most men will acknowledge themselves to be in my case** as far as what they can and cannot imagine goes. **The generality of men**—the unschooled multitudes **which are simple and illiterate—never pretend to** have *abstract notions* or to be capable of 'abstracting' in either of the philosophical senses. Such fictions have no relevance to the rough and tumble of their lives. **It is said** of such abstractions that **they are difficult** to perform **and not to be attained without** some effort, **pains and study. We** ascend to abstract ideas degree by degree, moving stepwise from the idea of a particular thing to the idea of a general thing (Arnauld and Nicole, *Logic*, Part I, Chapter 5). It **may therefore reasonably** be concluded **that, if such** exertions are required for the framing of abstract ideas, they are not to be had by everyone. If **there** are any such things, I'd say they must **be rare,** and the common man will find **they are** out of his reach—lofty notions being generally **confined only to the** minds of **learned** philosophers.

Abstractionists see a close link between the capacity for framing abstract ideas and the capacity for language: The existence of language in humans implies the presence of abstract ideas; the lack of language in animals suggests their absence. Locke makes the ability to form abstract ideas the distinguishing mark of human—as opposed to animal—cognition. Berkeley won't count as human on this criterion, since he can't form abstract ideas. That words become general, according to Locke, by picking out general ideas is further confirmation that his argument for abstract ideas is just an inference from the existence of language in humans to the existence of abstract ideas as a necessary condition of making universal claims. In contrast, Berkeley holds that universal claims can be made without reference to general ideas: The generality of a term consists solely in the fact that it can pick out any one of a number of ideas in a range.

11. I will now **proceed** to evaluate the evidence that can be offered for this doubtful supposition. I want **to examine** without prejudice **what**ever arguments **can be alleged** and put forward **in defence of the doctrine of abstraction, and** I will **try** to see **if I can discover what it is that** leads so many philosophers to posit abstract ideas, what high-minded confusion **inclines the men of speculation to embrace an opinion** such as this, when the opinion is **so** much at odds with popular convictions and so **remote from common sense as that** one **seems to be.** I suspect that some groundless assumption lies behind the error. What that assumption is may perhaps be discerned in the arguments of a prominent abstractionist. Let's have a look and see. **There has been a** lot of discussion **lately** about a **deservedly esteemed** and famous **philosopher, who, no doubt, has** increased the public profile of this false doctrine, **given it very much countenance,** in other words, **by seeming to think** that **the** capacity for **having abstract general ideas is what** distinguishes us, cognitively speaking, from animals. This capacity is what **puts the widest difference in point of understanding betwixt man and beast,** as far as this famous philosopher is concerned. My reader will by now have guessed that I am speaking of John Locke (1632–1704). In his own words:

> **The having of** abstract **general ideas, (***says he***) is that which puts a perfect distinction betwixt** and marks the biggest difference between human beings **and brute** animals, **and is** a quality—indeed, **an excellency—which the** cognitive **faculties of brute** animals are not capable of reaching and **do by no means attain unto. For it is evident that we observe** in animals not even rudimentary efforts at abstraction, **no footsteps** tending **in that** direction, nothing in **them** or their behaviour suggestive **of their making use of general signs for universal ideas; from which we have reason to** imagine—indeed, more than sufficient grounds to infer—**that they have not the faculty of** *abstracting* **or making general ideas at all, since they**

have and make **no use of words or any other general signs** (*Essay*, Book
II, Chapter 11, Section 10).

And a little after this, he says:

> **Therefore, I think, we may suppose that it is in this that** all **the
> species of brutes are discriminated** and distinguished **from men, and
> 'tis that proper** and significant **difference wherein they are wholly
> separated, and which at last widens to so wide a distance** between
> them. **For if they** (the animals) **have any ideas at all, and are not bare
> machines (as some,** like Descartes, **would have them** be—*Discourse on
> Method*, Part 5), then **we cannot deny them to have some** faculty of
> **reason**ing, however weak it may be. **It seems as evident to me that they
> do**—or, at least, that **some of them do**—**in certain instances reason as**
> it is evident **that they have sense** and are capable of sensations, **but it
> is only in particular ideas** that they reason in their rudimentary way,
> **just as they receive them from their senses. They are**—even **the best**
> and smartest **of them, such as monkeys and dolphins**—**tied up within
> those narrow bounds** and restricted to thinking in terms of particu-
> lar ideas only, **and have not (as I think) the faculty to enlarge** their
> inventory of ideas as we do, to augment **them by** forming **any kind of**
> abstract ideas through any act of ***abstraction*** (*Essay*, Book II, Chapter
> 11, Sections 10 and 11).

I readily agree with this learned author on one point, in any case. I grant
that animals are not able to form abstract ideas, since no one can suppose
that **the** cognitive **faculties of** these **brutes** allow them to separate things
that cannot exist apart, and this is precisely what the process of abstraction
requires. So we are entirely agreed that animals **can by no means attain to**
the sort of ***abstraction*** that the author describes. **But then** that is the extent
of our agreement. For **if this** inability to form abstract ideas **be made the
distinguishing property of that sort of animals,** if the lack of abstract ideas
is the very thing that makes something an animal rather than a man, then
I fear a great many of those creatures **that** normally **pass for men** won't
even qualify as human and **must** therefore **be** grouped with the animals and
reckoned into their number. The reason that is given **here** for thinking
that animals are confined to particulars is that they neither speak nor write.
The very factor **assigned** by the author to explain **why we have no grounds
to think** that **brute** animals **have abstract general ideas, is that we observe
in them** no language, we see **no use of words** amongst them **or** indeed of
any other general signs; which clearly indicates that the author takes the
presence of language to imply the presence of abstract ideas. His whole case
is built upon this supposition. As the quoted material makes plain, Locke's
key assumption is this: that **to** communicate **with** signs is to rise above the
level of particulars, **that the making use of words, implies the having** of

abstract **general ideas. From which it follows,** according to him, **that men who use language are able to abstract or generalize their ideas. That this is** in fact what he means, that this is precisely **the sense and arguing of the author** should be clear anyway, but it **will further appear** even more obvious **by his answering the question** that he raises **in another place. He puts** it to us like this. **'Since all things that exist are only particulars, how come we by general terms?'** *His answer* betrays a commitment to the supposition just mentioned and *is* confirmed, unequivocally, in the following passage: **'Words become general by being made the signs of general ideas'** (*Essay*, Book III, Chapter 3, Section 6). **But it seems** to me, by contrast, **that a word becomes general by being made** to stand for something else: It acquires broad scope or universality through serving as **the sign, not of an abstract general idea but of several particular ideas, any one of which it** (the word) **indifferently suggests to the mind.** The word may suggest any one of those particular ideas as easily as any other—that's what I meant by 'indifferently'. **For example, when it is said 'the change of motion is proportional to the impressed force', or that 'whatever has extension is divisible', these propositions are to be understood** as applying to, or being said **of, motion and extension in general, and nevertheless it will not follow that they suggest to my thoughts an idea of motion without a body moved, or** without **any determinate direction and velocity, or that I must conceive an abstract general idea of extension, which is neither** the idea of a **line,** nor of a **surface, nor** of a **solid, neither great nor small, black, white, nor red, nor of any other determinate colour. It** merely follows that the rule holds for all motions. This **is the only** thing **implied** by the proposition: **that whatever motion I consider, whether it be swift or slow, perpendicular, horizontal or oblique, or in whatever object** the motion occurs, **the axiom concerning it**—that 'the change of motion is proportional to the impressed force'—**holds equally true. As does the other**—that 'whatever has extension is divisible'—**of every particular extension** we may perceive, or imagine. And as far as the principle goes, **it matters not whether** we are talking about a **line,** a **surface or a solid, whether** we are thinking **of this or of that magnitude or figure.** They are one and all divisible. The proposition can be asserted without presupposing any generality in things or ideas.

It is the existence of intrinsically general abstract ideas that Berkeley wants to deny. He does not deny generality of function: Certain words and ideas have a general function that can be explained without recourse to abstract general ideas. An idea becomes general by acquiring the role of general signification: It is made to stand for any particular ideas that resemble it in a specified way. And a word becomes general by assuming the same role: It is general to the extent that it picks out any individual ideas of a specified kind. Abstractions do not figure in this account of generality at all.

12. We have just seen that a word becomes general by virtue of having a certain role assigned to it—it is made to *stand for* or *signify* several particular ideas. The role of the word 'horse', for example, is to signify ideas of individual horses. Generality is thus a *function* of some words, rather than an inherent *property*. But perhaps this account is still a bit hazy. **By** changing tack for a moment and considering how selected *ideas* come to play a signifying role, we may acquire a better understanding of the process by which *words* do. I suggest that we try this, **observing** first **how ideas become general,** so that **we may then** be in a **better** position to **judge** exactly **how words are made so.** This should remove any remaining obscurity from what I have said. **And here it is to be noted that I do not deny** generality altogether and **absolutely:** I do not say that **there are** no **general ideas** of any kind, **but only that there are** no *intrinsically* general ideas formed by the process of abstraction. I deny, in other words, that there are **any** *abstract general ideas* of the kind described by philosophers. An individual idea may acquire the function of *general signification,* but no individual idea can be *made general* by abstraction: This is the very antithesis of Locke's view, **for in the passages** from him **above quoted, wherein there is mention of general ideas, it is always supposed that they are formed by** the process of *abstraction,* and *become general* themselves **after the manner set forth in Sections 8 and 9. Now if we** want to make ourselves intelligible we **will** annex a meaning to our words, and speak only of what we can conceive and understand clearly. The process described by Locke, however, is completely incomprehensible. My own view is very simple: **I believe we shall** readily **acknowledge that an idea, which considered in it self is particular,** nevertheless **becomes general** in terms of its function: An individual idea may—while *retaining its individuality*—come to perform the role of general signification **by being made to represent or stand for all other particular ideas** that resemble it and are thus **of the same sort. To make this** notion of general signification **plain by** way of **an example, suppose** that **a geometrician is demonstrating** to his students **the method of cutting** or bisecting **a line into two equal parts. He draws, for instance, a** single **black line of an inch in length** on a sheet of paper; **this** line, **which in it self is** only **a particular** thing (an individual **line** on a sheet of paper), **is nevertheless with regard to its signification** and meaning a **general** indicator, **since** it is referred to all lines and indicates the manner of bisecting them. The particular line **as it is there used** for the purposes of demonstration is of universal import, since **it** stands for and **represents all particular lines whatsoever** and shows what operations can be performed on them; **so that what is demonstrated of** this particular line—that **it** can be bisected—**is also demonstrated of all** other **lines or, in other words, of a line**

in general. That is all that is meant, or can be meant, by 'general idea'. **And** how then does a word, such as the word 'line', become general? The answer is that just **as that particular line** the teacher drew **becomes general, by being made a sign** referring to all lines, **so too the name** or word **'line' which, taken absolutely is particular, by being** treated as **a sign** of all lines, **is made** to function as a **general** signifier. **And as the former** signifier—the line—**owes its generality, not to its being the sign of an abstract or general line** formed by the process Locke envisions, **but** by being invested with the function **of** denoting **all particular right lines that** either exist or **may possibly exist, so** too **the latter** signifier—the word 'line'—**must** itself **be thought to derive its generality** in the same way and **from the same cause, namely,** by carrying out and serving a general function. And so **the** word 'line' is still a concrete thing—an individual mark on a paper or a specific sound spoken—though it be used to pick out **various particular lines which it indifferently denotes** and brings to mind.

An additional passage from the 'Essay' sheds some further light on Locke's theory and reveals the uses of abstract general ideas according to him: They are needed for communication and the acquisition of knowledge. Anyone who claims to have abstract general ideas as Locke describes them is impervious to counterargument: How could you ever prove that a person doesn't have an idea she claims to have? But an appeal to the reader's own experience will suffice: Do you have an abstract idea that combines parts of several inconsistent ideas and is all and none of them at once? If not, then you have no abstract general ideas.

---

13. To reject a doctrine before considering it from every angle, to dismiss a theory without affording it a hearing, is to do an injustice to its proponents and to commit a serious fallacy. That is something I should like to avoid. So I will endeavour to **give the reader a yet clearer view of the nature of abstract ideas** as conceived by Locke, **and** to explain **their** supposedly essential role in knowledge and communication (the two **uses** he assigns to them, and for which **they are thought** to be **necessary**). And thus, **to** round out the details of Locke's theory, **I shall add one more passage out of the** *Essay on Human Understanding,* **which is as follows.**

Abstract ideas are not so obvious or easy to form for **children, or the** as **yet unexercised** and uneducated **mind** of an illiterate youth, **as** are particular ones. **If they seem so** easily acquired and understood **to grown men, it is only because** adults have had much more practice with them: It is **by the constant and familiar use** of abstract ideas that **they are made to** appear **so** simple and readily produced. **For when we nicely** and carefully **reflect upon them, we shall find that** abstract **general ideas are fictions and contrivances of the mind.** They are inventions, rather than things discovered. Abstractions are useful tools **that,** having been worked up from experience with considerable effort, **carry difficulty with them, and do not so easily** appear in the mind or **offer themselves** up for our inspection, **as we are apt to imagine. For example, does it not require some** real mental effort to ignore the incidental discrepancies between various shapes and isolate the common element? Does it not require **pains and skill to form the general idea of a triangle (which is yet** nowhere near **one of the most abstract, comprehensive, and difficult** of abstractions to perform)? It is no easy matter to create the abstract idea of a triangle, **for it must be neither oblique nor rectangle, neither equilateral, equicrural, nor scalenon, but** must be *all* triangles *and yet none* **of these** particular kinds **at once. In effect, it is something imperfect** and incomplete, a fiction **that cannot** actually **exist, an idea wherein some parts of several different and *inconsistent* ideas are put together** to form something new that somehow corresponds to all of them. **It is true that the mind in this imperfect state** of childhood or mental immaturity **has need of** abstractions and must deploy **such ideas, and makes all the haste to** apply them wherever **it can, for the** ease and **conveniency of communication and** for the **enlargement of knowledge, to both of which it is naturally very much inclined.** Abstract ideas are required early on, since children are so naturally inclined to begin talking and learning. **But yet one has reason to suspect** that the existence of **such ideas** and our reliance upon them **are** both **marks of our imperfection** and reveal the limitations of our minds. **At least this** consideration of the great difficulty involved in producing abstractions **is enough to show that the most abstract and general ideas are not those** very things **that the** young **mind is at first and most easily acquainted with, nor** are they **such as at its earliest** stage **knowledge is** directed at and **conversant about** (*Essay*, Book IV, Chapter 7, Section 9).

If any man wants to claim that he **has the faculty of framing in his mind such an idea of a triangle as is here described,** there is no argument I can give to prove that he does not; though I am convinced that he is fooling himself, **it is** beyond my powers to set him right. I would try **in vain to** show that his opinion is false or **pretend to dispute him out of it.** I have not even attempted to deploy such an argument here, **nor would I go about** trying to do **it,** since I can hardly argue with a man about the contents of his own mind. **All I desire is, that the reader**—who is my sole concern—**would fully and certainly inform himself whether he has such an idea** of a triangle **or not. And this, methinks, can be no hard task:** I am not asking the reader to conduct a lengthy investigation, but to engage in a little reflection—the sort of introspective examination that is easy enough **for any one to perform,** even without training in philosophy. **What** could be **more easy than for any one to look a little into his own thoughts,** to run through the contents of his own mind, **and there try** to see **whether he has, or can** at least **attain to have, an idea that shall correspond with the** strange **description that is here given of the general idea of a triangle, which,** according to the author, **is 'neither oblique, nor rectangle, equilateral, equicrural, nor scalenon, but all and none of these at once'?** Is this not outright contradictory? If the reader is like me, he will find himself unable to contemplate the idea described in the passage just quoted. I do not dismiss Locke's theory summarily, therefore, but for the best possible reason: It ascribes to us an idea which even a fool may see is contradictory.

Locke maintained that abstract ideas are required for everyday conversation. We are also told that the process of forming abstract ideas involves considerable effort. Yet conversation does not. So it seems, contrary to Locke, that abstract ideas are not required for conversation. Locke replies that abstract ideas were originally formed with great effort, but that they come more easily later. We grow accustomed to forming them with practice. But this does not seem right. When, exactly, were they formed? It can't be during childhood, since children are incapable of such subtlety and effort as are said to be required for the framing of abstract ideas. It can't be during adulthood either, since we have no memory of exerting ourselves so strenuously, and surely we would if the process were as laborious as Locke makes it out to be. There is no time at which we formed abstract ideas, therefore, and so they are not needed for communication.

14. On the strength of the preceding analysis we may conclude that Locke's theory of abstraction is doomed, for any theory implying a contradiction is false. And Locke's theory implies many contradictions: that I possess an idea of a triangle that is both oblique and not-oblique, equilateral and not-equilateral, etc. But let's try coming at it from a different direction. On a charitable reading, Locke's principal argument is this: Abstract ideas are needed for communication and for extending the sphere of knowledge. Since we do communicate and we daily increase our stock of knowledge, abstract ideas exist. This is a bad argument. Consider communication first: **Much is here said of the difficulty that abstract ideas carry with them, and the pains and skill requisite to the**

forming **of them** in the mind. **And** yet this sits poorly with the claim that they are needed for communication, since communication is very easy. Locke is not alone in making these assumptions: **it is on all hands agreed that there is need of great toil and labour** to identify the common features **of** things, to lift **the mind** to broader views, **to emancipate our thoughts from** their focus on **particular objects, and raise them to** the elevated plane of **those** universal concepts—the abstract ideas—purportedly involved in speech. And it is not only **sublime** philosophical **speculations that are conversant about abstract ideas**: Even everyday claims like 'The horse is in the stable' presuppose a high level of abstraction, since 'horse' and 'stable' are general terms signifying general ideas. **From all of which** Locke wants to infer that we gradually work abstract ideas up from our sensations in order to convey our thoughts, despite the immense difficulty of the process. But **the natural consequence should seem to be** the opposite. We should infer, not the existence of universal concepts such as 'horse' and 'stable', but **that so difficult a thing as the forming** of **abstract ideas was not** at all **necessary for** ordinary *communication,* **which is so easy and familiar to all sorts of men.** The line of reasoning I want to push against Locke, therefore, goes something like this: It is assumed that abstract ideas are difficult to form. So if ordinary communication relied on abstract ideas, it would be difficult too. **But** ordinary communication is not difficult. Therefore, ordinary communication does not rely on abstract ideas. Locke seems to anticipate this objection and to deny that the dependence of communication on abstract ideas entails the difficulty of communication. The reason communication feels easy is that the difficulty of framing abstract ideas has been minimized through steady practice: **we are told** that, **if they seem obvious and easy to** produce in **grown men,** this is not because abstract ideas came easily at first, but **'it is only because by constant and familiar use** over time **they are made** to appear so simple and readily produced' (*Essay*, Book IV, Chapter 7, Section 9). **Now I would** like to pose a question to Locke and his defenders, though there's but a **faint** chance I will receive a satisfactory answer: I want to **know at what time** of life **it is** that they suppose abstract ideas are initially formed. I ask them to pin down, if they can, the age at which **men are employed in surmounting that** great **difficulty** of acquiring abstract ideas, **and furnishing themselves with those necessary helps** and indispensable tools **for** ordinary **discourse** and everyday conversation. **It cannot be** that the preliminary work occurs **when they are** already **grown up, for then** they would remember all the energy they expended in creating abstractions, whereas **it seems they are not conscious of** having undertaken **any such pains-taking** effort and industry; I, for one, do not remember **it.** Unless Locke is mistaken, the process of acquiring abstract ideas **remains therefore to be the business of their** very early **childhood.** That would at least explain why adults have no memory of the undertaking. **And** yet this cannot be correct either, for **surely, the great** struggle **and multiplied labour of framing abstract notions, will be found** an impossibly **hard task for that** young and **tender age of** childhood. **Is it not a hard thing to imagine, that a couple of children cannot** prate together in their familiar way, cannot talk of their sugar-plums and rattles and the rest of their little toys and trinkets, till they have mounted the heights of abstraction? Must they first have tacked together numberless inconsistencies—'oblique', 'not-oblique', 'equilateral', 'not-equilateral'—and so framed in their minds the *abstract general ideas* believed necessary for communication, and annexed them to every common name they make use of when speaking? Can we really suppose them to have associated a lofty abstraction with every general term employed in their banter? That exceeds all credibility. Abstract ideas seem no more to be formed during childhood than during adulthood. Since Locke cannot answer our question, the argument I'm pressing still holds: That abstract general ideas are needed for communication is belied by the fact that communication is easy.

The generality of scientific knowledge seems to imply the existence of abstract general ideas. How could we learn a universal truth if we didn't have universal concepts in which to express it? While Berkeley agrees that knowledge is general in one sense, he does not allow the inference to abstract general ideas as a necessary condition of learning or expressing a universal truth. Nothing is intrinsically general. Universality is a function of reference: One particular idea can be used to pick out—or refer to—any number of other particular ideas. Such ideas can be used to express universal truths.

---

15. Nor do I think that abstract ideas play any role in the acquisition of knowledge. Indeed, I find **them not a whit more needful for the *enlargement of knowledge* than** I find them required **for *communication*.** We learn, and we communicate, quite effectively without them. **It is, I know, a point much insisted on** by philosophers, **that all knowledge and demonstration are about universal notions,** since knowledge and demonstration are by their nature general; this is a point **to which I fully agree.** That my horse eats grains and vegetables rather than meat is not a matter of scientific interest, since it pertains only to a particular horse. Knowledge, properly understood, is general: That *all* horses eat grains and vegetables is a claim that has the requisite universality for it to count as knowledge. The same goes for demonstration: What matters is not my ability to show that *this* triangle has three sides, but my ability to prove that *all* triangles have three sides. So the philosophers are right that knowledge and demonstration pertain to universal notions rather than particulars. **But then it does not appear to me that those notions are formed by *abstraction* in the manner** described by Locke and **premised** by the other abstractionists; **universality, so far as I can comprehend** it, is **not** something **consisting in the absolute, positive nature or conception of any thing** (as if a notion could be universal in itself), **but in the relation** that it—the concrete sign—**bears to the particular** things **signified or represented by it, by virtue whereof** the individual notion becomes a general signifier. In other words, **it is** by way of this signifying relation **that things, names, or notions, being in their own nature *particular*** (since each one of these is an individual item), **are rendered *universal*** by the use they are put to. **Thus when I demonstrate any proposition concerning triangles,** the demonstration is meant to hold for all triangles, and so **it is to be supposed that I have in view the universal idea of a triangle; which ought not to be understood as if I could frame an idea of a triangle which was neither equilateral nor scalenon nor equicrural.** I don't have a universal notion of triangle in that sense. **But** this does not rule out universality in terms of function. I mean **only that the particular triangle I consider, whether of this or that sort it matters not,** has a universal role or function in that it **equally stands for and represents all rectilinear triangles whatsoever, and so is in that** harmless **sense *universal*. All of which seems very plain** and simple, **and not to include any difficulty in it.** Locke's argument from the expansion of knowledge to universality—from the fact that we learn things to the existence of abstract general ideas—thus fails to persuade, since knowledge presupposes no generality in things.

Philosophers suppose that abstract general ideas are needed for demonstration: We can demonstrate that the internal angles of every triangle sum to 180 degrees only by demonstrating it of the abstract general idea of triangle. The assumption is that the abstract general idea represents all particular triangles and that anything proven of it is thereby proven of its instances. This argument for abstract ideas will fail, however, if it can be shown that universal truths may be established without the use of abstractions. And this can in fact be shown: We may establish a universal truth on the basis of a particular instance so long as the distinguishing features of the particular used do not factor in the proof. For example, we can demonstrate that triangles of any size or colour have internal angles summing to 180 degrees by demonstrating it of a particular triangle, so long as no mention is made of its particular size or colour.

---

16. But here it will be demanded of me to explain how we come to know any general truths if the ideas in our minds are all particulars. Adverting to our previous example, it is not at all obvious **how we can** possibly **know any**

proposition to be true of all triangles whatsoever, if the only materials at our disposal are **particular triangles.** There is no way of rounding all the triangles up for inspection, **except** for the indirect method of unifying them under a concept. Can we know some proposition to be true of all triangles if we go at it piecemeal, collecting them one by one but never finishing? Must **we not have first seen it demonstrated of the abstract idea of a triangle** in general, **which** applies **equally**—as every abstractionist **agrees**—to all triangles? **For** it's not like all particular triangles are *identical.* Some triangles are big; some are small. Some are acute, right or obtuse, red, yellow or pink. Just **because a property may be demonstrated to agree to** whatever specimen you happen to have in front of you, just because it may be shown to belong to **some one particular triangle** you are considering, **it will not thence follow that** every other triangle—actual or possible—has that same property too. You may not infer that that quality of the triangle in front of you—whatever **it** happens to be—**equally belongs to any other triangle,** since other triangles may not resemble the one **which** you are looking at **in all respects.** There might even be good reason to suppose that some other triangle **is not** quite **the same** as the first triangle **with** respect to **its** basic geometrical properties. **For example,** after **having** first **demonstrated that the three angles of an isosceles rectangular triangle**—one with a right angle and two sides of equal length—**are** all together **equal** in degree **to two right ones** (two 90 degree angles), **I cannot therefore conclude** that **this** geometrical **affection**—this possibly incidental property of an isosceles rectangular triangle—reflects a universal truth about triangles. I can't know on this basis alone that it **agrees to** the properties of **all other triangles, which,** possibly differing from the isosceles rectangular triangle, **have neither a right angle, nor two equal sides. It seems therefore that,** for us **to be certain** that **this proposition** about the isosceles rectangular triangle **is universally true**—that the three angles of any triangle, regardless of its individuating features, are equal to two right ones—**we must either make a particular demonstration** of it **for every particular triangle,** or we must demonstrate it to be true of the abstract idea of triangle, an idea **which** comprehends all the particulars. But the first is not an option, since it **is impossible** for anyone to examine every particular, there being indefinitely many actual and possible triangles (far more than anyone can count). That leaves the second manner of proof—to **once** and **for all demonstrate it** to be true **of** the single *abstract idea of a triangle,* **in which** the abstractionists suppose **all the particulars do indifferently partake, and by which they are all equally represented.** This presents me with a challenge: I deny that there are abstract ideas, but they appear to be needed for proving general propositions. I must explain how we can know universal truths about triangles, squares, horses and so on, without resorting to the corresponding abstract ideas. **To which** challenge **I answer, that** even **though the idea** of a triangle **I have in view whilst I make the demonstration be, for instance, that of an isosceles rectangular triangle,** even though I am looking at or imagining a particular triangle **whose sides are of a** specific and **determinate length, I may nevertheless be**

certain that the proof has broader significance. I may be certain that **it extends** and applies **to all other rectilinear triangles, of whate**ver **sort** they are, **or** of whatever **bigness.** If it didn't hold for every triangle of every kind or size whate**soever,** it wouldn't be universal; **and** I can be sure **that** it does, **because neither the right angle, nor the equality, nor** the **determinate length of the sides** of the particular triangle I am considering play any part or **are at all concerned in the demonstration. It is true, the diagram** of the triangle **I have in view** has angles of definite degrees and sides of determinate lengths, and these differ from the degrees and lengths seen in many other triangles. My triangle **includes all these particulars, but then** that has no bearing here, since **there is not the least mention made of them in the proof of the proposition. It is not said** in the proof, that **the three angles are equal to two right ones, because one of them is a right angle, or because the sides comprehending it are of the same length,** or on account of any other special property belonging to the isosceles rectangular triangle in front of me. **Which sufficiently shows that the right angle might** instead **have been** an **oblique** angle, more or less than 90 degrees, **and** that **the sides** might have been **unequal** in length. Since the proof did not reference any peculiarities of the specific triangle I used**, the** measurements could have been different **and for all that the demonstration** still **have held good. And for this reason** I suppose **it is** established**, that** the three angles of any triangle are equal to two right ones, though I considered but one instance in the proof. We may safely **conclude that** proposition regarding angles **to be true of any** triangle, whether **obliquangular or scalenon,** or something else. The proposition **which I had** originally **demonstrated of a particular right-angled, equicrural triangle** is thus of general significance; **and not because I demonstrated the proposition** to be true **of the abstract idea of a triangle,** as the objection alleged was necessary. **And here it must be acknowledged that a man may consider a figure** or shape **merely as triangular, without attending** to any of its incidental features; he may simply regard the triangle before his mind *as triangular* without paying any special attention **to the particular qualities of the angles or relations of the sides** of that specific figure. **So far he may** be said to **abstract; but this** is not the kind of abstraction Locke has in mind, and it **will never prove that he can frame an abstract general** and **inconsistent idea of a triangle. In a like manner we may consider Peter,** who is both a man and an animal. Ignoring Peter's broad shoulders and his broken tooth, we may regard him simply as a man—focusing on those features that make him a man—without resorting to an abstract idea, 'man', to use as our standard. Ignoring his upright posture and the use of language, we may regard him simply as an animal—once again without invoking any abstract idea, 'animal', in order to make the identification. Moreover, we may think of him **so far forth as a man,** that is to say, we may think of him just in respect of his being a man, without focusing on the fact of his also being an animal; **or** alternatively we can think of him **so far forth as** an **animal,** without focusing on the fact of his also being a man. Selectively fixing the mind on a single aspect of Peter can indeed be called a kind of 'abstraction', and one which I readily admit. However, this sort of 'abstraction' is done **without framing the aforementioned abstract ideas, either** the abstract idea **of man or** that **of animal,** which would be an entirely different conception of abstraction and one which I totally reject. In short, 'abstraction' in the sense of paying selective attention to particular qualities of Peter is quite feasible, **in as much as** various aspects of him are left out of the account, and **all that is perceived** in him **is not considered** simultaneously.

Medieval philosophers spent centuries arguing about nothing, and very little good came of it. Mental resources were dissipated on a massive scale. Debates about abstract ideas—the bread and butter of medieval philosophy—carry on today in academic circles and far beyond. This breeds contempt for science and study. The way forward is to expose the doctrine of abstraction for what it is—hot air and baloney.

---

17. It would be of no real benefit for me to enter into a debate about the metaphysics of abstract ideas (if I **were** so foolish as to attempt it). I see it as **an endless, as well as an useless thing, to trace the** thoughts of the medieval philosophers—the **'Schoolmen',** as they are called—to try to follow the reasoning of **those great masters of abstraction, through all the manifold** and **inextricable labyrinths,** through the mazes **of** conceptual **error,** confusion **and** pointless **dispute, which their** false **doctrine of abstract natures and notions seems to have led them into,** corrupting philosophy and science like a terrible plague. **What bickerings and controversies they were involved in, and what a learned dust have been raised about those matters, and what mighty advantage has been from thence derived**—what instruments or inducements **to** the improvement of **mankind,** and the perfection of our species—**are things at this day too clearly known to need being** explained or **insisted on here.** For it is obvious to everyone that nothing useful ever came of these debates. **And it** would have been far better **had** the belief in abstract ideas not **been** destructive as **well** as useless and misguided. The arguments might have been safely ignored, at least, **if the** negative influence and **ill effects of that doctrine were confined to** ivory towers, affecting **those** philosophers and theologians **only** who participate in the controversies. The belief in abstract ideas could be treated with the same sort of indifference as we treat the belief in fairies, if it harmed only those **who make the most avowed**

or committed **profession of it** and did not spread so far beyond the colleges and churches in which it is forged. But when the most intelligent men spend their time arguing about nothing they are necessarily diverted from more useful intellectual undertakings; they neglect the projects which could possibly improve our situation. **When men consider the great pains, industry and parts** that have been expended, the enormous amount of effort, work and skill **that have for so many ages been laid out** and wasted **on the cultivation and advancement of the** various **sciences, and that, notwithstanding all of this** labour, **the far greater part of them remain full of darkness and uncertainty,** a very natural aversion to higher learning results. The sciences are full of confusion **and disputes that are likely never to have an end, and even those** few **that are thought to be supported by the most clear and cogent demonstrations** actually **contain in them paradoxes which are perfectly irreconcilable to the understandings of men.** This much is obvious at a glance, **and** when we notice further **that taking all** the sciences **together,** only **a small portion of them** is successful and **supplies any real benefit to mankind, otherwise than by being an innocent diversion and amusement**—a fun distraction from the humdrum of daily business: **I say, the consideration of all this** waste, the realization that so much talent is being squandered on disputation with so little success, **is apt to** turn people away from scientific pursuits and **throw them into a** state of **despondency and** despair, generating in the process a **perfect contempt of all** serious **study. But this** failure of the sciences **may perhaps cease, upon** acquiring **a** clearer **view of the false principles that have obtained** and now have currency **in the world,** and which have caused so much confusion. These false principles I want to expose, **amongst all which there is none, methinks, that has** had **a more wide**spread and pernicious **influence over the thoughts of** the speculative men of science, **than** has **this** theory **of abstract general ideas.**

The doctrine of abstract ideas is rooted in a mistaken theory of reference: On the received view, precision in defining terms requires that every noun be made to pick out some one definite idea. This includes both proper and common nouns. Thus, just as there is one definite idea corresponding to 'Peter', so there must be another corresponding to 'man'. The idea corresponding to 'Peter' is the idea of the individual in question—the guy called 'Peter'. But no definite particular idea can be found corresponding to 'man'. So abstractionists infer that it refers to an abstract general idea of man (just as 'woman' and 'horse' and 'battle' refer to abstract ideas of woman, horse and battle respectively). But this reasoning is flawed: A definition can be sufficiently precise without its tying the term defined to one determinate idea. The definition of 'woman' narrows the range of ideas to which that word applies without

restricting its reference either to an abstraction or to the idea of any particular woman, such as Victoria or Elizabeth.

18. I come now to consider **the source of this** false but **prevailing notion** that there are abstract ideas, **and that seems to me to be** found in our use of **language**, implying as it does the capacity for reason. **And surely nothing of less extent**, nothing less pervasive in our lives, **than reason it self could have been the source**—the underlying cause—**of an opinion so** popular and **universally received** among philosophers as the belief that we form general ideas through a process of abstraction. **The truth of this appears as** much **from** several **other reasons** that I won't go into, as it does from **some core** doctrines of the abstractionists themselves. I mean that it is **also** clear **from the plain** and explicit **confession of the ablest patrons of abstract ideas** that their belief is closely bound up with language. In particular, those **who** defend the theory of abstract notions **acknowledge that they are made in order to** communicate. They are required for the **naming** of things, they say; **from which it** follows (and this **is a very clear consequence), that if there had been no such thing as speech or** words, which are **universal signs,** then **there** would **never** have been any need for abstract ideas. If we **had** not been language users relying on signs, there could hardly have **been any thought of abstraction.** *See* Book III, Chapter 6, Section 39 *and elsewhere of the Essay on Human Understanding.* So to better understand how the theory of abstract ideas originated, we need to think a bit more about language. **Let us therefore examine the manner wherein** our use of language and **words have contributed to the origin of that mistaken** supposition. **First then, it is thought** by abstractionists **that every name** or word **has, or ought to have, one** and **only** one **precise** meaning **and settled signification;** each word must bring a certain idea to mind and no others. For example, 'Peter' must bring the idea of a particular man to mind—namely, Peter. By parity of reasoning it is thought that general terms such as 'man' must bring determinate ideas to mind as well. But 'man' doesn't call up an idea of Peter specifically, rather than of James or John; no individual ideas are picked out by such general terms as 'man'. And yet it is assumed that they still must refer, **which** assumption **inclines men to think** that **there are certain** *abstract, determinate ideas,* **which constitute the true and only immediate signification of each general name** or common noun, **and that it is by the** help and **mediation of these abstract ideas that a general name comes to signify** and apply to **any particular thing.** The thought is that the common noun 'man' characterizes an individual man, Peter, just because the term denotes the abstract idea of man which encompasses all the particular ideas from which it was derived—ideas of individual men like Peter, James and John. **Whereas** the assumption that every noun—including common nouns—must bring a certain idea to mind is false. For, **in truth, there is no such thing as the one precise and definite signification annexed to any general name,** and which

the term must in each case call forth. Rather **they** have a much looser connection with the things they stand for; **all** general nouns denote by **signifying indifferently** any of **a great number of particular ideas**, without being rigidly tied to any one of them. **All** of that **which** I spell out here **evidently follows from what has been already said** in Section 12, **and will clearly appear to** be true to **any one by a little reflexion** on how words seem to be related to ideas in one's own mind. **To this** account of the relation between general terms and ideas that I offer **it will be objected, that every name** or common noun **that has a definition** in a language **is thereby** limited or **restrained** by the definition **to** have **one certain signification**, one precise and definite meaning. **For example, a** common noun like **'triangle' is defined to be a 'plane surface comprehended by three right lines'; by which that** name—'triangle'—**is** connected with and **limited to** one definite thing: It **denotes** and brings to mind **one certain idea and no other.** This clashes with my view that general words stand for and suggest various particular ideas to the mind. **To which** objection **I answer, that** my account of general terms is perfectly consistent with the requirement that definitions narrow the range of ideas to which a certain word may apply. And nothing more is needed from a definition. For example, **in the definition** of 'triangle' **it is not said whether the** plane **surface** comprehended by the three lines must **be great or small, black or white, nor whether the sides are long or short, equal or unequal, nor with what angles they are inclined to each other;** but, rather, **in all which** features the definition allows that **there may be a great variety,** so that triangles may differ in their size, colour, proportion and degree. 'Triangle' can thus evoke any of a number of different particular ideas, **and consequently there is no one settled idea which limits the signification** and meaning **of the word 'triangle'. It is one thing for** us **to keep a name,** like 'triangle', **constantly to the same definition, and** by that means fixing the range or selection of ideas to which it applies. It is **another** thing **to make it stand every where for** one and **the same** particular **idea: the one** thing **is necessary** in a definition, **the other** is **useless and impracticable.**

The theory of abstraction gets a boost from the assumption that every meaningful term stands for some determinate idea: Any apparently meaningful term that fails to pick out some particular idea must therefore denote a general idea instead. Otherwise we'd have an apparently meaningful term that doesn't refer, contrary to the assumption. So general terms must stand for general abstract ideas, just as their proponents allege. But the argument is unsound: Words can be used significantly without suggesting definite ideas.

---

19. **But to give a farther** explanation and clearer **account of how** this understanding of **words** has led philosophers to postulate these non-existent entities, how the supposition that words have certain properties, in other words, **came to produce the doctrine of abstract ideas, it must be observed that it is a** common and widely **received opinion, that language has no other** purpose or **end but the communicating** of **our ideas, and,** in addition, **that every** word or **significant name stands for an idea.** These are two false assumptions about language that philosophers typically make—again, that the only purpose of language is to communicate ideas and that each meaningful term stands for some idea. **This being** the case (or **so** the philosophers suppose), **and it being** moreover assertable—**with all** the **certainty** of a principle—**that names** can be regarded as meaningful and yet not refer to anything, the inference to abstract ideas is invariably drawn. Let me put it differently: From the fact that those words **which yet are not thought altogether insignificant, do not always** refer to and **mark out particular conceivable ideas, it is straightaway concluded** by the philosophers **that they** must **stand for** something else. Since some apparently meaningful names do not stand for any particular ideas, in other words, and since it is assumed that every meaningful term stands for some idea or other, it is inferred that such names must stand for **abstract,** rather than particular ideas or **notions.** But the assumption here is mistaken: **That there are many** purportedly significant **names in use amongst speculative men, which do not always suggest to others determinate particular ideas** when they hear them spoken, **is what no body will deny.** It's easy to think of examples: Medievalists talk about 'intelligible species', for instance (Thomas Aquinas, 1225–1274—*Summa Theologica*, Part I, Question 85, Article 2), and their assertions are believed to be significant. But what particular idea is produced by the term 'intelligible species'? Nothing definite comes to mind. Less contentious examples will do as well: Philosophers speak of 'centrifugal forces' (see Section 111 below), and in this case I suppose they really do speak intelligibly. Yet I think of no determinate ideas when I hear the words. **And,** in addition, paying **a little attention** to our own experience **will** help us **discover, that it is not necessary (even in the strictest** chains **of reasoning** or the hardest **proofs) that significant names which stand for ideas should, every time they are used,** induce or **excite in the understanding the ideas they are made to stand for** by convention. Names often fail to produce in the mind any ideas other than ideas of the names themselves: **In reading and discoursing, names being for the most part used as letters are** used **in *algebraic* proofs, in which,** even **though a particular quantity** or number (such as 7 or 8) might **be marked by each letter** (such as *a* or *b*), **yet to proceed right** and do the proof correctly **it is not requisite that in every step each letter suggest to our thoughts that particular quantity it was appointed to stand for.** We might do the proof without even considering what 'a' or 'b' denote. Similarly, when we read a book or listen to someone talking, we don't always consider what every word we read or hear refers to, and yet we still might comprehend the overall meaning of the sentence. So there's no need to suppose that the names stand for abstract ideas just because they don't produce in our minds any determinate particular ideas.

It is also false that the only use of language is to convey ideas from one mind to another. Words may be used to stir up emotions or to motivate people to action. This is evidenced by the fact that certain common nouns can trigger a reaction without producing any definite ideas. For example, the word 'melancholy' can immediately instil a feeling of gloominess in a person without bringing a painful separation, a lonely existence or any other miserable thing to mind. What's more, we may even respond to certain names without forming any relevant ideas. For example, the proper noun 'Caesar' can provoke admiration and awe without occasioning any particular image—either of Caesar or of anything he achieved.

---

20. **Besides, the** belief that every meaningful term picks out some definite idea is not the only misconception fuelling the theory of abstraction. As I mentioned above, its advocates also show a tendency to assume that language has a single function—the **communicating of ideas marked** out **by words.** But calling up ideas in other people's minds **is not the chief and only end of language, as is commonly supposed** by these philosophers. **There are other ends,** such **as the raising of some** feeling or **passion** in another person, **the exciting** of others **towards** action, **or** the **deterring** of them **from an action, and the putting** of **the mind in some particular disposition;** none of these aims have much **to** do with communicating ideas, **which** has been the sole focus of philosophers in studying language. Indeed, **the former** purpose—that of communicating ideas—**is in many cases** far less important than the other objectives. Sometimes we use language both to communicate an idea and simultaneously to stir up a feeling or prompt an action. In such cases, the goal of conveying ideas will often be **barely** relevant at all; it may be **subservient, and** quite secondary to the goal of firing the passions or inspiring some action. Indeed, **sometimes** imparting ideas is not even a consideration, but is rather **entirely omitted, especially when these** other ends **can be obtained without it, as I think not infrequently happens in the familiar** and everyday **use of language. I entreat the reader to reflect within himself, I** urge him to consider his own involvement with language, **and see if it does not often happen either in hearing** a speech **or reading a discourse, that the** feelings and **passions of fear, love, hatred, admiration, disdain, and the like, arise immediately in his mind upon the perception of certain words, without any**

ideas coming to mind at all. Words may rouse your feelings without any ideas intervening between the words and the feelings. At first when we learn a language, indeed, the words that agitate our feelings and passions might have occasioned ideas that were fit and likely to produce those emotions; but, if I mistake not, it will be found that later, when the language is once grown familiar and we are more accustomed to them, the hearing of the sounds of the words spoken or the sight of the characters composing them on a page does not always bring to mind any idea. Rather, the word is often capable of stirring us and so is immediately attended with those passions, which at first relied on the intervention of the relevant idea as catalyst. When we were first learning to speak, things were obviously different. If you don't know what a word means, you won't have any emotional reaction when you hear it spoken. But once the meaning is grasped you come to associate it immediately with a feeling or characteristic response, and you may now get the feeling—or give the appropriate response—that would originally have been produced only by the intervention of ideas that are now quite omitted and bypassed altogether. For example, before you learn the meaning of the word 'oppressor', the sound or sight of it has no real impact on you and elicits no response. But once you understand the word, hearing it will bring to mind the idea of a bully beating up a weakling, or something similar, and this will in turn produce feelings of anger towards the oppressor and sympathy for the victim. Later, after you've heard or read the word many times, it will have the power to immediately and directly provoke the feelings of anger and sympathy without even bringing the image of the oppressor or the victim to mind. There are countless ways to illustrate this point: May we not, for example, be immediately affected with and excited by the promise of a *good thing*, though we have not any more specific idea of what it is we are being promised? I, for one, am delighted whenever anyone promises me a 'good thing', even when the words do not suggest anything definite like a cake, a trip to the country or any other particular idea I find agreeable. Or is not the being threatened with danger sufficient to excite a fearful dread all at once, though we think not of any particular evil likely to befall us? 'The footpath you're on is dangerous!' Might not that be enough to frighten you? May we not be shaken to hear that the path we're taking is a dangerous one, though we form no idea of any particular danger—such as an outlaw or a snake—nor yet frame to our selves an idea of danger in the abstract? If any one shall join ever so little reflexion of his own to what has been said and consider for himself what goes on in his own mind, I believe it will evidently appear to him, that general names and words are often used in the propriety of language without the speaker's designing or intending them for marks or signs of the ideas in his own mind, which he would have them raise in the mind of the hearer—he may simply have no intention of provoking like ideas in anyone else. Even proper names of particular people, like 'Peter' or 'Aristotle', themselves do not seem always to be spoken with a design to bring into our view and into the minds of our hearers the ideas of those individuals that are supposed to be marked and named by them. For example, when a medieval **Schoolman tells me** in support of some proposition that *Aristotle has said it,* I do not think he expects me to form an idea of Aristotle. Rather **all I conceive he means** to do by saying **it is to** positively **dispose me** towards the proposition and **to embrace his opinion,** given the authority Aristotle was taken to have on any subject. He wants me to agree **with** him and to show **the** respect, **deference and** unquestioning **submission which** medieval **custom has** accorded and **annexed to that** name, 'Aristotle'. **And this effect** of submitting **may be so instantly** and immediately **produced in the minds of those who are accustomed to resigning their judgment to** his, and to placing their faith in **the authority of that** esteemed **philosopher,** that no thought of the actual man, Aristotle, is so much as suggested. Indeed, we can be sure that no idea of Aristotle arises, **as it is impossible**—given the speed with which the listener agrees—that **any idea either of his person, writings, or reputation should go before** their agreement. **Innumerable** other **examples of this kind may be given, but** I do not need to pile them on. For **why should I insist on** showing **those things, which every one's** own **experience** and reflection **will, I doubt not,** easily and **plentifully suggest unto him?**

Though a linguistic confusion lies behind the belief in abstract ideas, that in no way implies that words are merely a source of trouble. The cumulative knowledge of the sciences is recorded in books and made available to everyone through language. Still, in the actual practice of most sciences sloppy and obscure writing is an impediment to progress and understanding. To compensate for this problem, Berkeley will focus on the content of ideas rather than on the words with which they are normally associated.

---

21. We have, I think, shown the impossibility of *abstract ideas* in Sections 10 and 13. **We have considered what has been said for them** in Section 11, what arguments have been offered **by** past philosophers (who are **their ablest patrons** and greatest supporters); **and** we have **endeavoured** in Sections 12, 14, 15 and 16 **to show** that **they are** entirely fictitious and **of no use** whatever for attaining **those ends to which they are thought necessary. And lastly,** in Sections 18 and 19, we have explained the origin of our belief in them. To put it figuratively, **we have traced them to the source from whence they flow, which** we identified as language. More precisely, this strange opinion **appears to be** grounded in a mistaken view about **language. It cannot be denied that words** are exceedingly helpful; they **are of excellent use, in that by their means** vast amounts of information—**all that stock of knowledge which has**

been acquired through scientific investigation, **purchased by the joint labours of inquisitive men in all ages and nations**—is recorded in books so that it **may be drawn into the view and** considered by anyone. Anything that has been written down, any body of knowledge or information, however broad in scope, can be **made the possession of one single person.** This is the great advantage of words. **But at the same time it must be owned**—I think any impartial observer would have to admit—**that most** branches or **parts of knowledge have been** obscured and **strangely perplexed,** they have been confused **and darkened by the abuse of** language, by the playing of **word** games, **and** by the **general ways of speech** and writing **wherein they**—the results obtained in the various sciences—**are delivered. Since therefore words are so apt to** mislead us, so likely to **impose on** and confuse **the understanding,** I will take the following precaution: **whatever ideas I consider** in this treatise, **I shall endeavour to** heed the content of the ideas alone. I will try to **take them bare and naked into my view,** in other words, focusing only on what appears before my mind. In doing so, I will be disregarding the words that are normally attached to such ideas, **keeping out of my thoughts** and blocking from my mind, **so far as I am able,** those names of ideas **which long and constant use has so strictly united with them;** this is an exercise **from which I may expect to derive the following** three **advantages.**

Directing our attention to ideas rather than words helps us avoid (1) point-less verbal disputes, (2) the pernicious theory of abstract ideas and (3) errors regarding the objects of thought. The last point follows from the transparency of ideas to the mind—in terms of their existence, nature and content: When it comes to our own ideas, we cannot misjudge their properties or the fact of their existence.

---

22. **First,** by focusing on ideas rather than words **I shall be sure to get clear of** any disputes over the meanings of terms and thus avoid **all** those philosophical **controversies** that are **purely verbal,** such as all that business about 'real' versus 'conceptual' distinctions and 'clear' versus 'distinct' perceptions much discussed by Descartes and his followers (see his *Principles*, Part I, Sections 45, 60 and 62). This marks a significant gain, since **the springing up of** verbal disputes—**which** multiply like **weeds in almost all the sciences—has been an** enormous obstacle to progress and is arguably the **main hindrance to the growth of true and sound knowledge. Secondly, this** method **seems to be a sure way to** disentangle and **extricate** the mind from that misguided

theory that an undue emphasis on words has caused philosophers to embrace. By fixing my attention on the ideas I actually perceive rather than the words that represent them, I may be able to pull **my self out of that fine and subtle net** they have spun. The theory **of** *abstract ideas* is a great web of confusion, **which has so miserably perplexed and entangled the minds of** learned **men,** that they have lost sight of the objects before their very eyes **and** forfeited thereby all claims to common sense. It is, moreover, a theory **that** comes **with this peculiar circumstance,** that the smarter the philosopher, the more likely he is to be wrapped up in its complexities. It is certainly an unexpected result, and much to be regretted, **that by how much the finer** were the mental powers, **and the more** probing and **curious was the wit of any man, by so much the deeper was he likely to be** immersed in the theory—more truly **ensnared** by the net, as it were, **and faster held therein.** Redirecting the mental gaze to ideas may get us out of this dreadful trap. **Thirdly, so long as I confine my thoughts to my own ideas divested of** any association with **words, I do not see how I can easily be mistaken** regarding their existence, nature or content. **The objects I want to consider** are ideas, which are things **I clearly and adequately know.** Does this or that idea exist? No difficulty there, for **I cannot be** mistaken or **deceived in thinking** that **I have an idea which** in fact **I have not.** Is this idea the same as that one? If I perceive a difference, there is a difference. Are these two ideas similar in this or that respect? My answer will have the highest degree of certainty. **It is** simply **not possible for me to imagine, that any** two or more **of my own ideas are alike or unlike** to each other, and for that not to be the case; if I perceive that they are similar, then it is impossible **that** they **are not truly** just as I imagine them to be. Generally speaking, if I clearly perceive things to be a certain way, then they are that way—**so** long as we're talking about ideas. **To discern the agreements or disagreements,** the similarities or differences **there are between my** various **ideas, to see what** simple **ideas are included in any** complex or **compound idea, and what** simple ideas are **not** included in them, I need only visualize and reflect carefully on what passes through my mind. In sum, to avoid philosophical confusion and to arrive at a proper understanding of the nature and content of my ideas, **there is nothing more requisite than an attentive perception of what passes in my own understanding.** The subject matter makes error unthinkable.

Getting a clear and accurate view of our own ideas requires disassociating them from the words they are linked with by convention. But this is difficult, since the links were forged in childhood and then cemented over time by habit. Philosophers who recognize the need to look beyond words to the ideas themselves have been unsuccessful, as many of the words they want to shake off are regarded as signs of abstract ideas. It's no wonder they can't drop the words and contemplate the ideas, therefore, since abstract ideas are nothing. How can you contemplate nothing?

23. **But the attainment of all these** benefits—the securing of the **advantages** I claimed would follow from studying ideas rather than words—**presupposes** that one has managed to get free of the distorting influence of language; it implies **an entire deliverance from the deception of words** on the part of the investigator. This is something **which I dare hardly promise** to have done **myself.** I can't just assume that I have been successful in separating ideas from the words they are normally tied to; **so difficult a thing it is to dissolve an union so early begun**—it started in our childhood, after all, when we first began to speak. Any bond that is reinforced **and confirmed by so long a habit as that betwixt words and ideas,** between signs and signified, is something **which** takes time and effort to dissolve. And the **difficulty** of breaking this link **seems to have been very much increased by the** philosophers' **doctrine of** *abstraction.* **For so long as** learned **men** mistakenly **thought** that **abstract ideas were annexed to their words, it** was perfectly natural for them to make language their object—they couldn't very well study abstract ideas directly and in themselves, since abstract ideas are impossible fictions. And so it **does not seem** very **strange that they should use words** as placeholders **for ideas, it being found an impracticable thing to lay aside the word and retain the abstract idea in the mind,** when an abstract idea is something **which in it self**—insofar as it was supposed to be abstract—**was perfectly inconceivable. This seems to me** to be **the principal cause** of Locke's inability to stick to his own advice and avoid the confusion of words (see his *Essay,* Book IV, Chapter 4, Sections 13 and 17). It explains **why those men who have so emphatically recommended to others the laying aside all use of words in their meditations, and contemplating their bare ideas** instead—the very recommendation I made above—**have yet failed to perform it themselves:** They could not contemplate abstract ideas independently of the words they took to signify them, since they in fact had nothing in mind beyond the words. **Of** the empirically inclined philosophers who have **lately** brought sensations to the forefront of philosophical inquiry, **many have** also **been very sensible of the** need to discount all those **absurd opinions and insignificant disputes, which grow out of the abuse of words. And in order to remedy these evils**—to do away with *a priori* speculations on words and to destroy the false opinions they produce—**they advise well that we** take less notice of the terms themselves so as to **attend** more closely **to the ideas signified.** This is the method of mathematicians, who contemplate circles **and** triangles rather than names (*Essay,* Book IV, Chapter 3, Section 30). We ought to imitate their method, **drawing the mind off** the signs and turning **our attention** towards the things signified, which is just to say, away **from the words** like 'circle' and 'triangle' **which**

signify them. **But how good soever this advice may be,** which **they have given** to others (indeed, I think it's very good advice), **it is plain** that **they could not have** followed their own recommendation and had **a due regard to it themselves, so long as they thought** that **the only immediate** and important **use of words was to signify** or stand for **ideas, and that the immediate signification of every** universal term—that the thing each **general name** stood for—**was a *determinate, abstract idea.*** You can hardly discard the word and focus on the idea signified, if nothing is actually signified—and abstract ideas I take to be nothing.

Dumping the doctrine of abstract ideas means avoiding the mistakes it has occasioned in the past. We won't waste any more time reflecting on abstract ideas or thinking about their relations, if we know that they are fictions. An emphasis on particular ideas will facilitate progress in philosophy and science. We'll see how central the rejection of abstract ideas is to Berkeley's case for idealism in Section 5.

---

24. But these two assumptions—that the sole purpose of language is to communicate ideas from one mind to another and that every general term designates some definite abstract idea—are not only unjustified. As we have seen, they are also false and, **being known to be mistakes, a man may** block the inferences their proponents wish to draw from them and he may thus **with that** much **greater ease prevent his being imposed on by** philosophical obscurities and perplexed by the constant mishandling of **words. He** who is aware **that** general terms refer indifferently to particular ideas within a range rather than to general notions, he who **knows** that **he has no other than particular ideas** in his own mind, **will not** likely find himself entangled in **puzzles** concerning abstractions. He will not exhaust **himself in vain** in trying **to find out** how the abstract idea of a genus is related to the abstract idea of a species, for instance, or how the 'real' essence of gold is related to the 'real' essence of silver. He knows that there are no such things. He will not waste his time **and** energy in attempting to **conceive the** relation that ties **abstract ideas** to the general terms that name them, or in trying to identify the abstract idea that is **annexed to any** given **name,** such as 'animal', 'man' or 'nurse'. Why should he do this, if he knows that general terms denote particulars? **And he that knows** that even particular **names do not always stand for** definite **ideas, will spare himself the** hard **labour of looking for** the ideas behind every word, **where there are none to be had. It** would be much better for the field—much better for human knowledge in general—if there **were** not so many philosophers obsessed with answering these non-questions about non-entities. But I believe this trend will continue, until philosophers learn to distance themselves a little from language and to apply their thoughts to things. It is **therefore** greatly **to be wished that every one would use his** mind rightly and apply it to the objects it is suited to know. If everyone would make the **utmost** effort to bring these pointless disputes about language to an end, if everyone would **endeavour, as** best he can, **to obtain a clear view of the ideas he would consider, separating from them all that** heavy **dress and encumbrance of words which so much contribute to** misunderstanding, **blind the judgment and divide the attention,** human knowledge would advance at an extraordinary pace. **In vain do we** try to **extend our view into the heavens, and pry into the entrails** and depths **of the earth, in vain do we consult the writings of learned men, and trace the dark footsteps of** progress through **antiquity;** all such inquiries will come to nothing, until philosophers return to things and ideas—the concrete individuals inhabiting the world—and treat abstractions, spoken sounds and characters written on a page as so much needless ornamentation. **We** scarcely **need** to abandon language altogether, of course, or pretend that it serves no purpose, but **only** to **draw** back **the curtain of words, to** some extent, that we may **behold the fairest tree of knowledge, whose fruit is excellent, and** hangs ripe for the plucking. How much can be achieved in science and philosophy? How many discoveries can we make? What new wonders lie **within the reach of our hands**? Should we confine our view to words, I'm afraid the prospects are narrow. Should we look beyond them to ideas, we may aspire to new heights.

Starting from false principles leads to error and confusion, since mistakes trickle down and multiply. Whether the principles put forth in this treatise are true or false may be determined by the reader herself; she need only reproduce the arguments in her own mind, considering at every step the ideas suggested by the words, rather than their outward form.

---

25. **Unless we take care to clear** up our understanding of **the first principles of knowledge,** and detach them **from the embarras**sing befuddlement **and delusion of** past philosophers who have focused too much on **words, we may** risk arguing endlessly about our starting points—the first principles—and **make infinite reasonings upon them to no purpose; we may** develop elaborate philosophical theories, **drawing** more and more **consequences from the consequences** we reach, **and** yet **be never the wiser,** for if our first principles are false, the things we derive from them may be false as well. **The farther we go** in our reasoning from faulty assumptions, the more likely it is that our conclusions will be false, and **we shall only lose our selves** and our prospects of discovering the truth **the more irrecoverably, and be the deeper entangled in** conceptual **difficulties and** philosophical **mistakes. Whoever therefore** wants to comprehend my system, and who thus **designs to read the following sheets** of paper, I ask him—I **entreat him** earnestly—**to make my words** merely **the occasion of his own thinking, and** to try to replicate my ideas and patterns of reasoning in himself, **endeavouring to attain** and follow **the same train of thoughts in reading** my words **that I had in writing them. By** adopting **this means** of reading **it will be easy for him to discover the truth or falsity of what I say** for himself. **He will be out of all danger of being deceived by my words, and I do not see how he can be led into any error by considering his own** ideas and striving not to be confused by language, whether mine or his own. The reader should do his best to view his ideas **naked,** and **undisguised,** simply as **ideas,** whose nature and contents he cannot possibly misjudge, as I explained already in Section 22.

Of the Principles of Human Knowledge: Part I

The objects of human knowledge are ideas—nothing else is or can be perceived. The proper object of perception differs for each sensory modality: Sight perceives light and colours, hearing perceives sounds, smell perceives odours and so on. Clusters of ideas regularly perceived in unison are treated as objects and typically given a name. They trigger positive or negative emotions in us depending on whether we find them pleasing or displeasing.

---

1. Let us reflect on what is present to the conscious mind. What sorts of things do we perceive? We'll call the things we perceive—the things that are immediately present to the conscious mind—the 'objects of human knowledge'. **It is evident to any one who** looks inside his own mind and **takes a survey of these objects of human knowledge** that they fall into three distinct groups. When I focus on the objects before me, it is clear **that they are either** (1) **ideas actually imprinted on** and coming from **the senses, or else** (2) **such** objects **as are perceived by attending to the passions** I undergo—such as a feeling of satisfaction or desire—**and** concentrating on the **operations of the mind** while it is working, **or lastly** (3) **ideas formed by** the **help of memory and imagination,** either uniting and **compounding** sensory data, or **dividing it,** or else reproducing through recollection—what you might call **'barely representing'**—those things **originally perceived in the aforesaid ways.** Here I am partly in agreement with my English predecessor, John Locke (1632–1704), who calls them (1) ideas of sensation, (2) ideas of reflection and (3) ideas of the imagination (which includes the ideas of memory). A point of disagreement concerns (2): As will become clear shortly, there are no *ideas* of reflection, but only what I will later call *notions* (see Sections 27 and 143). We'll talk about the third group in Sections 28 to 33. For now, we should direct our attention to the first group—the ideas of sensation. We have five senses and each of them gives us a certain type of idea. **By sight I have the ideas of light and colours with their several degrees** of intensity **and variations** in hue. **By touch I perceive, for example, hard and soft, heat and cold, motion and resistance, and of all these** qualities I perceive **more and less either as to** their **quantity**—the number of things moving, for instance—**or** their **degree**—more swiftly, say, or very slow. **Smelling furnishes me with odours; the palate** supplies me **with tastes, and hearing conveys sounds to the mind in all their variety of tone and composition.** And as several of these are observed to accompany each other regularly in my experience, **they come to be marked by one name, and so to be reputed,** or viewed as, one individual **thing. Thus, for example, a certain colour, taste, smell, figure and consistence having been observed to go together** on various occasions, **are accounted** and regarded as **one distinct thing, signified** and set off from all others **by the name 'apple'.** The object itself is just this cluster of ideas which we pick out with that word as a matter of convenience. **Other collections of ideas constitute a stone, a tree, a book, and** so on. For what I say of **the** apple holds, **likewise,** for all other **sensible things; which** things, insofar **as they are pleasing or disagreeable** to us, stir up and **excite the passions of love, hatred, joy, grief, and so forth,** causing us to seek them out or to avoid them, as the case may be.

The subject of human knowledge is the mind—also called the 'soul', 'spirit' or 'self'. It is the thinking thing which has ideas and in which they exist. It is neither reducible to ideas nor built up out of them. The mind is an active being that can perceive, will, imagine and remember.

---

2. But besides all that endless variety of ideas there are in the mind **or soul,** above and beyond all the **objects of** human **knowledge, there is likewise** the mind itself, **something which knows** ideas **or perceives them.** In addition to knowing and perceiving, moreover, the mind manipulates ideas in various ways **and exercises diverse operations, such as willing** (I may call up the idea of red), **imagining** (I imagine eating an apple), and **remembering** (I remember reading a book). The mind evidently has this power to perceive ideas, to recollect and think **about them** when they are no longer present in sensation, to break them apart, as it were, and reassemble them in new combinations (see Introduction, Section 10). **This perceiving, active being** that wills, imagines, recalls and reassembles **is what I call** a **'mind', 'spirit', 'soul'** or **'my self'.** Though others may invest these terms with different meanings, I use them interchangeably. **By which words**—'mind', 'soul', 'spirit'—therefore, **I do not** mean to pick out or **denote any one of my ideas, but a thing entirely distinct from them,** that very thing **wherein they exist.** The mind is thus the receptacle of ideas **or,** putting it more plainly, it is that **which** 'has' them. To say that the mind 'has' ideas **is the same** as saying that it is the **thing, whereby they are perceived; for the existence of an idea consists** solely **in being perceived** by a mind.

No one supposes that a mere thought, an emotion or something imagined can exist outside the mind and unperceived. The same thing holds for sensations: They cannot exist outside of a mind perceiving them. In order to grasp this truth—that no idea of sensation can exist unperceived—we need only understand what an idea is. Understanding what an idea is involves—at least in part—understanding the existence conditions for ideas. And since sensible objects are collections of sensory ideas (see Section 1), their existence conditions are the same as those for ideas. To understand that the being of sensible objects consists in their being perceived, therefore, you need only understand what it means to say that an idea—or a collection of ideas—exists. Berkeley identifies three existence conditions here in support of his idealist principle that no sensible object can exist outside of a mind perceiving it.

---

3. Consider a thought (that 12 is greater than seven, for instance), a passion (say, a feeling of happiness) and an idea formed by the imagination (maybe the idea of Medusa or Pegasus). **That** none of these things—**neither our thoughts, nor passions, nor ideas formed by the imagination,** whether we take the examples just given or others—**exist without the mind, is what every body** believes and **will** certainly **allow** to be true. For who could suppose that bare ideas like these exist outside the mind independently of being perceived? Their existence is reducible to our perception of them—they are mere ideas, after all. **And it seems no less evident** to me that the same thing must hold for ideas of sensation, taken individually or in combination. What I mean to say is **that the various sensations or ideas imprinted on the** mind by the five **senses, however** they are **blended or combined together (that is, whatever objects they compose**—an apple, a tree, a book or whatever) **cannot exist otherwise than in a mind perceiving them.** Some truths are as clear as daylight to anyone who thinks them through. That ideas cannot exist outside of minds perceiving them is a case in point. **I think** a clear **and intuitive knowledge may be obtained of this** obvious truth, **by any one that shall attend to** his thoughts carefully and consider **what is meant by the term 'exist' when** it is **applied to sensible things.** I ask you, what does it mean to say that a sensible object exists? What are we asserting when we claim that something sensible *is*? Here I am in my study with papers spread out before me. **The table I write on, I say, exists,** and to say **that is** no more than to say that I perceive it, **that I see and feel it; and** even **if I were** to go **out of my study** and head downstairs to the kitchen, **I should** still **say it existed, meaning thereby,** not that I perceive it now, but **that if I was in my study I might perceive it,** indeed, that I *would* perceive it, **or that some other spirit actually does perceive it**—it could be God or just some other person, such as my maid or my servant. It's not as if there's a table perceived and a table unperceived. I don't even understand the expression 'a table unperceived'. And I doubt that my reader does either. Consider the claim: **'There was an odour'.** By this, I mean only that I had a perception of smell—**that is** to say, that **it,** the odour, **was smelled;** when I say **there was a sound,** I mean only that I perceived something by hearing—**that is to say,** that **it,** the sound, **was heard;** and when I say there was **a colour or figure,** I just mean that I had a visual or tactile sensation **and** thus that **it,** the colour or figure, **was perceived by sight or touch. This is all that I can understand by these and the like expressions**—they are simply reports on perceptions I had. They make no reference to things existing apart from the mind or perception. **For as to what is said** by some philosophers **of the** material or **absolute existence of unthinking things** outside the mind and **without any relation to their being perceived, that seems** to me **perfectly unintelligible** and totally meaningless. For sensible objects, to be is to be perceived, plain and simple. **Their** *esse* **is** *percipi*, in other words, **nor is it possible they should have any existence,** outside **of the minds or thinking things which perceive them.** So I am not denying that a table exists. I am explaining what it means to say that a table exists. And the only sense I can put on that expression is in terms of actual and possible perceptions. That's what we all mean, and the only thing we can mean, by 'exist' when applied to objects of the senses.

Philosophers believe that the things around us—ordinary objects such as apples and oranges, tables and chairs—exist outside our minds. But this is a mistake. For the objects around us are what we perceive by sense. And what we perceive by sense are ideas, as explained already in Section 1. Thus, the objects around us are ideas. And ideas cannot exist outside of minds, as is clear from Section 3. Therefore, the objects around us exist in the mind. Apples, oranges, tables and chairs—and all other objects of perception—exist in the mind and nowhere else.

---

4. Many philosophers have seen things differently. **It is indeed** a widespread error of the educated class, **an opinion strangely prevailing amongst** learned **men** and defended fiercely in their schools, **that houses, mountains, rivers, and—in a word—all sensible objects** whatever **have an existence** that is **natural or real** in itself, an existence outside of the mind, completely **distinct** and apart **from their being perceived by the understanding. But with** however **great an assurance and acquiescence soever this** lofty **principle may be entertained** by philosophers and propounded **in the** academic **world;** however unchallenged outside the halls of learning, **yet whoever shall find** it **in his heart to call it into question, may, if I mistake not,** come to **perceive it to involve** an obvious and appalling absurdity—indeed, the most **manifest contradiction** imaginable. **For** what are houses and mountains and rivers—**what are** any of **the aforementioned** sensible **objects—but the things we perceive by** our **senses?** No truth could be more evident: Sensible objects are things perceived by sense, **and what do we perceive** by sense **besides our own ideas or sensations?** It is therefore certain that sensible objects are ideas or sensations; **and is it not plainly repugnant** to reason and very ridiculous to suppose **that any one of these** ideas or sensations, **or any combination of them** (such as a house, a mountain or a river), **should exist unperceived** outside the mind? The argument is undeniable: If sensible objects are things perceived by sense, if things perceived by sense are ideas, and if ideas exist in minds alone, then sensible objects exist in minds alone. To suppose they exist anywhere else is to suppose a contradiction.

The hypothesis that sensible objects exist outside the mind and unperceived— popular amongst philosophers—is based on the doctrine of abstract ideas, the primary target of Berkeley's attack in the Introduction. There appear to be two arguments here: First, a sensible object is composed of sensible qualities (light, colours, figures, etc.). These are ideas and the existence of an idea consists in being perceived. And so a sensible object—a collection of ideas—cannot be conceived apart from perception. Second, just as it is impossible to see something without having a visual sensation of it, it is likewise impossible to conceive of a sensible object without conceiving of some sensible qualities it has. Putting both arguments together, the point is this: Supposing that a sensible object exists outside the mind requires abstracting an idea from the perception of it, and abstracting the conception of a sensible object from the perception of its qualities. Both are impossible.

---

5. That houses, mountains, rivers and books exist outside of minds is a strange opinion indeed—a tenet of the learned, rather than the common man. **If we thoroughly examine this tenet, it will, perhaps, be found** confused and **at bottom to depend on the doctrine of** *abstract ideas*—a theory I showed to be false in the Introduction. **For can there be a**nything more futile than the attempt to separate an idea from a mind perceiving it? Only a philosopher, poisoned by the theory of abstract ideas, could suppose that such a thing is even possible. There's nothing less tangible, no **nicer strain of abstraction, than** the learned philosopher's misguided effort **to distinguish the existence of sensible objects from their being perceived, so as to conceive them** apart. Can you even imagine a sensible object—a mere collection of ideas—**existing unperceived?** What would that be like? Try to picture it in your own mind. **Light and colours, heat and cold, extension and figures, in a word the things we see and feel, what are they?** They are nothing **but so many sensations, notions, ideas or impressions on the sense;** these qualities are perceptual through and through. If you reflect on this, you'll surely agree, **and so I put it to you, is it possible to separate, even in** your **thoughts, any of these** qualities **from perception,** given their status as ideas? **For my part I might as easily divide a thing from it self,** since an idea is a mental thing and I can't divide a mental thing from a mind—I can't dislodge an idea from the mind it is in. It would be like trying to divide colour from shape. Where there is colour there is shape. And where there are ideas, or clusters of ideas, there is a mind containing them. **I may indeed divide in my thoughts or conceive apart from each other those things which, perhaps, I never perceived by sense so divided,** but which really can come apart. **Thus I imagine the trunk of a human body without the limbs, or conceive the smell of a rose without thinking on the rose it self. So far,** but no further, **I will not deny that I can abstract, if that** straightforward, cut and paste sort of division **may properly be called 'abstraction'.** I guess you can call it 'abstraction', but it's a very simple process of mental division **which extends only to the** act of **conceiving separately such objects as it is possible may really exist or be actually perceived** separately, the adjacent parts of such things just being pulled **asunder** in the mind (see Introduction, Section 10). **But my conceiving or imagining power does not extend beyond the possibility of real existence or perception,** which I equate with each other. For I can conceive, or think, apart only what I can either perceive or imagine apart. Conception, perception and reality are for me one and the same. **Hence, just as it is impossible for me to see or feel any thing without an actual sensation of that thing**—I clearly can't see something without a visual sensation or feel something without a tactile sensation— it is similarly impossible for me to consider an apple independently of the sensation of it. My conception of the apple *consists* in the perception of its qualities. The point can be generalized, **and so** I infer that it **is** beyond my power of abstraction—**it** is strictly speaking **impossible**—for me **to conceive in my thoughts any sensible thing** whatever, **or** any perceptual **object, distinct from the sensation or perception of it.**

The idealist principle that the being of sensible objects consists in being perceived has a profound implication: The continuity of sensible objects requires the presence of a mind. When you close your eyes, or go outside, you do not perceive the desk in your study or the books on your shelves. So either your desk and your books cease to exist in such moments or else they are perceived by some other mind. If sensible objects continue to exist when no human minds are there to perceive them, they must exist in some ever-present mind which sustains them. Berkeley equates this ever-present mind with God.

6. Some truths are rather difficult to make out and hard to accept, but **there are** others which force themselves on the intellect and compel our assent. Truths such as these are **so near and obvious to the mind,** so plausible and apparent, **that a man** need but reflect on them once in order to be convinced. If they are not amongst his beliefs already, it is only because he has never yet contemplated them. He **need only open his eyes to see** that they are true and to place his confidence in **them. Such** a truth **I take this important one to be,** that existence and perception are absolutely inseparable, or, **to** express it **with** more precision, **that** all sensible objects whatsoever, **all the choir of heaven and furniture of the earth, in a word, all those bodies which compose the mighty frame of the world, have not any** being or **subsistence without** the mind. Their being consists solely in being perceived by **a mind.** To make such a bold and sweeping claim about sensible objects, to say **that their** very **being is to be perceived or known** by a mind, will perhaps astonish some of my readers; but **that** it is true and, **consequently,** that it has some very profound implications, I have not the slightest doubt. It follows, for instance, that when we are not perceiving them ourselves sensible objects must either cease to exist altogether or else exist in the mind of God; **so long as** none of us are looking at them—when **they are not actually perceived by me, or do not exist in my mind or that of any other created spirit,** whether human, angel or whatever—**they must,** as I say, **either have no existence at all** (a view too absurd to maintain), **or else** they **subsist in the mind of some** uncreated, eter-**nal spirit.** All of this follows from the conclusions of the last three sections: **it being perfectly unintelligible and involving all the absurdity of abstraction** (which we have exposed in the Introduction), **to attribute to** any sensible things, or **any single** sensible **part of them, an existence** outside the mind **independent of a spirit** which perceives them. **To be convinced of** that truth **which** I have brought into focus here, **the reader need only reflect** a little on his experience **and try to separate in his own thoughts the being of** any **sensible thing from its being perceived** by a mind. I trust he will find that this is not within his power and that, accordingly, he can make no sense of the view that sensible things exist without the mind. But then where do sensible things exist when there are no finite minds around to perceive them? There is but one possibility: They exist in the mind of God.

A substance is a bearer of properties. Sensible qualities—things like a round shape, a red colour and so on—are properties rather than bearers of properties. So they must exist in substances. Are the substances that bear sensible qualities perceptive or non-perceptive? Are they minds, in other words, or matter? We know from Section 1 that a red colour and a round shape are ideas—indeed, we know that all qualities of any kind are ideas. We know from Section 3 that ideas cannot exist outside of perceivers. And we know from Section 2 that minds are mental substances or perceivers. It follows that the bearers of sensible qualities are minds—perceptive mental substances rather than non-perceptive matter. That minds are the only substances follows, presumably, from both the unstated assumption that a substance must have some properties in order to exist and the fact that all properties are qualities or ideas.

---

7. The discussion so far has centred on the sensible qualities of things—the colour, shape, texture, odour and taste of an apple, for instance. But I've said very little about the substances in which these qualities exist. Are the substances in which sensible qualities exist perceptive or non-perceptive? Are they minds that perceive or are they mindless matter—something that doesn't perceive? **From what has been said, it follows, that there is not any other substance than *spirit*, or** mind—**that which perceives**, in other words. **But** it may help to spell out the argument. So **for the fuller proof of this point, let it be considered, that the sensible qualities** of things **are colour, figure, motion, smell, taste, and such like, that is** to say, **the** sensible qualities are simply **ideas perceived by** the **senses.** Ideas can't float around on their own, of course. They must exist in a substance—either perceptive or non-perceptive. **Now for an idea to exist in an unperceiving thing,** a nonperceptive substance, **is a manifest contradiction; for to have an idea is all one as to perceive**—they're the same thing: **that** substance, **therefore, wherein colour, figure, and the like qualities exist, must perceive them.** And only mental substances, or minds, perceive. It would be contradictory to suppose that a non-perceptive thing could contain qualities that must be perceived in order to be had. **Hence it is clear** that **there can be no unthinking substance or** *substratum* **of those ideas.**

Locke held that ideas can—and often do—resemble things outside the mind. Indeed, he thought that the ideas we perceive are caused by things that are not ideas but that resemble ideas in respect of their large-scale quantitative features. But Locke is mistaken, for ideas can resemble only other ideas. This is known as the 'Likeness Principle'. Berkeley offers two (not entirely distinct) arguments for it here. The first is a straightforward appeal to introspection: Can you even imagine any sort of resemblance obtaining between an idea and something that is not an idea? The second deploys an exhaustive disjunction: Either we can perceive the external objects that supposedly cause our ideas or we cannot. If we can perceive them, then they must be ideas, as explained in Section 1 (there being no distinction between direct and indirect perception for Berkeley). If we cannot perceive them, then they are not ideas. And if they are not ideas, then they cannot resemble ideas, as reflection on examples illustrates: a colour can resemble only another colour, not something colourless; a sound can resemble only another sound, not something soundless. Since the sensible qualities—colour, sound, taste and so on—are ideas, it is evident that ideas can resemble only other ideas—specifically, ideas in the same sensory modality. Contrary to Locke, therefore, ideas cannot resemble anything outside the mind and so there are no 'pictures' of extra-mental reality.

---

8. **But say you** object to these views of mine that the only substances are spirits, and that bodies do not exist outside of minds: **though the ideas themselves**—the sensible qualities composing the objects we see—**do not exist without the mind,** you will say, there may **yet** be other things that do. For all I have shown, **there may be things** entirely distinct from perception—not ideas, but things very much **like them.** Indeed, following Locke (*Essay*, Book II, Chapter 8, Sections 7–26), you might suppose there are things outside the mind which impress themselves on our senses and cause our ideas, things **whereof** we have no sensory perception but which we imagine to bear some similarity to our perceptions: **they**— our ideas—**are** like **copies, or resemblances,** of things **which** are not themselves ideas, **things existing without the mind** and unperceived. These things we are supposing to resemble our ideas, on this story—whatever they are—you regard as existing **in an unthinking substance,** in mind-independent *matter.* You are assuming here that an idea can resemble something that is not an idea. To this **I answer,** there can be no resemblance between an idea and a non-idea. Indeed, I treat it as a principle that **an idea can be like nothing** else **but** another **idea; a**

colour or figure can be like nothing but another colour or figure. This is clear from introspection: **If** we each **look but ever so little into** our own **thoughts, we shall find it impossible for us to conceive** of any **likeness** or resemblance to obtain between things—**except** when comparing ideas. The **only** similarities we can even imagine are **between our ideas. Again, I ask whether those** external objects—the things you have **supposed** to be the **original** causes of our ideas—are perceivable or not? Are they, **or** any other **external things, of which our ideas are** merely **the pictures or representations,** supposed to **be themselves perceivable or not? If they are, then they are ideas,** since only ideas can be perceived, **and** in that case **we have** a relation of resemblance between ideas, rather than between ideas and non-ideas. If you grant that the originals are perceivable, therefore, we have **gained** you over to **our point** of view; **but if,** on the other hand, **you say** that **they are not** perceivable, you have said something incomprehensible. For **I appeal to any one** to tell me **whether it be** intelligible, whether it makes any sense at all, **to assert** that an idea of **colour**—a red sensation, for instance—**is like something which is** not a colour, not an idea, and therefore **invisible;** or whether an idea of **hard**ness **or soft**ness, say, is **like something which is** totally **intangible**—as a non-idea would have to be. The answer is clearly 'no'; **and** I can ask questions of this **sort** for ideas **of** taste and **the rest** of our senses. We may thus conclude that an idea can never resemble a non-idea existing outside of the mind.

Locke distinguishes the primary qualities of bodies from their secondary qualities. The primary qualities are those that are utterly inseparable from bodies, even in thought—their extension, figure, solidity and motion, etc. Secondary qualities of bodies are mere powers to produce ideas in us by virtue of their primary qualities. Ideas of primary qualities—our quantitative sensations, such as extension, figure, solidity and motion—are said to resemble their external causes, whereas ideas of secondary qualities—our qualitative sensations, such as colours, sounds, odours and tastes—are said to bear no resemblance to their external causes. Collapsing the distinction between qualities and ideas allows Berkeley to collapse the distinction between primary and secondary qualities as well. Since extension, figure, solidity and motion are ideas, they cannot exist without the mind in unthinking matter. And as ideas can be like nothing but other ideas, there can't be anything like extension, figure, solidity or motion existing outside us either.

---

9. Some philosophers **there are who** want to **make a distinction betwixt** the **primary and secondary qualities** of objects. **By the former,** the primary qualities, **they mean extension, figure, motion, rest, solidity or impenetrability and number; by the latter,** the secondary qualities, **they denote** and mean to include **all other sensible qualities,** such **as colours, sounds, tastes, and so forth. The ideas we have of these** secondary qualities **they acknowledge not to be the resemblances of** or have any similarity to **any thing existing without the mind or unperceived; but,** in contrast, **they will have our ideas of the primary qualities to be patterns or images of**—the very likeness of—**things which do exist without the mind,** allegedly **in** and as properties of **an unthinking substance**—a mindless sort of stuff **which they call 'matter'. By 'matter' therefore we are** meant **to understand an inert,** inactive and **senseless**—which is to say, a non-perceptive—**substance, in which** the qualities of **extension, figure, and motion do actually subsist** quite independently of their being perceived. **But it is evident from what we have already shown** in the previous sections **that extension, figure, and motion**—as things perceived by sense—**are only ideas existing in the mind, and that an idea can be like nothing but another idea,** a colour like a colour, a shape like a shape. This means that extension, figure and motion—which are ideas—can resemble only other ideas and **that consequently neither they** (the ideas) **nor their archetypes** (the things they are supposed to resemble) **can exist in** matter, **an unperceiving substance.** For perceptible qualities (which is what ideas are) cannot exist in non-perceptive substances and, of course, cannot resemble them. **Hence it is plain** to anyone who thinks about it **that the very notion** or concept **of what is called 'matter' or 'corporeal substance' involves a contradiction in it,** for it is supposed to be a non-perceptive thing in which ideas (extension, figure, motion) exist, when ideas by their very nature can exist only in perceptive things, which is to say, in minds.

Some philosophers—Locke, Bayle, Malebranche—want to place the quantitative features of things outside the mind and the qualitative features within. The shape and motion of a carriage, for instance, exist outside us, while its colour resides in the mind. But this partitioning of qualities into distinct realms cannot be maintained, as it is impossible to abstract shape and motion from colour. Wherever the one is, so is the other. And since the philosophers acknowledge that colour—a mere sensation—can only exist in a mind, the same must be true of motion and shape. The insight from Section 10 of the Introduction— that certain qualities are inseparably mixed in perception, conception and reality—is employed here to further undermine the traditional distinction between primary and secondary qualities. A limitation on the argument is that it does not apply to the common sense view that colours exist outside us.

10. **They who assert that figure, motion, and the rest of the primary or original qualities do exist without** being perceived, **they** who regard them

as **mind**-independent properties of matter, placing them **in unthinking substances** outside us, evidently reject one part of my view: They deny that all qualities exist in the mind. However, they **do at the same time** agree to the other part of my view: They **acknowledge that colours, sounds, heat, cold, and** other **such** qualitative features of things—what they **like** to call the 'secondary qualities'—**do not** exist outside the mind. On the contrary, these are features **which, they tell us, are** inseparable from perception, **sensations existing in the mind alone.** They insist, further, **that** the primary and secondary qualities are related: the secondary qualities, the sensations in the mind, **depend on and are occasioned** or caused **by the different** primary qualities of **size, texture and motion of the minute,** unobservable **particles of** mind-independent **matter. This** view about the relation between primary and secondary qualities, and the manner of their existence, **they take for an undoubted truth, which they** believe they **can demonstrate** for all cases and **beyond all exception. Now** I must object: The supposition that primary and secondary qualities exist in distinct realms—one set of qualities existing outside the mind, the other set in it—will not work **if it be certain that those** primary **original qualities are** inextricably connected to the secondary qualities. If the primary qualities are **inseparably united with the other** set of sensible **qualities,** if they are firmly conjoined with the secondary **and so not, even in thought, capable of being abstracted** and considered apart **from them, it plainly follows that** the primary qualities do not exist outside the mind apart from the secondary qualities: **they exist only in the mind** alongside them. Placing the two sets of qualities in distinct realms clearly presupposes the possibility of separating them. **But** simple introspection shows that they are not separable: **I desire**—indeed, I challenge—**any one** of my readers **to reflect and try,** and see **whether** or not **he can by any abstraction of thought, conceive of the** primary qualities, such as the **extension and motion of a body, without** at **all** conceiving of any **other sensible qualities.** Just try to picture for yourself an extended, moving body, say, an apple falling from a tree, without giving it a certain colour, say red. **For my own part,** when I attempt anything like this, **I see evidently that it is not in my power to** conceive or **frame an idea of** the primary qualities of **a body extended and moved,** without relying on the secondary qualities. I try to picture a colourless apple falling from a colourless tree, **but** find that **I must, with all** the primary qualities of the body in the image, also **give it some colour or other sensible quality, which is** the sort of thing **acknowledged** by all **to exist only in the mind. In short,** the primary qualities of **extension, figure, and motion, abstracted** and isolated **from all other** secondary **qualities, are inconceivable. Wherever, therefore, the other sensible qualities are**—wherever colour, sound, heat, cold and so on exist—**there must these** primary qualities **be also.** Since we've established already that the secondary qualities exist in the mind and we've now established that the secondary and primary qualities are inseparable, we must conclude that they both exist in the same place—namely, the mind. I appeal again **to the** reader's own experience for the proof: Since primary qualities can never be conceived **without** the secondary, it follows that they both exist **in the mind and no where else.**

Relational qualities such as the size and speed of an object exist in the mind, since their values depend on the position of the perceiver, the condition of her sense organs, her own relative motion and so on. So if extension existed without the mind, it would be distinct from all the relational qualities in the mind: It would be neither great nor small, neither swift nor slow, etc. But extension without size or motion is nothing. A materialist might retort that extension in general has no size or motion and can therefore exist outside the mind, apart from relational qualities. This move clearly relies on the theory of abstraction, which has been discredited already in the Introduction. Solidity must also exist in the mind, since it cannot be conceived apart from extension and extension exists within.

---

11. Let's consider the primary qualities now one by one, starting with extension, motion and solidity. **Again,** the modern philosophers admit that colours and sounds, odours and tastes exist only in the mind. Similarly, **great and small, swift and slow, are allowed** by everyone, not just by philosophers, **to exist no where without the mind, being entirely relative, and changing as the frame** of reference **or position of the organs of sense varies.** Whether something is big or small, whether a motion is swift or slow, depends on our perspective. The moon looks small from the earth, but it would look very big up close. Days go by slowly compared with minutes but swiftly compared with years. **The extension, therefore, which** philosophers say **exists without the mind, is neither great nor small,** since great and small are relative determinations existing only in the mind. And **the motion** they think exists outside the mind is **neither swift nor slow,** since swift and slow are also relative. This won't do, however, since extensions that are neither great nor small, motions that are neither swift nor slow aren't real—**that is** to say, **they are nothing at all. But say you** claim, rather, that **they are** talking about **extension in general, and motion in general,** rather than particular extensions and motions: **thus we see how much the tenet of extended, moveable substances existing without the mind, depends on that strange doctrine of *abstract ideas*,** which I refuted in the Introduction. For here you are trying to abstract extension and motion from everything concrete. **And here I cannot but remark** on a close resemblance between two very obscure notions, **how nearly the vague and indeterminate description of matter or corporeal substance,** which you invoke and **which the modern philosophers are** always **running into by** the use of **their own principles, resembles that antiquated and so much ridiculed notion of** prime matter (*materia prima*), **to be met with in Aristotle** (384–322 BC—*Metaphysics*, 1029a11–26) **and his followers.** Both notions amount to nothing. Now what about the primary quality of solidity? **Without extension, solidity cannot be conceived**—a solid thing necessarily takes up space; **since therefore it has been shown that extension exists not** outside **in an unthinking substance, the same must also be true of solidity.** They are mental things existing within.

Objects have numerical properties. For example, a book can have the property of being 1 inch thick and the property of being 1 pound in weight. But we might just as accurately have described the book as being 2.54 centimetres thick and weighing 0.453592 kilograms, since an inch is 2.54 centimetres and a pound is 0.453592 kilograms. We needn't even consider the thing as one book at all; we could view it as a thing of 100 pages or 100 000 words. Numerical properties clearly depend on our measures and perspectives. So numerical properties are qualities in the mind.

---

12. This holds for numbers as well. **That the number** of anything **is** an invention based **entirely** on **the** measure or method of counting, a **creature of the mind alone,** is perfectly obvious. To be sure, **even** if the reader disagrees with everything else I've said about primary qualities, he will accept my reasoning here. For **though these other qualities be allowed to exist without** a perceiver, it **will be evident to** everyone upon reflection that numbers depend on perspective. After all, **whoever considers that the same thing bears a different denomination of number, as the mind views it** differently, that it can be counted or measured **with** varying standards and in **different respects,** will see that there is no such thing as a number outside of a mind. **Thus,** take something whose length we can easily gauge—a yardstick, for instance. Now consider the different ways the stick can be measured: **the same extension**—the very same piece of wood—**is** properly valued at **one or three or thirty six, according as the mind considers it with reference to** the different units of length—**a yard, a foot, or an inch,** there being thirty six inches, or three feet, to every yard. Whether a thing is valued at one or three or thirty six, therefore, depends on our perspective. **Number is** indeed **so visibly relative and dependent on men's understanding, that it is strange to think how any one should give it an absolute existence without** and apart from **the mind.** And this is the case whether numbers are being used to measure extensions or qualities, or to count particular things. **We say,** for example, that there is **one book, one page,** one paragraph or **one line; all these** items **are equally units** and may be treated as one thing, but **though some** of them **contain several of the others:** The one book might contain 100 pages, 1 000 paragraphs, 10 000 lines, etc., so that we could just as easily have counted the thing as one book or 100 pages, as 1 000 paragraphs or 10 000 lines. **And in each instance** of measuring or counting **it is plain** that the same relativity obtains, since **the unit** we choose to count by **relates to** and is wholly dependent upon **some particular combination of ideas arbitrarily put together by the mind.**

Locke placed special emphasis on unity, believing it to be a simple idea accompanying all of our other perceptions. But he was wrong about this. If an idea of unity were always present, it would be the most familiar idea of all. Reflection reveals no such idea, however. So unlike solidity, extension, motion and number, which are ideas in the mind rather than properties of matter, unity is not even an idea.

---

13. Unity I know some philosophers **will have to be a simple or uncompounded idea, accompanying all other ideas into the mind** and suggested by them. This is the view of Locke (*Essay,* Book II, Chapter 16, Section 1). **That I have any such idea, answering to the word 'unity', I do not find; and if I had** an idea of unity, I would surely know it—**methinks I could not miss finding it** alongside all my other ideas by simply looking inside. **On the contrary, it should be the most familiar** idea **to my understanding** and the easiest to locate, **since it is said to accompany all other ideas, and to be perceived by all the ways of sensation and** in every act of **reflexion. To say no more, it is an** *abstract* **idea** corresponding to nothing in reality.

Several materialist philosophers have argued for the perceiver-dependence of certain sensible qualities such as hotness, coldness, colours and tastes. Their arguments take the fact of perceptual relativity as their starting point. For example, try soaking your left hand in cold water and your right hand in hot water. Then dip both hands into a bucket of water at room temperature. The left hand will now feel hot and the right hand will now feel cold. If hotness or coldness were properties of the water existing outside the mind, then we would be forced to conclude that the water has contradictory properties—it is both hot and cold at once. But this is impossible. So hotness and coldness are sensations in the mind of the perceiver. If arguments like this are valid, then the perceiver-dependence of primary qualities follows as well. The letters on this page look clear to your good eye and blurry to your bad eye; they appear small at a distance and large up close. The letters would have contradictory properties, if shape and size were mind-independent. So we infer that they are sensations. Materialist philosophers must accept this inference, on pain of inconsistency.

14. As for the primary qualities discussed in Section 10, **I shall farther add, that** in the same way and **after the same manner, as** Locke and the other **modern philosophers prove certain sensible qualities to have no** external **existence in matter, or without the mind, the same thing may be likewise proved**—making use **of** exactly the same arguments—to hold for **all other sensible qualities whatsoever** (see Locke's *Essay*, Book II, Chapter 8, Section 21). This includes the primary qualities these philosophers want to locate outside the mind, independent of perception. The very reasoning they employ to show that the purely qualitative features of things exist in the mind alone—I mean colours, tastes, smells, etc.—show that the quantitative features do as well—figure, shape, motion and so on. **Thus, for instance, it is said that heat and cold are** qualities merely felt, **affections only of the mind, and not at all** properties outside it. For no one acquainted with modern physics thinks our sensations of hot and cold are **patterns of real beings existing in the corporeal substances which excite them**; no philosopher supposes the felt quality of heat, or coldness, to exist in the fire, or the snow. They exist in the mind alone, **for that** is the only way to make sense of the fact that, under certain circumstances, **the same body which appears** to be **cold to one hand seems warm to another.** This happens, for example, when you touch a body after soaking one hand in warm water and the other in cold. On this point, the philosophers are entirely correct. **Now,** I ask, **why may we not as well argue** in precisely the same way **that** the primary qualities, which philosophers take to exist outside the mind, in fact exist in it? We could reason that **figure and extension are not patterns or resemblances of qualities existing in matter,** but rather exist in the mind only, **because to the same eye** placed **at different stations, or** to **eyes of a different** strength or **texture,** placed **at the same station, they appear** to be different figures having **various** extensions. A coin viewed from the side will look elliptical, for instance, whereas viewed from above it will seem circular; the yardstick will appear longer when viewed at one angle than at another. Our reasoning concerning heat and cold applies here too, **and** so do we not have a similar proof that figure and extension **cannot therefore**

be the mental **images of any thing** that has an absolute, **settled and determinate** existence **without** and apart from **the mind?** How could anyone who accepts this line of reasoning in the one case deny it in the other? **Again, it is proved** by modern philosophers **that sweetness is not really in the sapid thing because, the** sweet **thing,** even while **remaining unaltered** in itself, can take on a different flavour: **the sweetness is changed into bitter, as in the case of** someone who has **a fever or** an **otherwise** damaged and **vitiated palate** (compare Locke's *Essay*, Book II, Chapter 8, Section 19). **Is it not** just **as reasonable to say that motion is not** anything existing **without** and apart from **the mind?** Surely it's more reasonable**, since if** you start thinking more quickly, if **the succession of ideas in the mind** were to **become swifter, the motion** you experience**, it is acknowledged** by all**, shall appear slower without** there being **any alteration in any external,** moving **object.** What grounds could there be for applying these arguments selectively, for allowing the inference sometimes but not always?

The determinate qualitative features one perceives a sensible object to have— its colour, for instance, or its taste—vary with the conditions, relative to the perceiver, under which the object is perceived. Materialists infer from this fact that the perceived qualitative features of sensible objects do not exist without the mind. Berkeley points out that the same relativity holds for the perceived quantitative features of objects—their shape and size, for instance, also vary with the conditions of perception. So, by parity of reasoning, materialists should infer that the perceived quantitative features of sensible objects do not exist without the mind either. This doesn't prove that all existence is mind-dependent, but Berkeley thinks his earlier arguments do.

---

15. In short, let anyone consider those arguments, which are thought by materialists **manifestly to prove that colours and tastes exist only in the mind, and he shall find** that **they may** just as easily and **with equal force be brought** in and used **to prove the same thing of extension, figure, and motion**—that they too exist in the mind alone. **Though it must be confessed that this** demonstration from the relativity of perception is of limited significance. The **method of arguing** I employ here fails to establish that materialism is false: it **does not so much prove that there is no extension or colour in an outward object, as that we do not know by sense which is the true extension or colour of the object.** For all that is said here, there could be extension or colour of some sort in external objects. It just couldn't be the same extension or colour that we perceive through the senses, since these latter change depending on our perspective or the condition of our sense organs, and it's perfectly inconceivable that the properties of external objects could change simply as a result of changes in us. **But the arguments** offered previously in the **foregoing** sections do **plainly show** that materialism is false. For we have seen that colour and extension are bare ideas and have therefore acknowledged **it to be impossible that any colour or extension at all, or other sensible quality whatsoever,** could exist unperceived. That ideas **should exist in an unthinking subject without the mind, or in truth, that there should be any such thing as an outward object,** is totally beyond my comprehension.

In traditional ontology, the 'modes' or 'qualities' of a thing are distinguished from its 'substance' or 'substratum'. Qualities like 'redness' and 'roundness' cannot exist on their own. They must inhere in, and be supported by, a substance. 'Substratum' is the name for the supporting element of things. Materialists sometimes take matter to be the substratum of extension and the other qualities. But this reveals nothing about matter, since we have no conception at all of what a substratum is beyond the everyday meaning of the word 'support', which doesn't apply here. More precisely, to understand 'substratum', we must either (1) understand what it is in itself without reference to the qualities it supports, or (2) understand how it relates to those qualities. But (1) can be ruled out: Try to picture or otherwise conceive the substratum of an apple without adverting to its redness, roundness or any other quality; you will not succeed. And (2) can be ruled out as well: No one has managed to explain in plain terms how it is that a substratum 'supports' its qualities. Talk of 'substratum' is therefore empty. So if 'matter' is construed as 'substratum', we don't know what matter is.

---

16. **But let us examine a little** more closely **the received** and common **opinion** amongst philosophers, even though I have already exposed it as unintelligible. **It is said** that **extension is** a quality, **a mode or accident,** of mind-independent **matter, and that matter is** the stuff that underlies the extension—**the *substratum* that** takes it on and **'supports' it. Now I desire that you would explain** to me **what is meant by matter's 'supporting' extension,** because I find it meaningless and incomprehensible. I really have no idea what you're saying: Worse, I suspect that you don't either. But **say you** respond, more or less, as follows: **I have no idea of** what **matter** is like in itself. I characterize it only by reference to the qualities it supports, **and**

therefore **cannot** describe or **explain its** inner nature. **I answer,** that we can conceive of things either as they are in themselves or as they are in relation to other things. So, **though you** admit that you **have no positive** conception of the nature of matter, **yet if you have any meaning** in mind **at all** when you speak of it, **you must at least have a relative idea of matter; though you know not what it is** like in itself, **yet you must be supposed,** if we're going to allow you any understanding of matter, **to know what relation it bears to** extension and other **accidents, and what is meant by its 'supporting' them. It is evident that 'support' cannot here be taken in its usual** meaning or lit‑ eral **sense,** which is to prop or hold something up, **as when we say,** for exam‑ ple, **that pillars 'support' a building,** or that wheels 'support' a carriage: For matter doesn't rest beneath extension, or prop it up. **In what sense therefore must it be taken?** I doubt that you will find any sense here, and so the views of my opponents remain obscure.

When pressed for an account of 'material substance', philosophers will say that all they have in mind is the general idea of 'being' and the relational notion of 'support'. This is unhelpful, as 'being' is the least intelligible idea going and no explanation is offered of 'support'. And matter is an impossible thing anyway, since it is supposed to support outside the mind what can only exist in it— figure, extension, motion and so forth being qualities or ideas.

---

17. If we try to spell this out and **inquire into what the most accurate phi‑ losophers declare themselves to mean by 'material substance',** we won't get very far. On the contrary, **we shall find them acknowledge** that, when they say the words aloud, **they have no other meaning annexed to those sounds, but the idea of being in general, together with the relative notion of its supporting** the various sensible qualities or **'accidents'** that we perceive. But this explains nothing. **The general idea of being appears to me** to be **the most abstract and incomprehensible of all others;** it is just the empty idea of existence stripped of every individuating property. If that's what you mean by 'being', you haven't told me anything; **and as for its supporting accidents, this** phrase, **as we have just now observed, cannot be understood in the common sense of those words. It must therefore be taken in some other sense, but what that** sense is they who use the phrase **do not explain.** So that I am left to figure it out on my own. And **when I consider the two parts or branches which** go to **make up the signification of the words 'material sub‑ stance'** (namely, 'being' and 'supporter of accidents'), **I am convinced that**

they signify nothing, as **there is no distinct meaning annexed to** either of **them. But why should we trouble ourselves any farther, in discussing this** mysterious **material** *substratum* **or support of figure and motion, and other sensible qualities?** We have already shown it to involve a contradiction. **Does it not** conflict, after all, with what we've said before about figure and motion, which are bare ideas? Is it not to **suppose** that **they have an existence without the mind** in this hypothesized material substratum? Is that not equivalent to supposing that something mind-dependent is mind-independent? **And is not this a direct** contradiction, a **repugnancy, and altogether inconceivable?** We might as well talk about a square circle or a string quartet with five players. Such things cannot exist.

Even if material objects were possible, we could never know that they're actual. We would have to either (1) perceive them directly, or (2) reason to their existence from what we perceive directly. But (1) is a non-starter: We perceive ideas in our minds; we do not perceive matter. (2) is not viable either: We cannot deduce the existence of material objects from our perceptions, for everything we experience perceptually is perfectly consistent with there being no objects outside the mind. Dreams, hallucinations and radical sceptical scenarios show that we can have ideas corresponding to no external reality. So even if all the previous arguments fail, we'll still lack a decisive reason for believing in material objects.

---

18. But incoherence is not the only problem with materialism: **though** my arguments showed the hypothesis of material substance to be incomprehensible, there is, in addition, an epistemological worry to consider. Suppose **it were possible that solid, figured, moveable substances may exist without the mind** and unperceived. Suppose, moreover, we know what it means to say that there are external objects **corresponding to** and resembling **the ideas we have of bodies.** Even so, we still wouldn't have any reason for supposing it's true. Mind-independent material substances correspond to our ideas, according to materialists. And **yet how is it possible for us to know this?** There are just two possibilities: **Either we must know it by** direct **sense** perception, **or else** we know it **by reason**ing from sense perception. **As for our senses, I** have already shown in Section 1 that **by them we have the knowledge only of our sensations, ideas, or those things that are immediately perceived by sense, call them what you will. But they do not inform us that** any **things exist on** their own **without the mind, or** that there are **unperceived** things, bearing some **likeness to those** things **which are perceived. This** is a point **the materialists themselves** are willing to **acknowledge.** So the first manner of coming to know the existence of mind-independent things is ruled out. **It remains therefore that, if we** come to **have knowledge at all of external**, mind-independent **things, it must be** indirectly, **by** means of **reason**ing. The mind makes a step, in other words, from the observed to the unobserved, from sensations to substances, **inferring their existence from what is immediately perceived by sense. But what** process of **reason**ing **can** point us beyond our own perceptions and **induce us to believe in the existence of bodies without the mind,** completely independent of perception? How could any deduction **from what we** directly **perceive** prove demonstratively that there are mind-independent things? Isn't it rather unlikely there could be any such proof**, since** even my opponents, **the very patrons of** mind-independent **matter themselves, do not** pretend that **there is any necessary connexion betwixt them and our ideas,** no strict link such as would be required for a proof? For there to be a demonstrative proof, after all, a necessary connection must obtain between the start and the end points: it must not be possible for the premises to be true and the conclusion false. This is a basic principle of logic. And so, for there to be a demonstrative proof taking us from ideas—that which is perceived by sense— to the existence of mind-independent things—that which is not perceived—it would have to be impossible for the ideas to exist and the mind-independent things not to exist. However, **I say** that **it is granted on all hands (and what happens in dreams,** or delusional **phrensies, and the like, puts it beyond dispute) that it is possible** that **we might be affected with all the ideas we have now,** even **though no bodies existed without us, resembling them.** Dreams alone bear this out, as Descartes (1596–1650) made clear, since everyone agrees that in dreams we have ideas—say, of talking plants or flying turtles— without any such external things corresponding to them. **Hence it is evident** that **the supposition of external**, mind-independent **bodies is not necessary for the producing of our ideas, since it is granted** that **they are produced sometimes** from within, as in dreams**, and might possibly be produced always,** as in some elaborate delusion, **in the same order we see them in at present, without their** involvement, or there being any **concurrence** between the ideas and external things.

Positing material substance has no explanatory power. Though external bodies are not necessary for explaining the occurrence of sensations in us—we could have all of our perceptual experiences without them—materialists might think they provide a better explanation of perception than any competing hypothesis. But the problem of mind–body interaction is intractable, according to Berkeley, and so we gain nothing by postulating bodies. In addition, the materialist hypothesis is theologically dubious, since it has God creating a whole class of beings that are seemingly redundant.

19. We are granting for the sake of argument that external bodies are possible—though we have already shown that they are not—and we have pointed out that we could conceivably have all of the sensations we do have even if bodies did not in fact exist. **But though we might possibly have all our sensations without them,** we cannot conclude on *this* ground alone that they do not exist, only that they *might* not. And **yet** there is another argument for materialists to make, based on the fact that we do have sensations. For **perhaps it may be thought easier to conceive** the occurrence of our sensations **and explain the manner of their production by supposing** the existence of **external bodies in their likeness**—bodies resembling our ideas—**rather than otherwise; and so,** one could argue, **it might be at least probable** that **there are such things as bodies that excite their ideas in our minds** by acting on the senses. This would not be a demonstrative proof, but a sort of inference to the best explanation: while they can't be *proven* to exist, unseen bodies can be shown to *probably* exist because they are the best way of explaining the occurrence of sensations in us. **But neither can this be said. For though we give the materialists their external bodies**—just pretending that they are possible—a great mystery then arises, which no philosopher can explain: the problem of mind–body interaction. How could a body—which is material—affect a mind—which is not? What mechanism could possibly link two such disparate substances? The materialists don't tell us, for **they by their own confession are never the nearer to knowing how our ideas are produced, since** the causal connection **they** assume between bodies in space and ideas in the mind is completely opaque. Bodies can't push minds, or pull them. So how are they connected? Even the materialists **own themselves unable to comprehend in what manner** a **body can act upon a spirit, or how it is possible** that **it should imprint any idea in the mind. Hence** the inference to bodies as causes falls flat and no explanation is offered for how a body could even be a cause of ideas. So **it is evident** that **the production of ideas or sensations in our minds, can be no reason why we should suppose** the existence of **matter or corporeal substances, since that is acknowledged to remain equally inexplicable with, or without, this supposition. If, there-fore,** the materialist wants to posit bodies, it can't be for the purpose of explaining the occurrence of our sensations. Rather, he would have to just suppose that **it were possible for bodies to exist without the mind, and yet** without causing any ideas. But **to hold that they do so must** be a last resort. At the very least, it **needs to be** acknowledged that this is **a very precarious** and ill-supported **opinion, since it is to suppose, without any reason at all, that God has created innumerable beings**—the materialist's external objects—**that are entirely useless, and serve to no manner of purpose.** This supposition is not only unwarranted, but also an affront to God's intelligence. Why would God create something that serves no purpose? Why establish an order of totally superfluous beings? I modestly maintain that God is too wise to be wasteful.

There can be no conclusive arguments for the existence of mind-independent things, since any possible argument you can advance could also be advanced by a person living in a dream world. Imagine two possible worlds, A and B. A is a world where ideas are caused by external objects; B is a dream world with no external objects where ideas are caused by something immaterial— say, an evil demon. Suppose you live in A. Give your best argument for external objects. Someone living in B whose experiences are identical to yours could give the very same argument, for any difference in evidence could only come from a difference in experiences, and we are supposing that you and the person in B have indistinguishable experiences. This casts some doubt on the cogency of your arguments for external objects, since your experiences do not discriminate decisively between world A and world B.

---

20. In short, even **if there were external,** material **bodies, it is impossible** that **we should ever come to know it; and if there were not** any such bodies, **we might have the very same reasons to think there were that we have now.** Just consider it: **Suppose** there could be some subject having the very same conscious experiences that you do, but without those experiences being caused by external, material objects. In a vivid dream or an elaborate delusion, which is **what no one can deny** is **possible, an intelligence** could, **without the help of external bodies,** have the same kinds of sensations as you; it is as easily imaginable as it is possible for the intelligence **to be affected with the same train of sensations or ideas that you are, imprinted in the same order** or sequence, **and with like vividness** and clarity **in his mind.** Now **I ask whether that intelligence has not all the** same **reasons to believe in the existence of** external, **corporeal substances, represented by his ideas and exciting them in his mind, that you can possibly have for believing the same thing?** I think you must admit that in such a scenario the subject has the very same body of evidence that you have for the existence of external, material things. Indeed, on the basis of your evidence, how can you tell that it's not *you* who is in that scenario? **Of this there can be no question; which** means that the evidence we have fails to discriminate between there being external, material objects and there being no such objects. Whatever arguments you give for the existence of external bodies—however clever those arguments may be—can be produced with equal force by someone in the scenario just described. So what force can they possibly have? This **one consideration is enough to make any reasonable person suspect** his reasoning and doubt **the strength of whatever arguments he may think himself to have for the existence of bodies without the mind** causing his ideas. But I am being too generous in even considering the arguments a materialist might give, since I have shown materialism to be impossible.

Aside from all the theoretical reasons for rejecting materialism, there are also compelling practical reasons. Belief in the existence of matter has many unwelcome consequences, each one of which gives us a practical reason to resist it. Berkeley does not spell out the consequences here, since he will do so later, and because the theoretical reasons are more than sufficient.

---

21. Anyone who has followed the course of reasoning up to this point will agree that matter is impossible and that, even if it were possible, there would be no good reason to assume it. **Were it necessary to add any farther proof against the existence of matter, after what has been said, I could** cite, for instance, **several of those errors and difficulties (not to mention** the religious impieties) **which have sprung from that** strange **tenet** of the materialists— that there are bodies existing behind our ideas. **It has occasioned numberless controversies and disputes in philosophy**—about time, space, real existence, scepticism **and** many other things. As for our moral well-being, it has caused **not a few** controversies **of far greater** harm to the soul, and positively **momentous in religion**, including atheism, fatalism and the denial of immortality. **But I shall not enter into the details of them in this place,** both because I will do so later, **as well** as **because I think** that **arguments *a posteriori*,** which draw out the troubling implications of a view, **are unnecessary for confirming what has been, if I mistake not, sufficiently demonstrated** directly, or *a priori*. But, **as** I said, there's no need to dwell on the unwelcome consequences of postulating matter any further now, **because I shall hereafter find occasion to say somewhat** more **of them,** starting in Section 85.

Berkeley sets the bar for his opponents surprisingly low: If they can just conceive the possibility of matter's existence—if they can coherently imagine even a single material substance existing—he will grant them everything. No argument is required: *Without receiving the slightest reason for believing that there actually are any material beings, he would concede an entire world of them.*

22. I am afraid that **I have** been rambling on without reason and may have **given** my readers **cause to think me needlessly** wordy and **prolix in handling this subject. For** how is it going **to** help, and **what purpose is it** going to serve, if I continuously expand and **dilate on** a view **that** may be proven quite simply? Should I carry on trying to establish by elaborate argumentation that there are no mind-independent things when I know this to be a simple truth **which may be demonstrated with the utmost** clarity, on the basis of irrefutable **evidence, in a** single **line or two, and to any one that** has any intelligence at all or **is capable of the least reflexion? It** is surprisingly easy to show that there are no mind-independent things. Nothing **but** a little introspection is required, simply **looking into your own thoughts, and in so** doing **trying to see whether you can conceive it possible for a sound, or figure, or motion, or colour, to exist without** any connection to **the mind, or** whether you can imagine it existing **unperceived.** So? Can you? **This easy trial may make you see, that what you contend for** in insisting on the existence of mind-independent things **is a downright contradiction,** as explained earlier in Sections 5 to 7. I am confident that this proof is decisive. **Insomuch that I am content to put the whole** debate in the following simple terms and to rest my entire case **upon this** single **issue: if you can but conceive it possible for one extended moveable substance** to exist independently of the mind, **or in general, for any one idea or any thing like an idea, to exist otherwise than in a mind perceiving it, I shall readily give up the cause** and consider myself refuted. **And as for** that imagined collection of material substances lurking behind our sensations, **all that** *compages* **of external bodies which you contend for, I shall grant you its existence** too. Just show me that it's *possible* for a mind-independent thing to exist and I'll agree that it does, even **though you cannot either give me any reason why you believe it** actually **exists, or assign any use to it**—though you can think of no role for it to play—**when it is supposed to exist. I say, the bare possibility of your opinion's being true shall pass for an argument that it is so.** This is generosity indeed! Could you imagine, by comparison, someone granting you that a centaur exists just because you convinced them that centaurs are *possible*, though you produced not a scrap of evidence for their *actual* existence? I'm stacking the deck strongly in favour of materialism here. But I am positive that materialists will be unable to show even the possibility of mind-independent things.

The materialist may want to push back like this: 'I can picture a pair of red shoes existing unperceived in my suitcase. In fact, I'm picturing them there *right now. So there is more to being than being perceived. There is also existing unperceived'. Berkeley's response is to point out that the materialist herself is perceiving the shoes—she perceives them inasmuch as she frames ideas of their qualities in her mind. This has been called the 'master argument', since Berkeley is willing to place all his money on it.*

23. But say you argue like this: If I can imagine something, it must be possible. And **surely there is nothing easier than to imagine trees, for instance, in a park, or books existing in a closet, and no body** nearby **to perceive them.** Since I can imagine them, therefore, external bodies are possible. To that **I answer, you may** do so: You can imagine trees in a park, or books in a closet, without imagining that someone else is there to perceive them. I admit that **there is no difficulty in it; but** this won't get you any closer to proving that external bodies are possible. For **what is all this** imagining of trees in a park or books in a closet, **I beseech you, more than framing in your mind certain ideas which you call 'books' and 'trees', and at the same time omitting to frame the idea of any one that may perceive them? But** though you may contemplate books and trees without forming the idea of an observer, an observer is always present. Did you fail to notice your own presence? Are the books you are imagining all alone in the closet? Are the trees all alone in the park? Or **do not you your self perceive or think of them all the while? This** imagining of books without a perceiver, **therefore, is** beside the point and **nothing to the purpose; it only shows** that **you have the power of imagining or forming ideas** of books **in your** own **mind. But it does not show that you can** imagine, or **conceive it possible,** that **the objects of your thought may exist without the mind.** Picturing trees in a park is not the same thing as picturing absolute, material existence, after all, which is what I am challenging you to do. What you will find, if you attempt it, is actual and possible perceptions—but no matter. **To make out** the possibility of your opinion's being true, **this** much, at least, is required: **it is necessary that you** picture external objects perceived by absolutely no one, to **conceive them existing unconceived or unthought of, which is a manifest repugnancy** and the most obvious contradiction. **When we do our utmost to conceive the existence of external bodies, we** must resort to sensible images of such things—we picture coloured, shaped things located in the vicinity of other coloured, shaped things. We **are** thus **all the while only contemplating our own ideas.** For what are colour and shape, if not ideas in the mind? **But the mind, taking no notice of itself** and overlooking its own presence, **is** tricked, even **deluded, into think**ing that **it can and does conceive bodies existing unthought of or without the mind; though at the same time they are apprehended by or exist in** the mind it self—the very mind that set out to conceive them. **A little attention** to your own ideas should make this plain. Try to picture books in the closet and you **will discover** that you are there too, perceiving them from one perspective or another. Simple reflection will reveal **to any one the truth and evidence of what is here said, and make it unnecessary to insist on any other proofs against the existence of material substance.** What other proof do you expect after it has been shown that you can neither sense nor imagine matter?

The materialist insists on the 'absolute existence' of things outside the mind. There are only two ways of understanding this 'absolute existence' outside the mind: either (1) we are to imagine some particular thing existing outside the mind, or (2) we are to imagine something or other in general existing outside the mind. But (1) won't work: it would mean having in mind a thing that is not in mind—a patent contradiction. And (2) won't work either: it would mean having an idea with no content. Just try to form the idea of something or other in general existing outside the mind—you will come up with absolutely nothing. What the materialist insists on is either a contradiction or meaningless. There is thus no coherent way of understanding the 'absolute existence' of things outside the mind.

---

24. It is very obvious that words are sometimes used without any meaning. And we should be able to tell, **upon the least inquiry into our own thoughts,** whether or not we're using a term sensibly. The question we must ask is simply this: Do we have anything definite, or coherent, in mind when we use the term? Here we want **to know** specifically **whether it be possible for us to understand what is meant by the 'absolute existence of sensible objects in themselves, or without the mind'.** The expression could be taken in one of two ways: Either I'm trying to imagine the absolute existence of some *particular* sensible object without the mind, or else I'm trying to conceive the existence of *something or other in general* that exists without the mind. **To me it is evident that those words make out either a direct contradiction, or else** they are completely empty and so mean **nothing at all.** When we try to picture some *particular* object existing without the mind, we run into the contradiction: There we are perceiving the thing in our mind, though we were trying to imagine something existing independently of minds. When we try to conceive of *something or other in general* existing without the mind, we find that we cannot supply the supposed idea with any intuitive content. The only way to flesh the thought out is in terms of actual or possible perceptions, but we can't do that without bringing in a mind to hold the perceptions—which of course doesn't get us beyond the mind. So we really can't flesh it out. We thus have a completely empty thought—in other words, no thought at all. **And to convince others of this, I know no readier or fairer way, than to entreat** them to reflect on what's happening in their own mind when they utter these words. All I ask is that **they would calmly attend to their own thoughts** and tell me what, if anything, comes to mind when they say 'absolute existence of sensible objects'; **and if by this attention** to their own thoughts **the emptiness** or inconsistency—the utter hollowness **or repugnancy—of those expressions does appear,** then **surely nothing more is requisite** to convince them that the words mean nothing: **for their conviction** will be based on their own inability to make any sense of them. **It is on this therefore that I insist, to wit, that 'the absolute existence of unthinking things' are** either (1) **words without a meaning, or** (2) words **which include a contradiction. This is what I** want to instil in your mind, so I **repeat** the point **and inculcate** it. Try to attach any clear meaning to the words that doesn't implicate actual or possible perceptions, **and** that doesn't involve the presence of your own mind in the background. I **earnestly recommend** this exercise **to the attentive thoughts of the reader.**

Atomistic or 'corpuscularian' materialists believe that our sensations are caused by tiny bits of matter impacting on our sense organs. But the atomistic theory is untenable. The atoms they envision are extended particles of various shapes and sizes moving about in space and affecting our senses. But extension, figure and motion cannot cause sensations, since they are ideas and ideas are causally inert. Were ideas capable of acting or doing anything, we would know it, since the existence, nature and content of our own ideas is transparent to the mind. This is Berkeley's famous transparency thesis. Attending to our ideas, then—whose properties we can gauge accurately—we find that they are passive and therefore incapable of producing sensations. So the atomistic theory of perception can't get off the ground.

25. All our ideas, sensations, or the things which we perceive, are completely inert. Rocks, trees, water, houses—**by whatsoever names they may be distinguished**—these things are, in a certain sense, dead. They **are visibly inactive; there is nothing of power or agency included in them, so that one idea or object of thought cannot produce, or make any alteration in another.** Ideas possess no causal powers whatever. **To be satisfied of the truth of this** claim, **there is nothing else requisite but a bare** observation of our own **ideas.** Just think about what an idea is—call one up and inspect it. You will instantly recognize that ideas are passive. **For since they and every part of**

them exist only in the mind, it follows that they are open to mental scrutiny and have no properties inaccessible to our mental gaze; so **there is nothing in them but what is perceived.** How could there be, if they are only ideas? Ideas are, in this sense, *transparent* to us. **But whoever shall attend to his ideas, whether of sense or of reflexion, will not perceive in them any power or activity; there is therefore no such thing contained in them**—and therefore no such power or activity in sensible objects either, which are just collections of ideas. **A little attention will discover to us that the very being of an idea implies passiveness and inertness in it, insomuch that it is impossible for any idea to do any thing, or, strictly speaking, to be the cause of any thing;** the idea of red doesn't *do* anything to the idea of blue, and the idea of a rock doesn't *do* anything to the idea of a window. It's just one idea following another. A boat goes down the stream. Where is the power? I don't see any. I can't even imagine what it would be like for one idea to *affect* another. Furthermore, since *representation* occurs only by way of resemblance, and since ideas resemble only other ideas, there is no way for an idea to represent anything other than an idea. So an idea can **neither** cause anything, nor **can it be the resemblance or pattern of any active being, as is evident from Section 8,** where I introduced my likeness principle. **Whence it plainly follows that** the corpuscularian philosophers are mistaken in identifying **extension, figure and motion** as the external cause of sensation; they **cannot be the cause of our sensations,** since extension, figure and motion are just ideas and ideas are wholly passive. To attribute causal efficacy to ideas, to posit a vital principle in bodies, is to ensoul them—a category mistake committed most famously by Gottfried Wilhelm Leibniz (1646–1716). **To say, therefore, that these** sensations **are the effects of powers resulting from the configuration, number, motion, and size of corpuscles** makes no sense, and **must certainly be false.**

Ideas succeed each other constantly in our minds. Their existence and variation require an explanation. There are three candidate explanations: Ideas might be caused by (1) other ideas, (2) a material substance, or (3) an immaterial substance. (1) is defeated by the reflection that ideas cannot be causes; (2) is excluded on the grounds that material substances are impossible. We may thus infer by elimination that the cause of our ideas is (3) an immaterial substance or mind.

---

26. We perceive a continual succession of ideas in our minds, like a current of moving images. This is what it is like to be conscious. For example, you might now be undergoing various sensations—seeing the dark surface of your table, hearing a bird chirping in the tree, perhaps tasting the sweetness of your tea. In the stream of your sensations, **some** are like flashes, some **are** like bangs— **anew excited,** and appearing suddenly; **others are** like fading pictures, colours or sounds that dwindle and are gradually **changed, or** that **totally** die away and **disappear** from consciousness, only to be replaced immediately by others. They don't come from nowhere. **There is therefore some cause of these ideas,** something that brings them into being and coordinates them. This is simple causal reasoning: Ideas exist and pass before the mind, so I posit some stable foundation **whereon they depend, and which** continually **produces and changes them. That this cause** which I infer **cannot be any quality or idea or combination of ideas, is** already **clear from the preceding section** where it was shown that ideas, being wholly passive, are powerless to produce anything. **It must therefore be a substance** that creates our ideas and varies them. **But it has been shown** in Section 17 **that there is no corporeal or material substance** and so material substance cannot be the cause of our ideas; **it remains therefore that the cause of ideas is an incorporeal active substance or** disembodied **spirit.** In short, the succession of ideas in our minds must have a cause. The cause must be either (1) some other ideas in ours or another mind, (2) a material substance, or (3) an immaterial substance. But we have shown that ideas cannot be causes— that rules out (1)—and that material substances are impossible—that takes care of (2). So the cause of ideas is (3), an immaterial substance or spirit.

To have an idea of mind or spirit is impossible. One thing, A, can represent another thing, B, only if A bears at least some resemblance to B. The mind is an essentially active thing—its nature consists in the activities of understanding and willing. An idea is an essentially passive thing—its nature consists in being perceived. A wholly active thing and a wholly passive thing are utterly disparate; there is no resemblance between them. So an idea cannot represent a mind. We infer other minds from their effects. And we know our own minds— we have some 'notion' of them—just insofar as we engage in mental activity.

---

27. A spirit, or mind, **is one simple, undivided, active being**—a substantial unity and a centre of force—but it manifests its activity in two different forms. **As it perceives ideas, it is called the 'understanding'.** When I look around my study, I see my desk, my books **and** my teapot. In taking all of this in, my mind exercises its power of *understanding*. This is one form of mental activity. The other form of mental activity occurs when the spirit exercises its power of *willing*. I can call up and manipulate ideas at will: Right now I'm thinking of a church; now I'm thinking of a church on fire. As the spirit controls ideas, **as it produces or otherwise operates about them, it is called the 'will'.** Its essence, in understanding and in willing, is *activity*. **Hence,** according to our likeness principle, **there can be no idea formed of a soul or spirit; for all ideas whatever, being** essentially **passive and inert, they cannot represent unto us, by way of** an **image or a likeness, that which acts. A little attention will make it plain to any one that to have an idea, which shall be like** a mind—that **active principle of motion and change,** that manipulator **of ideas**—defies the nature of each, **and is absolutely impossible.** A spirit is by nature active. An idea is by nature passive. To *represent* a spirit, an idea would need to *resemble* it. But an active being and a passive being are as diverse as any two things can be, and an idea can only be like another idea. And thus it is readily understood why there can be no idea of spirit. **Such is the nature of *spirit*, or that which acts, that it cannot become its own object,** a passive thing, and so cannot **itself be perceived.** A mind is never *perceived* directly, **but only** indirectly, **by the effects**—that is to say, by the ideas—**which it produces.** We make a very quick inference to other minds, in other words, and the process is called 'perception' only by courtesy, since to perceive is to have an idea and we have no idea of mind (see Section 145). **If any man shall doubt of the truth of what is here delivered, let him but reflect and try if he can frame the idea of any power or active being;** let him try to *picture* power **and** *imagine* a spirit. Let him ask **whether he has ideas of the two principal powers** of the mind, **marked** above **by the names 'will' and 'understanding', where those ideas are distinct from each other as well as from a third idea of substance or being in general.** Does he have the idea of a mental substance, **with a relative notion of its supporting or being the subject of the aforesaid powers,** 'willing' and 'understanding'? He must try to picture this willing and understanding thing, **which is signified by the name 'soul' or 'spirit'. This is what some hold** can be done; **but so far as I can see, the words 'will', 'soul', 'spirit', and 'mind' do not stand for different ideas or, in truth, for any idea at all, but for something which is very different from ideas, and which** is always the *perceiver*, rather than the *perceived*. This being, as **an agent, cannot be like unto, or represented by, any idea whatsoever. Though it must be owned at the same time, that,** lacking **an idea, we still have some notion of soul, spirit, and the operations of the mind, such as willing, loving, hating;** we know the active powers of the mind in the exercise of them, but no further. Mental pictures of active beings are simply not possible. We therefore know spirit only **in as much as we know or understand the meaning of those words** 'willing', 'loving' and 'hating'.

The mind is a powerful, active being: It conjures up ideas in the imagination by a simple act of will, and does away with them just as easily. We know this from experience. It makes no sense to speak of something other than a mind acting, or of something acting by any means other than will.

28. The extent of my will—the scope of its power—is fairly broad indeed. **I find I can excite ideas in my mind at pleasure:** I call them up on a whim, **and vary and shift the** perceptual **scene as often as I think fit. It is** an easy and effortless performance: The whole thing requires **no more than willing** some idea into being, **and straightway this or that idea arises in my** imagination exactly as I **fancy it; and by the same power** I can lay the idea aside and redirect the mind. Thereupon the image is whisked away: **it is** immediately **obliterated, and makes way for another** idea which promptly takes its place. Say I want to imagine a golden carriage: The image pops into my mind. And the carriage turning white? There it is already. Now I want to think of a church: The carriage is gone and a church appears. **This** remarkable feat of the mind, in the **making and unmaking of ideas, does very properly denominate** *action*: It is **the mind** considered as an **active** being. **Thus** we may say that this **much is certain:** The mind has a power to conjure up various ideas, **and** also to suppress them. Knowledge of this fact is **grounded on** our own **experience** of the mind's activity: We feel this power over ideas all the time. Minds alone have power, however. Activity, it must be remembered, is limited to mental substances; **but when we** speak loosely and **talk of unthinking agents** doing things, **or of** their **exciting ideas** mechanically (calling them up **exclusive of volition**), we're talking a lot of rubbish—**we only amuse our selves with words** that literally don't mean anything.

Though the mind is able to call up and eliminate ideas of the imagination, it has no control over what it perceives in sensation. When conditions for perception are favourable—when the organs are working properly and the perceiver is suitably positioned—sensations occur automatically. No act of will is required, and none can prevent the ideas from appearing. So there is a cause distinct from the agent. But that cause is neither an idea nor a material substance. It is therefore an immaterial substance.

29. But whatever power I may have over my own thoughts through the use of imagination, **I find** that I have no power over **the ideas actually perceived by sense.** They occur without my help, and **have not a like dependence on my will.** I can keep my eyes closed, if I like, or stop up my ears. But remove the obstruction and ideas pour in. **When in broad daylight I open my eyes,** for instance, **it is not in my power to choose whether I shall see** something **or not, or to determine what particular objects shall present themselves to my view.** Trees, rivers, clouds—there they are in front of me whether I want to see them or not; **and so likewise as to the** faculty of **hearing and the other** three **senses, the ideas imprinted on them are not** a matter of choice. Were they **creatures of my will,** I could control them. So where do the ideas of sense come from? They don't come from other ideas, since ideas are passive and passive things produce nothing. They don't come from matter, since matter is impossible. And my will has no effect on them at all. **There is therefore** an immaterial cause, **some other will or spirit** distinct from me **that produces** and sustains **them.**

The final step in Berkeley's 'sensation generator' argument for the existence of God is introduced. In Section 26, we learned that only a mind can generate ideas. In Section 29, we learned that the mind generating ideas of sense must be distinct from our own. The strength and supreme coordination of sensations suggest that this mind is exceedingly wise and good—attributes associated with divinity.

---

30. **The ideas of sense,** which strike us immediately when we open our eyes, **are more strong, lively, and distinct than** memories and **those** creations **of the imagination** that depend on our will. The rocks and trees I see when I walk to the church are much sharper and better defined than the kitchen or closet I remember or the dungeons and dragons I imagine. **They have likewise a steadiness, order, and coherence, and are not** brought about or **excited at random, as those** ideas **which are the effects of human wills often are.** When I think back to dressing in my bedchamber this morning, my mind darts from one thing to another. I remember tying my shoes and then suddenly I'm thinking about my breakfast. Without warning I picture myself in a chariot race or clashing with a Roman soldier. These ideas come and go in only partly discernible patterns; they are never wholly systematic. The ideas of sense, by contrast, are neither fleeting nor erratic, **but** occur **in a regular train or series, the admirable connexion** and beautiful coordination **whereof sufficiently testifies to the** great **wisdom and benevolence of its Author,** who, we infer, is God. **Now the set of rules or established methods, wherein the** divine **mind we depend on excites in us the ideas of sense** and according to which they are ordered, **are called the 'laws of nature'; and these** laws **we learn by** everyday **experience** as well as by more systematic empirical investigation, **which teaches us that such and such ideas are** always **attended** and go along **with such and such other ideas in the ordinary course of things.** Consider a

simple example: I toss my hat on the floor. What really happened here? One cluster of ideas—those composing my hat—moved towards another cluster of ideas—those composing the floor. How did I know that the hat would tend towards the floor rather than towards the ceiling? Experience taught me the rules by which God coordinates sensations.

The rules in accordance with which sensations are governed are learned through experience. We can make predictions on their basis and thus organize our lives rationally. Without regularity and the ability to recognize patterns in nature we would be unable to perform even the simplest of tasks.

31. **This** orderliness in the stream of sensations **gives us** a means of navigation. On its basis we produce **a sort of** guidebook to nature in which we record her laws and chart her effects. We observe the patterns and remember them. We gain **foresight** with experience, and start to predict **which** sensory ideas will be followed by which others. This **enables us to regulate our actions for the benefit of life**—to pilot our ship, as it were, and to plot our own course. **And without this** predictive power **we should be** unable to plan—unable even to move—**eternally at a loss** for what to do. **We could not know how to act** so as to bring about **any thing that might procure** for us the least pleasure, or **remove the least pain of sense. That food nourishes,** we must learn. That **sleep refreshes, and** that **fire warms us** is a matter of experience; **that to sow in the seed-time is the way to reap in the harvest** is something we ascertain through trial **and** observation. To know, **in general, that to obtain such or such ends, such or such means are** required or **conducive; all this we know, not** in advance, but **by** studying nature carefully. It is not through **discovering any necessary** or fixed **connexion between our ideas** that we learn, since there is none, **but only by the observation of the settled laws of nature, without which we should be all in uncertainty and confusion.** If there were no orderliness in our ideas and no laws, then you couldn't build a carriage **and** you couldn't cook your food: **a grown man** would **no more know how to manage himself in the affairs of life than an infant just born** can tie a shoe.

The total synchronization of sensations in an orderly system of nature is strong evidence for the existence of God, according to Berkeley. But many people misconstrue this evidence: They look for causes of order within the order of nature itself.

One idea, B, is observed to follow another idea, A, with strict regularity. Instead of attributing this regularity to God's will, there is a tendency to regard A as the cause of B. But this is an error, since no idea can have any effect upon any other.

32. And yet this consistent uniform working of the settled laws of nature can often prove a distraction. The regularity and flawless coordination of our experiences, **which so evidently displays the goodness and wisdom of** God—and should satisfy us beyond doubt with regard to providence—will often divert our thoughts from God rather than pointing us to him. Surely God is **that governing spirit whose will constitutes the laws of nature,** and whose concern for us is evidenced most clearly in the order and constancy of our experiences. But owing to weakness of the intellect, this order and constancy **is so far from leading our thoughts to** the contemplation of **him,** and to appreciation of his goodness, **that it rather sends them** off in another direction, **wandering after** material causes. Rather than seeing God's hand at work in arranging our experiences so wisely, we attribute the order to material things, which are meant to be **secondary causes,** intermediate between God (the original cause) and our ideas (the effects). **For when we perceive certain ideas of sense** to be **constantly followed by other ideas** of sense, **and when we know** that **this** uniformity **is not of our** own **doing,** we hesitate to invoke a designer. Instead, we immediately and **forthwith attribute the power and agency** behind the regularity **to the** relevant **ideas themselves**—construed, normally, as material things—**and make** the **one** idea **the cause of another.** But as I explained in Section 25, this is a view **than which nothing can be more absurd and unintelligible,** for ideas are totally inert, and so one idea can never produce, or make a change, in any other. But the passivity of ideas escapes our notice. **Thus,** we have a tendency to reason as follows: After undergoing experiences of a uniform kind—**for example,** after **having observed that when we perceive by sight a certain round luminous figure, we at the same time perceive by touch the idea or sensation called 'heat'**—we try to identify connections, and **we do from thence conclude,** incorrectly, the round luminous figure—I mean, of course, **the sun—to be the cause of heat. And in like manner,** after first **perceiving the motion and collision of bodies to be attended** always **with** a banging or thumping **sound, we are inclined to think the latter**—the banging or the thumping—is **an effect of the former**—the collision of the bodies. But as we have seen, ideas—such as motion—are incapable of producing other ideas—such as sound—and so this way of thinking, though natural, is fallacious.

Subscribing to an ontology of ideas does not prevent one from drawing a principled distinction between appearance and reality: We encounter real things

in sensation and contemplate illusory things in the imagination. The marks of reality to be found in sensation are greater intensity and stability, greater coordination and less dependence on individual volition.

33. Perhaps we should clarify our ontology by drawing a distinction. I recognize two classes of perceptible things: **The ideas imprinted on the senses by the Author of nature are called 'real things'; and those excited in the imagination** are mere appearances: **being less regular, vivid, and constant, these** latter **are more properly termed 'ideas', or 'images of things', which they copy and represent. But then our sensations, be they never** mistaken for ideas of the imagination, since they are **so vivid and distinct** by comparison, still have something essential in common with them. Despite their greater force and vivacity, sensations **are nevertheless *ideas*, that is, they exist in the mind, or are perceived by it,** just **as truly as the ideas of its own framing** do. Though everything perceptible is ultimately mental, there are good grounds for insisting on this distinction between *sensations*, or real things, and *ideas*, or images of things. **The former—ideas of sense—are allowed to have more reality in them, that is, to be more strong, orderly, and coherent than the** latter—the **creatures of the** human **mind; but** though sensations have more reality than images, **this is no argument that they exist without the mind.** The distinction between *real things* and *images of things* can be drawn *within the mental realm*. Indeed, it must be, since no objects exist without the mind. We have identified two criteria of reality thus far: (1) ideas of sense are more forceful and steady than ideas of the imagination; (2) ideas of sense exhibit greater coherence and order than ideas of the imagination. But we can add a third real-making feature possessed by the ideas of sense: **They are also (3) less dependent on the spirit or thinking substance which perceives them.** They are less subject to our voluntary control, in other words, **in that they are excited by the will of another and more powerful spirit.** We cannot just call them up and shake them off as we do with ideas of the imagination. **Yet still they are *ideas*,** their greater reality notwithstanding, **and certainly no *idea*, whether faint or strong, can exist otherwise than in a mind perceiving it.**

The principal arguments for idealism are now complete. To further corroborate his claims, Berkeley next considers objections—12 in total—which he explains and answers in turn. The first objection is that idealism does away with the ordinary objects of sensory experience: If sensible objects are clusters of ideas in the mind, then they are not real and everything is reduced to illusion. There

are no real things, on this interpretation of idealism—no tables, no chairs, no apples, no snakes. In response, Berkeley observes that the intra-mental existence of perceptual objects in no way implies the ontological equality of all ideas, or that none of them qualify as real. Though real things are clusters of ideas in the mind, they are distinct, highly organized, interrelated clusters existing independently of our will. In these respects, they contrast sharply with ideas merely imagined.

34. Before we proceed any farther with our investigation, **it is necessary to spend some time in answering** the various **objections which may probably be made against** our system: **the principles** we have **hitherto laid down** are certain, but I must consider how they might be attacked. **In doing of which** I must apologize a little, **if I seem too prolix** and long-winded **to those** learned readers **of quick apprehensions** who have already grasped my meaning and can answer objections themselves. However, **I hope it may be pardoned** if I spell the objections out and formulate solutions, **since** I am hoping to reach a wider audience and **all men do not equally apprehend things of this** philosophical **nature.** Those who misunderstand my position may reject it in view of some difficulty they can't get around; **and I am willing** to spend some time addressing their worries, since I am eager **to be understood by every one. First then,** is the worry that our ontology is too sparse: **it will be objected that, by** assuming **the foregoing principles** to the effect that there are no mind-independent things, we have surrendered the world around us. If there is nothing mind-independent, **all that is real and substantial in nature is banished out of the world, and instead thereof** we find a global illusion; a counterfeit, **chimerical scheme of ideas takes the place** of the real world of things. **All things that exist,** according to our principles, turn out to **exist only in the mind, that is, they are purely notional** and imaginary. **What therefore becomes of the sun, moon, and stars? What must we think of houses, rivers, mountains, trees, stones; nay, even of our own bodies? Are all these** objects nothing **but so many chimeras and illusions of the** mind, mere creatures of the **fancy?** Since the sun, the moon, houses and rivers are all real things, according to the objection, principles implying otherwise must be false. But I reject this line of reasoning. **To all that which the objection alleges, and** against **whatever else of the same sort may be objected,** there is indeed a ready reply: **I answer, that by** assuming **the principles premised** above, **we** are not denying the existence of the world around us, and we **are not deprived of any one thing in nature. Whatever we see, feel, hear, or any wise conceive or understand,** all the choir of heaven and furniture of the earth, **remains as secure as ever, and is as real as ever. There is** what is called in Latin a *rerum natura,* a nature of things, and a natural order, independent of thought, **and so the distinction** that everyone recognizes **between realities and** illusory **chimeras retains its**

full force in our system. **This is evident from Sections 29, 30, and 33, where we have shown what is meant by** *real things* **in opposition to** *chimeras,* **or ideas of our own framing.** Though both are mind-dependent, real and imaginary things are easily distinguished; real things impress themselves more forcefully upon us, they are more orderly and fixed in their relations, and they have no dependence on our will for their existence. The criticism goes wrong in thinking that the distinction between the real and the imaginary collapses if all things exist in the mind; **but then** the objection is right to suppose that **they both** do **equally exist in the mind, and in that sense,** while real and imaginary things are different kinds of ideas, they **are** each **alike** in being *ideas.*

***

The ontology of idealism and the ontology of common sense are precisely the same. Ask a farmer what exists: She will point to things like cows, wagons, churches and tomatoes. Ask a philosopher: She will say, 'Matter'. Berkeley sides with the farmer. Dropping matter from our ontology means dropping a word. Not a single object is lost.

***

35. I do not argue against the existence of any objects postulated by common sense. Are there trees? Yes. Churches and rivers? Of course. Not **one thing that we can apprehend, either by sense or reflexion,** is lost on my principles. **That the things I see with mine eyes and touch with my hands do exist, really exist,** I admit fully and **make not the least question. The only thing whose existence we deny is that which philosophers call 'matter' or 'corporeal substance'.** It is their special delusion. No farmer believes in unperceived corporeal substances—no blacksmith, no priest, no barrister. Here I gladly part company with the philosopher and assert that matter is an impossible fiction. **And in the doing of this,** the repudiating of matter, **there is no damage done to the rest of mankind, who, I dare say, will never miss it.** For how can they miss what they never thought was there? The mill keeps on turning and the grain is still ground. The trees scratch the gables and the sun warms the road. Do we need matter for any of this to happen? Rubbish! **The atheist indeed will want** to retain **the** word, **colour**ing his rejection **of** God and immortal souls with **an empty name,** trying everything he can think of **to support his impiety**—proclaiming loudly, 'Nothing but matter! Everything perishes!' This is utter foolishness; **and the philosophers,** who are no better, **may possibly find,** that **they have lost** an opportunity for making noise about nothing—**a great handle,** or lever, **for** their **trifling and disputation.** But I'm not going to bother about people who propound absurdities.

Berkeley summarizes the idealist conception of reality. A real thing is a combination of vivid, constant and well-ordered ideas impressed on our minds by God. An imaginary thing is a combination of faint, fleeting and disordered ideas concocted by us. The tables, chairs, apples and snakes we encounter in sensation are every bit as real on Berkeley's system as they are on the view of any other philosopher.

---

36. If any man thinks that **this detracts from the existence or reality of things,** he is mistaken. Anyone who equates the denial of matter with the denial of reality distorts my words and puts a new meaning on them: **he is so very far from understanding what has been premised** above **in the** simplest and **plainest terms I could think of** that I question his competence as a reader. **Take here** a moment to consider **a** recapitulation or **abstract of what has been said** above. What I've proposed, in a word, is this: **There are spiritual substances,** immaterial **minds, or human souls,** which freely **will** ideas into being, **or excite ideas in themselves at pleasure; but these** ideas **are faint, weak, and unsteady** in comparison to those that impinge on the senses without prompting. Finite minds are passive **in** this **respect,** conscious **of** these **other** ideas as things coming in from elsewhere. The ideas **they perceive by** their five **senses** are altogether more powerful than those they will into being themselves, **which** plain fact is the result of these sensory ideas **being impressed upon them according to certain rules or laws of nature** established by God. Indeed, the brightness, constancy and power of sensations **speak** for **themselves,** as it were, and signal the nature of their cause: Sensory ideas are so forceful and well coordinated that they could only be **the effects of a** divine **mind,** infinitely **more powerful and wise than** the mind **of human spirits. These latter** ideas—those impressed on us by God—**are said to have more** *reality* **in them than the former** sort of ideas—those produced by us. But we must avoid misunderstanding: **by** saying that the sensations produced by God are more real than those ideas **which** are produced by us, we do not mean that the objects we perceive by sense are ever anything other than ideas. All that **is meant** by this claim is **that they are more affecting, orderly, and distinct, and that they are not** like the **fictions** which depend on our will, the imaginary products **of the mind perceiving them.** They are stamped on our meagre minds by a greater mind. **And** it is only **in this sense** that I assert their reality, their actual being in the world. I can thus say with confidence that **the sun that I see by day is the 'real' sun, and that** the sun **which I imagine by night is** not, merely being **the idea of the former** sun. **In the sense** that is **here given of** the word 'reality', **it is evident that every vegetable, star, mineral, and in general each part of the**

mundane system of nature, **is as much a** *real being* **by our principles as by the** principles of **any other** philosophy, including the materialist. **Whether others mean any thing** else by the term 'reality' different from what I do is doubtful, and I entreat them to look into their own thoughts and see whether they do in fact understand something else by the term. I am sure they will find it impossible to articulate any better conception of 'reality' than the one I offer here.

Perhaps the objection is not that idealism eliminates the ordinary objects of sense perception but that it takes away 'corporeal substance'. In one sense, this is true: Idealists deny the existence of an unknown support of sensible qualities existing without the mind. This is the philosophical sense of 'substance', which has been rejected previously on the grounds of incoherence. But idealists do not deny the existence of 'corporeal substance' in a more pedestrian sense: If you want to call bundles of sensible qualities 'substances', then idealists are committed to substances.

---

37. It will be urged against our principles at this point **that** we do deny the existence of something philosophers are fond of discussing—the hidden support of sensible qualities. The materialists will cry foul, insisting that **thus much at least is true, to wit, that we take away all corporeal substances. To this my answer is, that** we need to draw a distinction: **if the word 'substance' be taken in the vulgar** or everyday **sense,** according to which it stands **for a combination of sensible qualities, such as extension, solidity, weight, and the like** ideas, then the objection misfires, since I hold these things to be real. 'Substance' in **this** non-technical sense **we cannot be accused of taking away.** Does the farmer believe that his plough exists? Yes, he does. So do I. For we both believe in a certain combination of properties—a distinctive colour, shape, texture, weight and so on, which together comprise a plough. Neither of us denies the existence of *that* substance. **But** there is another use of 'substance' we need to consider: **if it be taken in a philosophic sense,** as standing **for the** unknown **support of accidents or qualities** existing **without the mind, then indeed I acknowledge that we take it away, if one may be said to take away that which,** being impossible, **never had any existence, not even in the imagination.** To turn one's back on a philosophical fiction is not to surrender reality.

On the idealist picture, everyday objects are clusters of ideas. But it sounds strange to say that we eat clusters of ideas, or that we wear them. This is an awkward consequence of bringing the sensible world into the mind. That a view sounds strange, however, is no argument against it. And it may help to bear in mind that ideas are the immediate objects of sense: So eating and wearing 'ideas' is really a matter of eating and wearing the things we perceive in sensation. Berkeley even admits that calling sensible objects 'things' is more in keeping with conversational norms.

38. But, say you raise the following objection: If the things around us are composed of sensations—if that bonnet, and this apple, are just clusters of ideas in the mind—then that lady over there is wearing ideas on her head and I am eating them! This is ludicrous. To put it mildly, **it sounds very harsh to say that we eat and drink ideas, and are clothed with ideas.** In response, **I must acknowledge** that **it does** sound quite odd to say so. However, this is because of the difference in meaning between **the word 'idea'** as it is used in everyday contexts and its use in philosophical or scientific contexts. The word 'idea' is **not being used** here in the loose and vulgar way to signify something imagined, but in a sense now **common** in more accurate **discourse**s, where it refers to the immediate object of perception. Observing this trend, I use it **to signify the several combinations of sensible qualities** that we immediately perceive and which together make up the apple or bonnet. To put it bluntly, the farmer or baker uses 'idea' to stand for mental fictions of our own creation, whereas for me it refers to those particular combinations of sensible qualities, **which are** normally **called 'things'**. My usage is thus at odds with common parlance; **and it is certain that any expression which varies** in meaning **from the** everyday, **familiar use of language will seem harsh and ridiculous. But this** admission that my view sounds funny is insignificant and it **does not concern the truth of the proposition** I propose, that we eat and wear ideas. If you can just forget about how weird it sounds, and try to understand my meaning, then you will see that we do indeed eat and wear ideas. What I am claiming is that we eat and wear the things **which** we *experience*, **in other words**, and this **is no more than to say, that we are fed and clothed with those things which we perceive immediately by our senses.** This follows from what we have established above: **The hardness of the apple or softness of the bonnet, the colour, taste, warmth, figure, and such like qualities, which, when combined together, constitute the several sorts of** delicious **victuals and** cosy **apparel, have been shown to exist only in the mind that perceives them.** In *this* respect the apple and bonnet are like 'ideas' in the everyday sense. **And this is all that is meant by calling them 'ideas'; which word, if it was as ordinarily used** to pick out things such as apples and bonnets **as the word 'thing' is, would sound no harsher nor more ridiculous than it.** But **I am not** overly concerned with sounding one way or another. I don't care much **for disputing about the propriety** of my use of the word 'ideas', **but** I do care about **the truth of the expression** that we eat and wear ideas. **If therefore you agree with me that**

we eat and drink, and are clad with the immediate objects of sense, which cannot exist unperceived or without the mind, then you essentially agree that we eat and wear ideas. If you would rather not call such things 'ideas', that doesn't really bother me: We will agree on the philosophical point and the remainder of our dispute will be verbal. Let's come to an understanding: if you will grant me the philosophical point, that all the things around us are clusters of ideas, then I shall readily grant you the verbal point, that it is more proper in everyday conversation, or more conformable to customary ways of speaking, that they should be called 'things' rather than 'ideas'.

Why would Berkeley flout conversational norms and call sensible objects 'ideas' rather than 'things'? One reason is that 'thing' has misleading connotations: It is often used in reference to external objects. Another reason is that 'thing' is less specific than 'idea': It applies to minds as well as bodies.

39. The reader may be puzzled: If apples and bonnets truly exist on my system, if churches and carriages are fully real, then why not speak according to custom? I think it could be justly demanded of me that I explain a little more clearly why I make use of the word 'idea', and do not rather in compliance with customary ways of speaking call them 'things'. To alleviate the reader's perplexity, I answer: I do it for two reasons: First, because the term 'thing', in contradistinction to 'idea', is generally supposed to pick out or denote something non-mental—at least by philosophers. It will be somewhat easier to understand my preference for 'idea' if the reader reflects that sensible objects are not 'things' existing without the mind; secondly, because 'thing' is strictly universal and thus has a wider scope and more comprehensive signification than 'idea'. Whatever exists is a thing, including spirits or thinking things as well as ideas. But apples and bonnets are a specific kind of thing. They are sensible objects, not spirits. They are passive in nature, not active. Since therefore the objects of sense exist only in the mind, and are, with all their colours, shapes, motions and textures, completely thoughtless and inactive, I chose to mark them by the word 'idea', which implies those properties of inertness and lack of sentience.

The materialist might want to fall back on her senses: No philosophical argument is ever going to convince her to doubt what she sees. The sensory *evidence for the existence of a material world will always outweigh whatever evidence Berkeley can marshal against it. But no one is being asked to abandon their senses or to sacrifice any sensible objects. No one sees matter or any other mind-independent objects, and the things we do see—clusters of ideas—provide no evidence for anything unseen. Indeed, an idealist places more confidence in her senses than does a materialist: If everyday objects are just the ideas we perceive, then we can be certain of their existence; if they are material things beyond them, then we can never confirm their presence.*

---

40. **But say what we can** to reassure our materialist opponent that taking matter out of the picture does not destroy apples and bonnets, that equating them with collections of sensible qualities does not turn them into illusions, **some one perhaps may** still **be apt to reply,** that the evidence of the senses is all **he** needs for believing in matter. He sees apples and bonnets—he calls them 'material things'—and concludes that matter must be real. In spite of everything I have said, he **will still believe** what **his senses** tell him, **and** so he'll still believe in matter. Given the strength of his sensations, he will **never suffer** from doubts about matter. He will never allow **any arguments** against the existence of apples and bonnets, no matter **how plausible soever** the arguments may be, **to prevail over the certainty of** his belief in **them.** Seeing is believing, he will say, and no philosophical subtlety will ever move him to stop believing in the existence of what he sees. To such a stupid and stubborn critic I reply: **Be it so, assert the evidence of** the **senses as highly** and confidently **as you please, we are willing to do the same.** The critic has missed my point entirely, and does not realize that we are basically in agreement. When I declare that apples and bonnets are ideas, I do not mean to say that they do not exist, or that he does not see them, or anything else so obviously false. **That what I see, hear, and feel does** really and fully **exist,** I do not dispute; **that is to say,** I have no doubt about the existence of anything that **is perceived by me**—indeed, **I have no more doubt** about what I see, hear or feel **than I do of my** very **own being.** My opponent and I are of the same opinion when it comes to the existence of sensible objects. **But** if he should go on to say that the senses deliver any more than this—that they reveal any beings outside the mind—then I take exception. As I've explained repeatedly, **I do not see how the testimony of the senses can be alleged, as a proof for the existence of any thing, which is not perceived by** the senses, and we certainly do not perceive matter with the senses. We perceive sensible qualities with the senses, and matter was supposed to be the underlying support of sensible qualities, not itself a sensible quality. **We are not for having any man turn** into a *sceptic,* **and** asking him to **disbelieve** what **his senses** show him; **on the contrary, we** trust the senses entirely and **give them all the stress**

and assurance they deserve—no greater confidence is **imaginable. Nor are there any** philosophical **principles more opposite to scepticism, than those we have laid down** in this book. Dropping material substance is arguably the most powerful antidote to scepticism, **as shall be hereafter clearly shown,** in Sections 86 to 91.

The second objection is that idealism cannot accommodate the everyday distinction between a real thing and the idea of a thing. A real fire, for example, is quite different from the idea of a fire. But if everything reduces to ideas, that distinction cannot be maintained. As we saw in Section 33, however, even ideas are divided into the real and the imaginary. Moreover, the criteria we use to distinguish a real fire from an imaginary fire are equivalent to the criteria we use to distinguish a real pain from an imaginary pain. But no one supposes the pain to exist without the mind. So why suppose that the fire does?

---

41. That takes care of the first objection. **Secondly, it will be objected that there is a great difference betwixt real fire, for instance, and the idea of fire, betwixt dreaming or imagining one's self burnt, and actually being so: This** distinction **and the like may be urged in opposition to our tenets.** We allegedly collapse the distinction between the real and the imaginary. **To all which the answer is evident from what has been already said.** The real fire has no dependence on our will; it is caused by the will of another. Though it has no existence without the mind, the real fire is a stronger and steadier presence than a product of the imagination. And like all real things, it coheres with the natural order laid down by God. These three criteria of reality—dependence on the will of another, strength of appearance and coherence with the order of nature—suffice to distinguish the real from the imaginary, **and I shall only add** one counterargument **in this place,** though none is actually needed. You must admit, **that if real fire be very different from the idea of fire, so also is the real pain that it occasions** when you burn yourself **very different from the idea of the same pain** when you recall it afterwards. The parallel is exact: real fire is more forceful than imagined fire just as real pain is more forceful than imagined pain. You infer that real fire exists in an unperceiving thing outside the mind while the idea of it does not. **And yet no body will pretend that real pain either is, or can possibly be, in an unperceiving thing or without the mind, any more than its idea** can. This is inconsistent: If the inference fails in the case of pain, it must fail as well in the case of fire. Both real pain and real fire exist only in the mind.

The third objection is that sensible objects appear at a distance: They look like they are outside us rather than in our minds. So the idealists must be mistaken. Suppose you see a lamppost on the corner. It can't be composed of ideas in your mind, since you see it over there—across the street, in front of the bank. Berkeley offers two replies: The first is a counterexample to the assumption that apparent distance implies actual distance. Consider seeing a lamppost in a dream: Though it appears to be several paces from you, you know that it is not. It is nothing outside your mind.

---

42. Thirdly, it will be objected that sensible objects do not exist in the mind since **we** actually **see** them outside us. Some things appear far away and others in close proximity. I see trees dotting the hillside and a flower at my feet. I see clouds overhead and a button on my sleeve. But whether near like the button or far like the clouds, such **things actually** *look* like they exist **without or at a distance from us.** In fact, the appearance of distance is common to all sensible objects**, and** I have no reason to suspect any error in my senses. But ideas—**which** exist in the mind—are not at any distance: The feeling of warmth is in me when I walk in the sunshine, as is the feeling of joy. The sun itself, however, appears outside me. I can infer, **consequently,** that sensible objects **do not exist in the mind** as clusters of ideas. It is perception of distance that marks the difference for us between external objects and ideas**, it being absurd** and therefore impossible to believe **that those things which are seen at the distance of,** say, **several miles, should** turn out to **be as near to us as our own thoughts. In answer to this** objection, **I desire** my reader to think about other cases where objects appear to be far off when they are actually very near: **it may be considered,** for instance, **that in a dream we do often perceive things as existing at a great distance off** from us, **and yet for all that,** no one thinks that in the dream we are perceiving objects outside us. Rather, **those things are acknowledged** by everyone to be mere ideas, and **to have their existence only in the mind.** So *appearing* at a distance is clearly insufficient for *being* at a distance. By invoking dreams in my defence, I do not mean to imply that the real world is a dream. I have already explained the difference between real things and mere ideas in Sections 34 to 41. The point is just that we can account for the phenomenon of apparent distance without supposing externality.

The second reply to the objection that sensible objects appear at a distance is outright denial: We do not perceive objects at a distance. We learn to associate visual sensations with tactile sensations and take the former as 'distance cues' suggestive of the latter. The response relies heavily on Berkeley's theory of vision.

---

43. But for the fuller explanation and **clearing** up **of this** important **point,** perhaps a few comments on the nature of vision would help. In particular, **it may be worth while to consider, how it is that we perceive distance and things placed at a distance by sight. For that we should in truth see external space, and bodies actually existing in it, some** of them **nearer** to us, **others farther off, seems** contrary to my principles. I look out my window and see a tree, along with many other sensible objects. They seem to be *out there* in the yard. That such things appear at a distance might be thought **to carry with it some opposition to what has been said of their existing no where without the mind:** if they *appear* to be outside of us, perhaps they really *are*. **The consideration of this difficulty it was, that** prompted me to reflect on the process of seeing and eventually **gave birth to my *Essay towards a New Theory of Vision*, which was published not long since. Wherein it is shown that *distance* or outness is neither immediately of it self perceived by sight, nor yet** deduced from any intrinsic features of ideas—say, if distance were **apprehended or judged of by lines and angles, or any** other **thing that has a necessary connexion with it: But** rather, my theory proves **that it is only suggested to our thoughts, by certain visible ideas and sensations attending vision** (like strain on the eyes), **which in their own nature have no manner of similitude or** predetermined **relation, either with distance, or things placed at a distance.** Speaking precisely, we do not see objects at a distance but read *outness* into our visual experience. I glance across the room at a frame on the wall and get the visible idea of a square. Were I to walk over and run my hand around the edge, the sense of touch would furnish me the idea of a tangible square as well. But do I *see* the tangible square? No. I have learned through experience to associate visible squares with tangible squares. So it is with everything that *looks* to have a certain physical shape or to be at a certain distance from me: their tangible shapes and distances are merely suggested. The visible shapes and colours of things are *signs* of the tactile sensations I would have if I reached out and touched them. They are not *perceptions* of them. **But by a connexion taught us by experience, they come to signify**

and suggest apparent distance and various bodily sensations. To draw a comparison, they suggest **them to us, after the same manner that words of any language suggest the ideas they are made to stand for.** The word 'church' doesn't look like a church. The association between the word and the thing is extrinsic. Similarly, the association between visible space and ideas of touch is something we learn rather than perceive or deduce. **Insomuch that a man born blind, and afterwards made to see, would not, at first sight, think the things he saw to be without his mind, or at any distance from him**: the sun and stars would seem to be in his mind—as, in fact, they are—no more distant from him than a feeling of pain. **(See Section 41 of the aforementioned treatise** for details.) He learns to regard them as distant, or outside the mind, without their really being so. The objection mistakes *suggested* distance for *absolute* distance.

The same word is often used in reference to an idea of sight and an idea of touch. For example, when we see and feel a book the idea we acquire by sight and the idea we acquire by touch can each be called 'rectangular'. But this does not imply that ideas of sight resemble ideas of touch—they are actually nothing alike. Nevertheless, ideas in the one sensory modality are linked with ideas in the other: God coordinates visual and tactile sensations such that we can make predictions on the basis of what we see—a rectangular shape, a coloured surface, etc.—concerning what we will feel if we undertake certain actions—a straight edge, a sharp corner and so on.

---

44. Some of the words we use to denote specific ideas furnished by the faculty of sight are the same as the words we use to denote certain ideas furnished by the faculty of touch: For example, when we see an apple we describe what we see as 'round', and when we feel the apple in our hands we also describe what we feel as 'round'. You might attribute this coincidence of names to the similarity of visible roundness to tactual roundness. But this would be a mistake: There is no similarity. **The ideas** furnished by the faculties **of sight and touch** are of radically different kinds; they **make two species,** as it were, which are **entirely distinct and heterogeneous. The former**—ideas of sight—**are** only **marks and prognostics of the latter**—ideas of touch. In other words, the ideas we have while *viewing* something help us predict the ideas we will have while *touching* it. For example, if I see an apple *looking* round, I anticipate that it will *feel* round. The association of visual and tactile perceptions is discussed at length in my *New Theory of Vision*, though I skirted round one important issue in that work. **That the proper objects of sight neither exist without the mind, nor**

are the images or resemblances **of external things, was shown even in that treatise** on optics. However, I did not extend the point to include the objects of touch; **though** I argued that everything we see exists in the mind alone, **throughout the same** treatise, **the contrary** might well have **been supposed** to be **true of tangible objects**—the reader might have just assumed that tangible objects exist outside us. **Not that** I myself endorsed such an absurdity! I mean only that my essay was neutral on the question. In an essay on vision, there was no need **to suppose** either **that** the objects of touch exist within the mind or that they exist without the mind. Exposing **vulgar error**s about the objects of touch **was** simply not **necessary for establishing** any of the points made in the essay or for defending **the notion** of vision **therein laid down;** I neglected to mention that the objects of touch exist within the mind alone, not because I believed otherwise, **but because it wasn't** relevant to the main point of the essay—it being **beside my purpose to examine** the materialist theory of the objects of touch **and refute it in a discourse concerning *vision*.** But let's return to the objection: It was alleged against my denial of mind-independence that we actually *see* objects outside us. But I have suggested that we *learn* through experience to judge of distance by correlating visual sensations with tactile sensations. **So we can reply that in strict truth the ideas of sight** (such as compose an apple or a carriage), **when we apprehend by them distance and things placed at a distance, do not suggest or mark out to us things actually existing at a distance.** They do not inform us of the presence of anything outside the mind, **but only admonish** or warn **us** about what is to come if we reach out and touch the things we see. Ideas of sight are signs of **what ideas of touch will be imprinted in our minds at such and such distances of time**—in one second, if I reach out for this apple; in 20 seconds, if I walk over to that carriage—**and in consequence of such and such actions**—picking up the apple; getting into the carriage. **It is, I say,** already perfectly **evident from what has been said in the foregoing parts of this treatise, and in Section 147 and elsewhere of the essay concerning vision, that visible ideas** do not *show* us distance or depth, but *suggest* it to us. They **are the language whereby the governing spirit, on whom we depend, informs us of what tangible ideas he is about to imprint upon us.** When God impresses ideas of sight on our minds, we are thereby informed of what ideas of touch he will impress **in case we excite this or that motion in our own bodies:** I see a round wheel on the carriage and I expect to feel a round wheel if I reach out my hand. There is nothing more to distance than this. **But for a fuller** account and for more **information in** connection with **this point, I refer** my reader **to the essay** on vision it **self.**

The fourth objection is that sensible objects exist intermittently on idealist principles: They disappear every time we look away and pop back into

existence when we look again. Presumably, the more reasonable stance is to
suppose that objects continue to exist when not perceived. Berkeley answers
this worry by referring back to the meaning of 'existence' as applied to ideas
discussed previously and by reminding the reader that the extra-mental exis-
tence presupposed by the objection is inconceivable. He picks up on this thread
in Section 48.

45. Fourthly, it will be objected that from the foregoing principles it follows,
that the **things** we perceive pop in and out of existence continually, that they
are every moment annihilated and created anew, depending on the presence
or absence of a perceiver. This seems to be implied by my doctrine that *esse* is
percipi—that to be is to be perceived. **The objects of sense exist**, according to
the objection, **only when they are perceived: The trees** I see when I look out
my window, **therefore, are** present **in the garden** only while I'm looking. And
the stove in the kitchen, **or the chairs in the parlour,** exist **no longer than**
while there is some body standing **by** in the kitchen or the parlour **to perceive**
them. Upon shutting my eyes all the furniture in the room is reduced to
nothing—it winks right out of existence. I open my eyes a second later, **and**
barely upon opening them it reappears where it was, and then **is** wiped out
again and **created** afresh every time I blink. Does this sound plausible? If my
principles have such strange consequences, then perhaps it is my principles
that need to be revised. **In answer to all which, I refer the reader** once again
to what has been said in Sections 3, 4, **etc.,** concerning the criteria of reality
and what it means for something to exist. In particular, I **desire** that **he will**
consider whether he means any thing **by the actual existence of an idea,**
other than (1) that he perceives it, (2) that he would perceive it were he in
the right perceptual circumstances or (3) that some other spirit perceives it.
Is there any other way for an idea to exist? The critic seems to think that for
an idea to be real it must exist without the mind, **distinct from its being per-**
ceived. For my part, this is like supposing that for an apple to be red it must
be invisible—sheer nonsense. The existence of an idea consists solely in the
actual or possible perception of it and **after the nicest inquiry I could make,**
the most careful consideration of my own thoughts, **I am not able to discover**
that any thing **else is meant by those words** than this. **And I once more**
entreat the reader to reflect on his experience and **sound his own thoughts,**
and not to wrack his brains and **suffer** over paradoxes, or allow **himself to be**
imposed on by the empty **words** of philosophers. The unperceived existence
of the things seen, touched and heard means nothing. **If** the reader disagrees,
if he can conceive it possible either for his ideas or their extra-mental **arche-**
types to exist without being perceived, then I give up the cause of idealism;
but if he cannot, he will acknowledge that it is unreasonable for him to
stand up in defence of non-mental existence when **he knows not what** it is,

and pretend to charge on me, as an absurdity, the principled rejection of an absurdity invented by him. On the contrary, **not assenting to those propositions which at bottom have no meaning in them** is the opposite of absurdity; it is common sense.

Berkeley's second way of dealing with this objection is to point out that his opponents face the very same problem. For on their view, what we perceive by sight is equally short-lived: light and colours cease to exist as soon as we close our eyes but return the instant we open them. There is also a precedent in medieval philosophy, since it was commonly held that God recreates things from moment to moment and that the existence of sensible objects is therefore intermittent.

---

46. **It will not be** at all **amiss** or out of place for me to turn this fourth objection back on my opponents. I just need **to observe** that it counts as much against their views as it does against mine. One can see just **how far the received principles of** materialist **philosophy are themselves chargeable with those** very consequences that they have **pretended** to be the special **absurdities** of my principles alone. **It is thought** to be one of the **strangely absurd** implications of my principles **that, upon closing my eyelids, all the visible objects round me should be reduced to nothing;** I simply shut my eyes **and** the lights and colours disappear. And **yet is not this** same consequence exactly **what** materialist **philosophers commonly acknowledge** to follow from the basic principles of optics which they accept? Indeed, they admit as much **when they agree on all hands that light and colours, which** are the only things we directly perceive, are just sensations. Of course, they differ from me when they then go on to suppose that sensations are caused by extra-mental objects. But aside from that difference, must they not also admit that what we perceive directly—the light and colours which **alone are the proper and immediate objects of sight,** as we have agreed—**are** nothing more than **mere sensations** in the mind **that exist** for **no longer than** the very instant when **they are perceived? Again, it may to some** of my opponents **perhaps seem very incredible,** that the **things** we perceive **should be every moment** going in and out of existence as they go in and out of our field of vision. While this constant annihilating and recreating of things might seem extraordinary**, yet this very notion** of recurrent creation over time **is commonly taught** by my opponents **in the** old-fashioned philosophical **Schools. For** even **the** medieval *Schoolmen,* **though they acknowledge the existence**

of matter, and affirm **that the whole mundane fabric** of the world **is framed out of it, are nevertheless** also **of the opinion that it cannot subsist** from one moment to the next **without the** help of God, who sustains it by his will. This is a kind of **divine conservation, which by them is expounded to be a continual** recreation **of the world.** My theory is thus no worse off in this respect than its rivals.

The materialist might try to get round the intermittency objection by citing matter as an object that continues to exist unperceived. But the intermittency objection pertains to the things perceived by sense, and even materialists must admit that the things perceived by sense exist only so long as we perceive them. Matter—were it even possible—could never be an object of sense, since it would be infinitely large and shapeless.

---

47. **Farther,** through **a little thought** we **will discover** that the foregoing objection, though designed **to** frustrate **us** in particular, will cause just as much trouble for the materialists. Suppose **that** we set our proofs against matter aside, and grant its existence for the sake of argument. Even so, **though we allow** the materialists **the existence of matter or corporeal substance, yet it will unavoidably follow from the principles of** perception **which are now generally admitted, that the particular bodies** we perceive by sense, **of what kind soever** they may be, **do none of them exist whilst they are not perceived.** For it is evident from Section 11 and the following sections, that the matter philosophers contend for is completely indeterminate, **an incomprehensible somewhat which has none of those particular qualities**—shape, figure, or colour—**whereby the bodies falling under our senses are distinguished one from another;** it is a purely hypothetical correlate of sensation, devoid of sensory content. So even if this material counterpart of our ideas were possible and continued to exist unperceived, the objects of sensation—the things we see and touch—would not, since they are simply ideas. With respect to the intermittency objection raised in Section 45, therefore, materialists have no advantage over idealists. The objects of *sensation* seem to go in and out of existence on their principles as well as on ours, whatever the status of matter. **But to make this more plain** I will demonstrate once again that bodies, in the *materialist* sense, are unperceived. And **it must be remarked that** materialists will not escape the charge of intermittency by citing *unperceived* objects, since it was the intermittent existence of *sensible* objects—the stove in the kitchen, the tree in the garden—that was imputed to us. To be persuaded that matter is neither seen nor felt, one need only consider that **the infinite divisibility of matter is now universally allowed, at least by the most approved and considerable philosophers** such as Leibniz, **who on the received principles demonstrate it** decisively and **beyond all exception.** And there is no difference between infinite division and infinite expansion, since infinity in one direction is the same as infinity in the other. **Hence it follows, that there is an infinite number of parts in each particle of matter, which are not perceived by sense.** The infinity of parts is incontestable, if matter is infinitely divisible. And anything with an infinity of parts must be infinitely large. **The reason, therefore, that any particular body seems to be of a finite magnitude** when we look at it, **or exhibits only a finite number of parts to sense, is not because it contains no more** parts than are seen, **since in itself it contains an infinite number of parts,** as we just agreed. The parts are all there, **but because the sense is not acute enough to discern them** we see only a finite number. **In proportion therefore as the sense is rendered more acute,** say by a magnifying glass or microscope, **it perceives a greater number of parts in the object**—the number of parts seen increases proportionately with the increase in magnification, or power of discernment. And **that is** why, no doubt, **the object appears greater, and its figure varies,** as more parts are revealed—**those** smaller **parts in its extremities,** or outer edges, **which were before unperceivable, appearing now to bound it in very different lines and angles from those perceived by an obtuser** or less refined **sense** organ, or a less sophisticated piece of equipment. **And at length,** if the magnification were to continue indefinitely, **after various changes of size and shape, when the sense** organ **becomes infinitely acute, the body shall seem infinite** in size. **During all** the magnification **which** more powerful senses or instruments would afford us, **there is no alteration in the body, but only in the sense** organ or magnifying equipment. **Each body, therefore,** each chunk of matter, **considered in it self, is infinitely extended and consequently void of all shape or figure,** since shape and figure are defined by *limits*, and an infinitely large thing has no limits. And if it has no shape, it has no colour, since there is no colour where there is no shape. Material things, therefore, having no shape and no colour, are neither seen nor felt. The intermittency objection brought against us by the materialists, therefore, applies no less to materialists than it does to us. They can't just point to matter as an unbroken object of sensation, if matter fails to be an object of sensation. **From which it follows, that though we should grant the existence of matter to be ever so certain, yet it is, with all** that has been said, **as certain, that the materialists themselves are by their own principles forced to acknowledge, that neither the particular bodies perceived by sense, nor any thing like them, exists without the mind,** since they are simply clusters of ideas. **Matter, I say, and each particle thereof, is according to them infinite,** colourless **and shapeless,** and consequently unperceived; **and it is the mind that** perceives ideas and so **frames all that variety of** sensible bodies which compose the visible world, any one whereof does not exist any **longer than it is perceived.**

Berkeley's chief reply to the fourth objection is that idealism is consistent with the continued existence of sensible objects. Though the existence of sensible objects depends on their being perceived, it does not depend on their being perceived by us. They would still exist if some other mind perceived them during the intervals when we do not. So the fact that no human mind perceives a sensible object does not imply its non-existence.

---

48. If we consider it more carefully, we'll see that **the objection proposed in Section 45** misses the mark entirely. It was said that things like trees and chairs would pop in and out of existence for the idealist, depending on whether or not they are perceived. But if we draw a distinction between being perceived *by us* and being perceived *by some mind or other*, then the objection **will not be found** to be **reasonably charged** against us **on the principles we have premised.** Actually, nothing I said implies that things pop out of existence when not perceived by us, if the criteria of reality I described in Section 33 are taken into account. We do not treat the ideas of sensation as isolated beings—as if they were mental atoms in a void—but as standing in thoroughgoing connection with one another according to the laws of nature laid down by God; **so** when sensible things are regarded as forming a *system* of nature, **as in truth** they do, the intermittency charge fails **to make any objection at all against our** philosophical **notions.** And if the systematicity of nature did not of itself provide adequate security against intermittency, the objection would still fall through, given the distinction just drawn. **For though we hold indeed the objects of sense to be nothing else but ideas** in the mind **which cannot exist unperceived**, that does not mean they must be perceived *by us* in order to exist. Trees and chairs are sometimes perceived by us and hence exist, at those times, in our minds; **yet we may not hence conclude** from this that **they have no existence except** when they are in our minds or **only while they are** being **perceived by us.** They may well exist while not being perceived by us, **since there may be some other spirit that perceives them,** even **though we do not.** There may be chairs in empty rooms, or trees in remote forests, where no humans are present to perceive them. But does God not perceive them at every moment? Then they exist in his mind. **Wherever** in this book I have maintained that the being of sensible things is to be perceived, wherever **bodies are said to have no existence without the mind, I would not** want to be understood to mean that they must be perceived by **this or that particular mind, but** that they must be perceived by *some* mind in order to exist. I mean to include **all minds whatsoever** in my claims about existence, even the mind of God. **It does not therefore follow from the foregoing principles that** any **bodies are annihilated and recreated every moment, or exist not at all during the intervals between our perception of them.** Another mind may perceive them all the while.

According to the fifth objection, idealism implies that the mind has spatial form. For if figure and extension exist in the mind, they will be properties of the mind. And if they are properties of the mind, the mind will be characterized by them—it will be extended and have a shape. But the mind does not have a shape and it is not extended. So idealism is false. In response, Berkeley points out that there is a difference between existing in something as a property and existing in something as an idea, and that the objection turns on an untenable distinction between substance and property.

---

49. Fifthly, it may perhaps be objected, that if extension and figure, which are ideas, **exist only in the mind, it follows that the mind** becomes spatial, and takes on a shape, when it contemplates spatial things. The reasoning goes something like this: A spatial object **is extended and figured;** and **since extension is** a property—a **mode or attribute**—of the spatial thing, extension must be a mode of the mind, **which** is just to say that the mind is extended in space. To put the objection a little more formally **(and to speak** more in keeping **with the** language of the **Schools):** (1) Spatial extension **is predicated of the subject in which it exists.** (2) Spatial extension exists in the mind. Therefore, (3) the mind is spatially extended. **I answer** as follows. To suppose that the mind becomes spatial, or extended, by virtue of contemplating spatial things, is like supposing that the mind becomes scaly when it contemplates a fish. This is absurd: **those qualities** of spatial extension and scaliness **are in the mind only as** ideas, not as properties—**they are perceived by it, that is, not by way of** *mode* **or** *attribute,* **but only by way of idea.** The mind is the agent, or perceiver, and the idea is the object, or perceived; **and it no more follows that the soul or mind is extended because extension exists in it alone, than it does that it is red or blue, because those colours are on all hands acknowledged to exist in it, and no where else.** This objection blends the agent of perception with the object of perception, runs the active principle into the passive. A further problem is that it relies on obscure terminology: 'subject'

and 'mode' are words I don't understand—at least as they occur here. **As to what philosophers say of 'subject' and 'mode', that** is of no help whatsoever and **seems** to me **very groundless and unintelligible. For instance, in this proposition, 'a die is hard, extended and square', they will have it that the word 'die' denotes a subject or substance, distinct from the** 'modes' of **hardness, extension, and figure, which are predicated of it and in which they are** said to **exist. This I cannot comprehend: To me a die seems to be nothing distinct from those things which are termed its** 'modes' or 'accidents'. Hardness, extension and a characteristic shape *constitute* a die. There is no need to posit anything further. **And to say** that **a die is hard, extended, and square, is not to attribute those qualities to a subject** somehow **distinct from and supporting them** mysteriously, **but only** to define it—to provide **an explication of the meaning of the word 'die'** by listing the various things that *make* a die the thing that it is.

The sixth objection is that denying the existence of matter brings idealism into direct conflict with the best scientific theories. The success of physical science— which affords a prominent place to matter—thus puts considerable pressure on the basic idealistic assumption. Berkeley has two responses. First, he argues that matter is not an essential commitment of science. It is an entirely useless hypothesis, for the goal of science is to track connections between ideas and it is an utter mystery how matter could affect a mind or produce any idea. Second, Berkeley observes that scientific theories explain natural phenomena not in terms of matter but in terms of qualities such as extension and motion. But such qualities are ideas and ideas cannot do or cause anything. So they play no role in scientific explanation.

---

50. Sixthly, you will perhaps want to oppose our system of nature to a more scientific view and thus reject it in the name of science. You will **say** that **there have been a great many things explained by** scientific theories about the existence and nature of **matter and motion;** in denying the existence of matter, my principles come into conflict with established scientific truths (which presuppose it), and indeed **take away** the very possibility of science. Abandon **these** scientific theories in favour of idealism, **and you destroy the whole corpuscular philosophy,** that is to say, all the work of Isaac Newton (1642–1727) and Robert Boyle (1627–1691), amongst many others. In rejecting the work of Newton **and** Boyle, they suppose that I **undermine those mechanical principles which have been applied with so much success to**

explain and **account for the** *phenomena* we see all around us. **In short,** my principles run counter to **whatever** progress and **advances have been made, either by ancient or modern** natural **philosophers, in the study of nature.** After all, these scientifically minded thinkers **do all proceed** in their inves-tigations **on the supposition that corporeal substance or matter does really exist,** whereas I assert the contrary. In a word, you object that my principles are at odds with science, despite the apparent success of science in explaining the phenomena of nature. So much the worse for my principles, you will say. **To this** objection **I answer, that there is not any one** natural *phenomenon* for which science needs to suppose the existence of matter. Nothing whatsoever in nature can be **explained on that supposition** which cannot be as easily explained without it. Even if we grant, for the sake of argument, that the postulation of matter may help to explain some natural phenomenon—**which** is what I have denied throughout—**may** we **not** conceive that it can **as well be explained without** supposing its existence? Science does not need the hypothesis of matter, **as might easily be made** to **appear by an induction** from experience; we could simply take a survey **of** various **particular** explanations that make no reference to it. **To explain the** *phenomena* of nature **is all one** and the same thing **as to show why, upon such and such occasions** and given such and such prior conditions, **we are** subsequently **affected with such and such ideas:** For example, science will explain why it is that whenever we put our hands in the fire, we experience pain. However, the hands that we see, and the pain that we feel, are composed of ideas, rather than matter. We have already observed in Section 30 that such phenomena are to be under-stood in terms of natural laws, and that natural laws are to be understood in terms of God exciting sensations in regular patterns. We can thus understand how another mind, such as God's, can act on us so as to produce ideas in our minds; we do as much on a smaller scale, after all, when we conjure up ideas in the imagination. **But** we haven't the foggiest notion how such radically different substances as mind and matter could interact; **how matter should operate on a spirit, or produce any idea in it, is what no philosopher will** even **pretend to explain. It is therefore evident** that appealing to matter will do nothing to explain why placing a hand near the fire is always followed by pain. More generally, I think we may conclude that the positing of matter has no explanatory power whatever and hence that **there can be no use of matter in** science or **natural philosophy. Besides,** when we consider the way Newton and Boyle actually go about their work, we discover that, contrary to the objection, **they** do not postulate mind-independent matter at all. In fact, those **who attempt to account for things** in nature, **do it, not by** positing the existence of **corporeal substance, but by** pointing to certain features, such as the **figure** or shape of things, their **motion, and other qualities, which are in truth** mind-dependent and incorporeal. Such features are **no more than mere** sensations—passive **ideas,** existing only in the mind—**and therefore cannot be the cause** or explanation **of any thing** in nature, **as has been already shown. See Section 25.** So we see that the hypothesis of matter, far from being necessary for science, plays no role in science at all. In contrast, my own principles comport with science perfectly.

If we were to adopt the idealist system, we would have to modify our expressions in curious ways: We could not say that fire burns wood or that water cools rocks. Accuracy would require us to say that a spirit burns wood and that a mind cools rocks. The seventh objection is that this sounds ridiculous. Berkeley answers that so long as we think accurately we may continue to speak inaccurately—avoiding, thereby, the appearance of ridiculousness.

---

51. Seventhly, it will be objected **upon** receiving **this** concession of ours— the open disowning of material causes and mechanistic explanations—that our theory of divine agency is very strange. For it may **be demanded** that we cleave more closely to common usage with our words and asked **whether it does not seem absurd to take away natural causes, and ascribe every thing** that happens **to the immediate operation of spirits? We must no longer say upon these principles** of ours **that fire heats, or water cools**—since these are ideas, and ideas cause nothing—**but that a spirit heats, and so forth. Would not a man be deservedly laughed at, who should talk after this manner? I answer, he would so; but in such things we ought to *think with the learned, and speak with the vulgar.*** Expediency requires that we sometimes use inaccurate modes of expression, and speaking with scientific rigour in everyday contexts may open us to ridicule. But this does not affect the truth of things. **They who** have come **to** accept on the basis of recent astronomical **demonstrations** that the earth orbits the sun—Galileo's (1564–1642) discovery of Jupiter's moons and the phases of Venus, for instance, support this hypothesis—do not renounce the ordinary ways of speaking. Though they **are convinced of the truth of the *Copernican* system,** which places the sun at the centre of our solar system, they **do nevertheless say, that the sun rises** in the east, **the sun sets** in the west, **or** that it **comes to the meridian at midday: And if they affect a contrary style in common** situations—if they **talk** about the earth setting in the east, or its hurtling round the sun— **it would without doubt appear very ridiculous** in some people's minds. **A little reflexion on what is here said will make it manifest,** though, **that the common use of language** remains intact on our system and **would receive no manner of alteration or disturbance from the** widespread **admission of our tenets.** The truth of my principles prevents no man from saying that the fire burned his hand or that water cools his feet. We may speak as if there were causal powers in things, though we know the real cause is volition—the universal will of a divine agent.

In everyday contexts it is often appropriate to speak loosely—to use inaccurate modes of expression—since the aim is to be understood. Many inaccurate phrases have been handed down to us and become ingrained in the language; we can't do without them if our audience is expecting us to speak according to custom. We should try to heighten accuracy in philosophical and scientific contexts, but even there, some imprecision is unavoidable.

---

52. In the ordinary affairs of daily **life, any** common **phrases that are not,** strictly speaking, true **may** yet **be retained, so long as** we follow custom and do not intend to deceive the listener. We may say things we know to be imprecise provided **they excite in us** the **proper** or expected **sentiments, or** produce **dispositions to act in such a manner as is necessary for our well-being.** For example, there is no harm in saying that the sun is about to set, even though it's actually the earth that is moving. We're not trying to mislead anyone in using this expression; we're just informing them of the time of day and trying to elicit some appropriate response, such as closing the shutters or leading the horses back to the stable. We may say such things, **how false soever they may be if taken in a strict and** literal sense. When engaged in scientific or philosophical investigations, where we want to be as precise and accurate as possible, it wouldn't be proper to describe the sun as setting. But in everyday life we don't have to speak in a scientific or **speculative sense. Nay,** not only *may* we speak more loosely in everyday contexts: **this** sort of verbal inaccuracy **is** completely **unavoidable.** The loose way of speaking is the right way of speaking, **since it is** the popular way of speaking, and the popular way of speaking is always preferable in an ordinary, non-scientific context. After all, if we want to be understood by others we must speak the way they do. The **propriety** of language—the rules concerning how we ought or ought not to speak—is determined by the popular vernacular, the popular way of speaking itself **being regulated** and determined **by** the received linguistic **custom** of past generations of speakers. For example, when the first speakers said that the sun sets in the west, they meant it in a strict and literal sense: They supposed that the sun dipped down into the ocean or dropped below the western horizon every night. From them we inherited this inaccurate phrase. And though we now know that it's false, we still speak as if it were true. Thus, even today, our **language is** shaped by and **suited to** express **the received opinions** and beliefs of our distant ancestors, **which are**

not always the truest or most precise. **Hence it is impossible, even in the most rigid philosophical reasonings,** to totally avoid the usual ways of speaking. We can only go **so far** as to aim for improved accuracy, **to** gently finesse or modify the English language, **alter**ing at points **the bent and genius,** the tendency and style, **of the tongue we speak.** In the end, **there is nothing we can do** so **as never to give an** opportunity or **handle for** petty faultfinders to object, those annoying **cavillers** who like **to** fuss about our choice of words and **pretend** that there are **difficulties and inconsistencies** between our principles and ordinary language. **But** this is mere pretence on their part: **a fair and ingenuous reader**—one who makes an honest effort to understand what he reads—will place odd sounding phrases in a broader context; he **will collect,** so to speak, **the sense** and meaning of what is said, **from the** whole **scope and tenor** of the work, **and** make relevant **connexions** between the various parts **of any discourse,** speech or book. He will interpret things more charitably, all the while **making allowances for those inaccurate modes of speech, which** the customary **use** of language **has made inevitable** for even the most accurate of speakers.

The rejection of material causation is not without precedent. Those who deny the causal efficacy of matter, however, generally still posit it behind our ideas— serving, on some theories, as the 'occasion' for God to produce contextually relevant sensations in our minds. But if God can produce the right sensations without relying on matter—as these philosophers themselves must admit— then the hypothesis of matter is needless and should therefore be dropped.

---

53. As to the opinion that there are no material or **corporeal causes, this has been heretofore maintained by some of the** medieval **Schoolmen,** such as al-Ghazālī (1058–1111), **as it is of late by others among the modern philosophers,** such as Nicolas Malebranche (1638–1715), **who, though they allow matter to exist** without the mind, **yet will have God alone to be the** source of change in nature and thus the only **immediate efficient cause of all** sensible **things. These men saw that, amongst all the objects of sense, there was none which had any power or activity included in it, and** on this point they were entirely correct: The things we perceive are passive. But then these philosophers took it a step further and argued **that** matter, too, is causally inert, providing only the *occasion* for God to exercise his infinite agency, without doing anything itself. In other words, **by consequence of this** lack of power or agency in the objects of sense it **was** by these *occasionalists* **likewise** held to be **true of whatever bodies they** mistakenly **supposed to exist without the mind,** behind the ideas—material things **like unto the immediate objects of sense** but having no effect on them. Impotent in themselves, material things were thought to 'occasion' God's willing of various effects: when my horse trips on a stone, it is God, not the stone, that makes him stumble. **But then, that they should suppose** all these material things to exist when they serve no natural purpose seems arbitrary in the extreme. They postulate **an innumerable multitude of created beings, which they acknowledge are not capable of producing any one effect in nature, and which therefore are made** for nothing and **to no manner of purpose, since God might have done every thing** just **as well without them** simply by willing it; **this** hypothesis, **I say,** that matter exists, is both groundless and redundant—**though we should allow it** to be **possible, it must yet be** completely useless. The positing of lifeless things behind the ideas of sensation is indeed **a very unaccountable and extravagant supposition**, and I see no good reason to allow it. The Author of nature would not be so wasteful.

The eighth objection is an argument from universal consent: Everyone believes in matter. Could we all be mistaken? That seems unlikely. So matter must exist. Berkeley offers two replies. The first is to deny that anyone does believe in matter. Talk of matter is unintelligible, and we can't believe what is unintelligible. Try to believe a meaningless string of words. It can't be done.

---

54. **In the eighth place,** there is an objection to be made from **the universal** agreement of all men that matter exists. Not only philosophers, but all people in all places and at all times have believed in matter. The **concurrent assent of mankind may be thought by some** to make for **an invincible,** knock-down **argument in behalf of matter, or** for **the existence of external things.** For if there is no matter, then everyone has been mistaken—badly mistaken, always and everywhere. **Must we suppose the whole world to** have gone so wrong in their judgements and **been** so gravely **mistaken** on such a fundamental point? Can we seriously believe that *everyone* is wrong? **And if so, what** could have brought all this confusion about? What **cause can be assigned** for the existence **of so widespread and predominant an error** amongst the people of every nation throughout all of history? This is all very improbable, according to the objection, and so we might as well drop our radical thesis and just admit the existence of matter like everybody else. However, there are two possible replies. **I answer, first, that upon a narrow inquiry** and investigation, **it will not perhaps be found** that there are **so many** people (**as is imagined** by our critic) who **do really believe in the existence of matter or things without the mind. Strictly speaking,** if my arguments are sound, then no one actually

believes in matter. For **to believe in that which involves a contradiction, or has no meaning in it, is impossible:** Something must be intelligible—it must make some sort of sense—before I can believe it. For example, I can't believe that 'the gorbler zeppled its borbler' because the words don't mean anything. But, as I have argued in Sections 16 and 17, the words 'matter' and 'material substance' don't mean anything either; **and whether the foregoing expressions**—'matter', 'material substance', 'external object', etc.—**are not of that** same **sort,** whether they are not just empty sounds with no significance at all**, I** can only **refer it to the impartial examination** and honest reflection **of the reader. In one** very limited and loose **sense indeed, men may** nevertheless **be said to believe that matter exists.** We can say that they believe in matter just insofar as they behave as if there were external, mind-independent things**, that is** to say**, they act** and talk **as if the immediate cause of their sensations, which affects them every moment and is so nearly present to them, were some senseless unthinking being.** Still, this isn't *real* belief. Belief, strictly speaking, is a psychological state of agreement—assent to a proposition that is meaningful and comprehensible. **But** I doubt there is any such agreement when people talk and act as if there were 'matter' or 'things outside the mind', since you can't agree to what you don't understand; **that they should clearly apprehend any meaning marked by those words, and form thereof a** belief or **settled speculative opinion, is what I am not able to** accept or even **conceive.** Rather, if talk of 'matter' amounts to anything, it is just the attempt to dispose the listener to experience certain emotions or to perform certain actions, as explained in Section 20 of my Introduction. **This is not the only instance wherein men** deceive and **impose upon themselves, by imagining** that they **believe those propositions they have often heard.** They might *claim* that they believe them**, though at bottom they** do not, since those 'propositions' really **have no meaning in them.** Take, for example, just one famous passage:

> Actual knowledge is identical with its object: in the individual, potential knowledge is in time prior to actual knowledge, but absolutely it is not prior even in time. It does not sometimes think and sometimes not think. When separated it is alone just what it is, and this alone is immortal and eternal (we do not remember because, while this is impossible, passive thought is perishable); and without this nothing thinks (Aristotle, *De Anima* iii.5).

Is it not obvious that this profound passage—over which so much ink has been spilt by philosophers—is simply rollicking nonsense?

Even if belief in matter were universal it could still be false. It is easy to think of propositions that were once embraced by everyone but which we know to be mistaken. The same could hold for belief in matter.

---

55. But secondly, even if belief in the existence of matter *were* common to all men, that would prove nothing. For **though we should grant a notion to be ever so universally** accepted **and steadfastly adhered to, yet this is but a weak argument** for it and falls short **of** establishing **its truth.** For all we know, our belief that letting blood is a principal cure for melancholy could prove to be false. That universal assent never passes for demonstration will be apparent **to whoever considers what a vast number of prejudices and false opinions are every where** taken for fact. Falsehoods and fables are defended vigorously in the schools and **embraced with the utmost tenaciousness, by the unreflecting (which are the far greater) part of mankind.** This is a symptom of human fallibility, and should make us wary of majority opinion. **There was a time when the** existence of the ***Antipodes***—opposite points on the planet— **and** the orbital **motion of the earth** around the sun **were looked upon as monstrous absurdities** with no basis in reality, **even by men of learning: And** now we know the common view was entirely wrong. Even today majority opinion is still against them. For **if it be considered** how few people are educated in the sciences, and **what a small proportion they bear to the rest of mankind, we shall find that at this day those notions** about the earth and the Antipodes just mentioned are widely rejected and **have gained but a very inconsiderable footing in the world.** Matter may well be a fiction, however numerous its adherents.

Supposing belief in matter to be universal, the ninth objection demands an explanation: Why would the belief be so widespread if it is false? Berkeley conjectures that it arises in response to sensations: A person notices that sensations occur independently of her will. She concludes that they exist externally. She calls those external things 'matter'. Philosophers, who are more sophisticated, realize that ideas cannot exist outside the mind, so they conclude that the cause of sensations exists externally—once again, they call it 'matter'.

---

56. But it is still **demanded** by those who raise the eighth objection (Section 54) **that we** explain how the belief in matter arose, that we **assign a cause of this prejudice, and account for its obtaining** so widely **in the world. To this** demand **I answer that** it has to do with the involuntary nature of sensory experience. Some ideas come to mind through an act of will, while others come from without. The apples on the counter, for instance, or the wagons in the street, are not called up by me, while my daydream of Bermuda is. And so **men,** aware of this difference and **knowing** that **they perceived several ideas in sensation, whereof they themselves were not the authors** or originators, had to account for their presence. But**, as** the ideas composing such things were **not being excited from within** the mind **nor depending on the operation of their wills,** they looked for a cause of the ideas outside their minds. And since it never occurred to them that the mind of God could be the cause, **this made them maintain,** that **those ideas or objects of perception had an existence** totally **independent of, and without the mind.** Thus they went along in ignorance, supposing that material things exist outside the mind, **without ever dreaming that a contradiction was involved in those words. But philosophers** have avoided this trap, **having plainly seen that the immediate objects of** sense **perception**—the aroma of the apple, the brownness of the wagon—exist within the mind. Philosophers having understood that what we see **does not exist without** being perceived by **the mind, they in some degree corrected the mistake of the vulgar,** unsophisticated man. To some extent this recognition marks an improvement over the common view, **but at the same time** these thinkers have **run into another** error, **which seems no less absurd** than supposing that what we perceive exists outside us. While they see that it is impossible for sensations, the immediate objects of perception, **to exist without the mind,** they still think **that there are certain objects really existing without the mind, or having a subsistence distinct from** their **being perceived.** In contrast to the common man, our modern philosophers take the things outside the mind to be perceived indirectly, by way of ideas in the mind. They are things **of which our ideas are only** copies, **images or resemblances, imprinted by those** external **objects on the mind. And** just as the involuntariness of sensory experience triggers the vulgar error, so too **this notion of the philosophers owes its origin to the same cause.** Here is a case, therefore, where the uneducated man and the philosopher suffer from the same misconception. I have tried to explain this fact by reference to what the latter have in common **with the former, namely, their** both **being conscious that they were not the authors of their own sensations.** They did not conjure up the sensations themselves, **which they evidently knew were imprinted** on their minds **from without, and which** they assumed, **therefore, must have some cause distinct from** and outside of **the minds on which they are imprinted.**

What explains our tendency to identify matter as the cause of sensations rather than the will of God? Three explanations are offered: (1) The incoherence of the supposition that material things exist outside the mind and affect the senses is not immediately apparent. (2) Since no particular subset of sensations is linked with God, those with a limited outlook are apt to miss him. (3) The regularity of sensations suggests a non-mental cause to those who misunderstand rational agency.

57. But what puzzles me is **why they should suppose the ideas of sense to be excited in us by** material **things in their likeness, and not rather** by minds. Why, in explaining the occurrence of ideas, do philosophers not **have** immediate **recourse to *spirit*, which alone can act,** invoking instead, by faulty inference, a set of non-perceptible things behind and supposedly like them? This **may be accounted for, first, because they were not aware of the repugnancy** or contradiction **there is,** both in holding that material things resemble ideas **as well** as **in supposing** that they have causal powers. It takes some effort to see that the notion of material **things like unto our ideas** and **existing without** the mind is incoherent, **as** it does to perceive the absurdity involved **in attributing to them** any sort of **power or activity.** And few philosophers are careful with their notions. **Secondly, because the supreme spirit, which excites those ideas in our minds, is** not associated with any sensations, He is 'invisible' to the senses. I mean that God is **not marked out and limited to our view by any particular finite collection of sensible ideas,** such **as** might compose a face or a body that could serve as proxy for him in our experience. And though we don't actually perceive the spirits of other men, we come to associate each finite spirit we know with a certain cluster of ideas that regularly go together. Since **human agents are** suggested to us **by their size, complexion, limbs, and motions**, we deduce their existence by analogy with our own, whereas we come to know God by contemplating nature as a whole—a sublime vision surpassing the typically narrow view of philosophers (see Sections 147 to 149). **And thirdly,** philosophers do not suppose our ideas are caused by minds **because** God is perfectly rational in **his** actions and so the **operations** of nature **are** exceedingly **regular and uniform**—whereas the free actions of minds are expected to be capricious and irregular. This is owing to a false conception of freedom. **Whenever the course of nature is interrupted by a miracle, men,** who mistake unpredictability for freedom, **are ready to own the presence of a superior agent** as cause of the marvellous occurrence. **But when we see things go on in the** steady and **ordinary course** characteristic of nature, **they do not** lead our thoughts to an unseen mind or **excite in us any reflexion** on the true nature of agency; **their order,** stability and lawful **concatenation, though it be an argument** in favour **of the greatest wisdom, power, and goodness in their Creator, is yet so constant and familiar to us, that we do not think them the immediate effects of a *free spirit*, especially since inconstancy,** arbitrariness **and mutability in acting, though it be an imperfection** borne of ignorance, **is looked on as a mark of *freedom*,** when precisely the opposite is the case: A mind is most free when it is compelled by reason.

The tenth objection says that idealism clashes with certain established scientific truths. For example, it is allegedly unable to account for the orbit of the earth around the sun. For if idealism is true, the orbit is composed of ideas. Since the existence of ideas depends on their being perceived, the orbit does too. But no one perceives the orbit from the earth. So the orbit doesn't exist. But astronomy says that it does. So idealism must be false. Berkeley answers that idealism is perfectly consistent with our never having perceived the orbit. Its reality doesn't depend on our actual perceptions. It is enough that we would perceive it in favourable perceptual circumstances. Although he doesn't mention it here, Berkeley's thought is presumably that the existence of such counterfactual truths about perception depends on God's actual perception of the relevant ideas.

---

58. Tenthly, it will be objected that the principles and **notions we advance** in this book **are inconsistent with several sound truths** that have been discovered **in** natural **philosophy**, especially in physics **and mathematics. For example,** take **the motion of the earth.** That the earth orbits the sun **is now universally** recognized and **admitted by astronomers, as a truth grounded on the clearest** evidence **and most convincing reasons; but on the foregoing principles** of my book, the critic alleges that **there can be no such thing** as the motion of the earth. **For** assuming that my principles are correct, **motion** is an idea in the mind, and **being only an idea, it follows that if it be** such that it is **not perceived,** then **it exists** nowhere, since ideas do **not** have any reality outside the mind and its perception; **but,** so the objection goes, **the motion of the earth** around the sun **is not perceived by** anyone—it is completely undetected by the **senses.** After all, no one is out in space looking down on the earth as it passes round the sun, and we can neither see nor hear it moving from where we stand. The critic thus alleges once again that my principles are out of step with science. **I answer, that** the well-founded scientific **tenet** according to which the earth orbits the sun, **if** properly and **rightly understood, will be found to agree with the principles we have premised** here. In fact, the point I want to make is general: My principles cohere perfectly with all established scientific truths, including this one, which may serve as an illustration. **For the** scientific **question, about whether the earth moves or not, amounts in reality to no more than this, to** determine whether or not certain counterfactual perceptual claims hold **wit**hout worrying about what perceptions we actually have or fail to have: The question, in other words, is **whether we have reason to conclude from what has been observed by astronomers, that if we were placed in such and such circumstances, and such and such a position and distance, both from the earth and sun, we should perceive the former to move among the choir of the planets, and appearing in all respects like one of them** as it orbits the sun. I needn't actually perceive the transit of the earth in order for it to exist, so long as I *would* perceive it in the appropriate perceptual circumstances. More generally, there are cases where we can say that something exists even if we don't observe it ourselves. In such cases, the thing exists in virtue of the fact that if we *were* properly situated we *would* perceive it. So, again, even if we don't actually see the motion of the earth around the sun, the motion is there so long as it's true that we would see it were we hovering above the earth: **And** that **this** is indeed what we would perceive is what astronomy teaches, for, **by the** scientifically **established rules of nature, which we have no reason to mistrust,** the hypothesis that the earth orbits the sun **is reasonably** inferred, being **collected,** as it is, **from the** astronomical **phenomena.** The earth orbits the sun, therefore—my principles allow it. And no other scientific truths will need to be sacrificed, should my system be generally accepted.

Accurate predictions concerning the perceptions we would have if placed in different perceptual circumstances can be made on the basis of known regularities. Idealism provides a solid foundation for the regularities and hence for the predictions they support. Objections pertaining to the distant or unobservable entities posited in science can be dealt with in terms of counterfactual perceptions.

---

59. We may, extrapolating **from the experience we have had of the train and succession of ideas in our minds, often make, I will not say uncertain conjectures, but sure and well-grounded predictions, concerning the ideas we shall be affected with,** if we were to undertake some particular course of action. This is a matter of inducing from our own experience how things would have appeared to us had we done something differently. Had I wandered down to the stables instead of up here to my study, I would be looking at horses and hay right now rather than books and papers. We may anticipate perceptions, **pursuant to a great train of actions, and be enabled to pass a right judgment of what would have appeared to us in case we were**

placed in circumstances **very different from those we are in at present. Herein consists the knowledge of nature** from induction, **which** teaches us its laws and allows us to plot our course wisely. Far from undermining this knowledge, our principles **may preserve** both **its use and** its **certainty,** and all the truths of natural philosophy and mathematics may be upheld **very consistently with what has been said here. It will be easy to apply this** response **to whatever objections of the like sort may be drawn from the magnitude of the stars, or any other discoveries in astronomy or nature.** We are told that the stars are very large—much larger than the earth—and yet they appear to be tiny candles in the sky. But to say that the stars are very large means only that if we were situated differently with respect to them than we are now, we should have very different perceptions. Why should I deny this?

The eleventh objection is that the internal complexity of natural objects is unaccountable on idealistic principles: If everything is composed of ideas, then the internal parts of sensible objects are ideas and ideas are causally inert. Since they can serve no purpose if causally inert, their existence is a mystery. Idealism is also at a loss to explain why natural objects appear to rely on their internal parts in order to function properly. Why the underlying structures if surfaces would do?

---

60. In the eleventh place, there is this objection: **it will be demanded** of me to explain why things have the internal complexity they do, **to** explain **what purpose** any interior part of anything **serves.** The critic alleges **that** on my principles there can be no reason for the **curious** internal **organization of plants, and the admirable** structure of moving components—those highly sophisticated **mechanisms** one finds—**inside the parts of animals.** For all we really need are surfaces. It makes sense for God to impress on our minds the green colour of a plant's leaves, and the length of its stem, or the black fur and imposing figure of a bear; but it makes no sense for him to go further and install organs and machinery underneath these surfaces. After all, **might not vegetables grow, and shoot forth leaves and blossoms, and** couldn't **animals perform all their motions,** just **as well without** any hidden complexity **as they do with all that variety of internal parts?** The inner workings appear **so elegantly** designed, so well **contrived and put together,** that one imagines them having some great purpose. They exhibit a degree of intricacy, **which** points beyond mere ornamentation. But we find instead on my principles that the internal parts do nothing. How could they? The internal parts, **being ideas, have nothing powerful or operative in them, nor have** they **any necessary** causal **connexion with the effects ascribed to them.** So the intricate machinery of nature is an empty display. Does this make sense? **If** my principles are right, and **it be a** divine **spirit that immediately produces every effect** we see **by a** *fiat,* **or act of his will, we must think all that is** fine, intricate **and artificial in the works, whether of man or of nature, to be made in vain,** for no purpose at all. Consider some particular work of man, say, a watch: **By this doctrine** of mine, that only minds have the power to produce anything, **though** an artistic watchmaker **has made the** internal **spring and wheels, and every movement of a watch, and adjusted them** precisely **in such a manner as he knew would produce the motions he designed,** they actually don't produce anything, since they aren't minds; **yet he must** instead **think** that **all this** precise arrangement of wheels and springs inside the watch has been **done to no purpose.** If he accepts my principles, he must admit that his efforts were wasted, **and that it is** instead a mind—**an intelligence** outside the watch—**which directs the index** hand, **and points to the hour of the day. If** this is **so,** however, **why may not the intelligence** that moves the hands of the watch **do it, without his being at the pains of making the** internal **movements** of the watch, **and putting them together** in perfect synchronization with the hour, minute and second hands? **Why does not** a watch without any internal mechanisms—**an empty case** or shell—**serve as well as another** containing elaborate machinery? **And how comes it to pass, that whenever there is any fault in the going of** the hands of **a watch, there is some corresponding disorder** or fault **to be found in the** internal **movements, which being mended by a skilful** watchmaker's **hand, all is right again?** In short, my principles seem to imply that the internal parts of the watch are unnecessary, since the motions of the hands are coordinated by God rather than machinery. But the critic insists that the parts are necessary: A watch won't work without them and their connection to the operation of the watch is what explains their presence. **The** objection is not limited to watches, of course: The world is somewhat **like** a watch, and so the same thing **may be said of all the clockwork of nature, a great part whereof** is hidden from view. Some of the intricacy can be exposed by dissecting things, but much of it **is so wonderfully tiny, fine and subtle as scarcely to be discerned by** even **the best of microscopes. In short, it will be asked** by the critic, **how upon our principles any tolerable account can be given,** any remotely plausible explanation put forward, **or any final cause assigned,** of the internal parts of **an innumerable multitude of bodies and** natural **machines** apparently **framed** and designed **with the most exquisite art**istry. To what purpose is all this show, if the parts are causally inert? The position of my opponents is apparently stronger, since they can account for the internal mechanisms, **which, in the common philosophy** they endorse, **have very apposite** and appropriate **uses assigned to them, and serve to explain** the functioning of the larger bodies that contain them, as well as an **abundance of** other natural **phenomena.** And hence my opponents seem to have the advantage over me when it comes to explaining why sensible objects are internally complex.

A preliminary response to the eleventh objection is provided. First, it has been demonstrated a priori that matter is impossible. That demonstration carries more weight than the worry that Berkeley has not been able to explain everything pertaining to the organization of the natural world and the workings of divine providence. Moreover, materialists face the very same difficulty: The idealist was challenged to explain the internal complexity of things. The materialist regards the possession of complex physical properties as necessary for the production of natural phenomena. But it has been shown already that 'physical' properties such as solidity, bulk, figure and motion are causally inert. So the materialist has no explanation either.

---

61. To all which I answer, first, that, though it would be preferable if my principles could explain everything, it is unreasonable to demand that they should. Suppose that **there were** in fact **some difficulties relating to the administration of providence, and the uses by it assigned to the several parts of nature, which** appear to be more intricate and multilayered than is strictly necessary. And suppose **I could not solve** this puzzle **by** invoking **the foregoing principles, yet this objection could** still **be set aside as one of** desperation and as carrying **small weight against the truth and certainty of those things which may be proved**, and have been proven, *a priori*, **with the utmost evidence.** For the incoherence of matter is at this point beyond dispute and the impossibility of sensible objects existing without the mind has been demonstrated conclusively. So even if we granted the challenge we face in explaining why God decided to make the inner workings and microstructure of sensible objects so elaborate, that would hardly overturn the demonstrative proofs we have offered in support of idealism. **Secondly, but neither are the received** materialist **principles free from the like difficulties; for** how do they explain the multitude of internal parts in sensible objects? I think **it may still be demanded, to what end God should take those round-about methods of effecting things by** way of **instruments and machines, which no one can deny might have been effected** more easily **by the mere command of his will, without all that** extra *apparatus* and layering of parts. **Nay, if we narrowly consider it, we shall find that the objection may be** turned around **and retorted with** even **greater force on those who hold** materialist principles and assert **the existence of those machines without the mind;** indeed, they who insist that the microstructure of plants and animals is corpuscular in nature are in an awkward position. The corpuscular theory explains natural processes in terms of the *physical* properties of atoms—their solidity, bulk, figure and motion. And therein lies the problem, **for it has** already **been made evident that solidity, bulk, figure, motion and the like, have no** *activity* **or** *efficacy* **in them, so as to be capable of producing any one effect in nature:** they are utterly incapable of *doing* anything. **See Section 25. Whoever therefore supposes them to exist** (generously **allowing the supposition** of physical atoms to be **possible) when they are not perceived, does it manifestly to no purpose, since** they are causally inert. The materialist hypothesis of physical atoms existing behind our ideas is therefore unmotivated, since **the only use that is assigned to them, as they exist unperceived, is that they produce** our ideas—**those perceivable effects, which in truth** can only be explained on our system. For power and agency **cannot be ascribed to any thing but** a **spirit.**

Though the presence of internal parts is not necessary for the proper function-ing of things, it is necessary for their functioning according to natural laws. And our pursuit of science and invention depends on the proper functioning of things in accordance with natural laws. So our pursuit of science and inven-tion depends on the presence of internal parts as well. Without the regular operation of natural laws and the internal complexity of natural objects, we could make no predictions and design no machines. Our creative and scientific endeavours thus depend crucially on God's setting the laws of nature, accord-ing to Berkeley, and on the systematic arrangement of internal parts.

---

62. But to come nearer to answering **the difficulty, it must be observed, that although the** complex design and **fabrication of all those** internal **parts and organs** of things may **be not absolutely necessary to the producing of any** visible **effect, yet** they are necessary for producing the effect in a certain way; that is, **it is necessary** for there **to** be internal machinery in order to ensure **the producing of things in a constant, regular way, according to the laws of nature.** Let me explain: **There are,** as we know, **certain general** rules, such as Newton's **laws** of motion, **that** govern all the interactions of things in the universe, and that **run through the whole chain of natural** causes **and effects. These** natural laws are exceedingly useful. They **are learned by** scientists in **the observation and study of nature, and are** then by blacksmiths, carpenters and other practically minded **men applied as well to the** design and **framing** of those **artificial** machines that promote our ease and comfort. Then there are the watchmakers, the bookbinders, the tailors and so on, who—studying these same laws—are able to produce for us those finer **things** which are, though not strictly required **for the** preservation of our species, still of great **use** in entertaining **and** diverting us, and which add much to the **ornament**ation **of life.** Knowledge of natural laws is **as** useful to science as it is to daily life. Indeed, the learning of natural laws is vital **to the** scientists in **explaining the various** observed *phenomena:* by **which** I mean that scientific **explication consists only in showing the conformity any particular phenomenon has to the general laws of nature or, which is the same thing, in discovering the** *uniformity* **there is in the production of natural effects.** There is nothing to scientific explanations beyond illustrating how what we observe conforms to natural laws**, as will be evident to whoever shall attend to the** writings of those who study nature. To take just one of **several instances,** there are recent works on optics **wherein philosophers pretend to account for appearances** just by describing the laws governing vision. Many other such works could be cited. **That there is a great and conspicuous** practical **use** for us **in** there being **these** perfectly **regular** laws, that the **constant methods of** providence **working** so predictably help us to order and organize our lives, should be beyond question. Indeed, that the patterns of willing generally **observed by** God, **the Supreme Agent,** are the precondition of our doing anything at all **has been shown in Section 31. And it is no less visible** or obvious **that a particular size, figure, motion, and disposition of** internal **parts are necessary** than that the corresponding, external features suggest them to us. For **though** the internal parts are **not absolutely** necessary **to the producing of any** external **effect, yet** they are necessary **to the producing of** it **according to the standing mechanical laws of nature** we learn through experience. **Thus, for instance, it cannot be denied that God, or the intelligence which sustains and rules the ordinary course of things might, if he were** inclined to do something out of the ordinary—if he were **minded to produce a miracle,** in other words—directly and immediately **cause all the motions** of the hands **on the dial-plate of a watch** without making use of machinery on the inside. The hands of the watch would go round, even **though no** cog, no spring, no internal **body** part **had ever made the movements, and put them in it. But yet**, the internal structure of a watch, and the constancy of the laws by which it works, are guides provided by God for *us.* Humans make watches by machinery, not miracles. With no regularities in nature and no microstructure of parts, we could do nothing; all science, all industry and all art would cease at once. For who could make a watch if there were no parts to put together? Or if the parts kept changing shape? Or if cogs produced motion one minute and porridge the next? The art of watchmaking exists only so long as there are parts to assemble and rules to follow. For God, **if he will act agreeably to the rules of mechanism,** which were **by him for wise ends established and maintained in the Creation,** must not remove the machinery that allows us to act. For watchmaking to be possible, **it is necessary that those actions of the watchmaker, whereby he makes the movements and rightly adjusts them** (such as tightening of the springs and aligning of the cogs), **precede the production of the aforesaid motions** in the hands of the watch; if the watchmaker couldn't take any such steps, he would be completely incapable of producing a watch. It is just **as** necessary to the art of watchmaking that malfunctions in the watch are **also** linked with mechanical failures in the parts, **that any disorder in them be attended with** an internal breakdown that the watchmaker can detect and set right. It is precisely **the** watchmaker's **perception of some corresponding disorder in the movements of the parts, which** allows him to make the necessary repair. The mechanical problem **being once corrected, all is right again** with the watch. This explains the admirable mechanism of nature and the steadiness of her laws.

An occasional miracle poses no threat to science and it may be necessary for promoting God's greater purposes. But God's preference seems to be for impressing us with regularity and order rather than surprising us with disruptions.

---

63. Uniformity in the production of natural effects does not preclude an occasional miracle, if God should think it fit for attaining some higher purpose. **It may indeed on some** historic **occasions** even **be necessary that the Author of nature display his overruling power in producing some appearance out of the ordinary series of things,** such as when a coin appeared at the right moment in the mouth of a fish, illustrating vividly for doubting men that what they owe to Caesar is not what they owe to God. **Such exceptions from the general rules of nature are** sometimes **proper** if used **to surprise and awe men into an acknowledgment of the Divine Being** or to mark out for them the path of virtue and piety. **But then they are** not **to be used** often, **but** only sparingly and **seldom; for otherwise** we shall become accustomed to them and **there is** an incoherence in the notion of 'frequent miracles'. This is **a** very **plain reason why** God should interrupt the course of nature with marvels only now and then: If **they** were common, they **should fail** to produce any **of that** wonder and admiration they are liable to **effect** in the minds of men. **Besides, God seems to choose** more steady indicators of his presence and divinity: **the** most **convincing** signs, which persuade **our reason of his** exemplary **attributes,** are orderliness and regularity. He proves himself **by the works of nature, in which we discover so much harmony and contrivance,** so much ingenuity **in their** design and **make, and** which **are such plain indications of wisdom and beneficence in their Author.** He wants to sway us rationally, **rather than to astonish us** fitfully **into a belief of his being by anomalous and**

surprising events. It is the constancy of the natural order, not the disruption of it, which speaks most powerfully to our understanding.

Berkeley reformulates the eleventh objection in terms of the regularity of nature: Ideas do not appear at random but occur in predictable patterns—the patterns suggesting causal relations. And many ideas come in highly regulated clusters, which suggest the existence of machines behind the appearances. These machines are thought to be responsible for producing the appearances.

---

64. **To** reformulate the eleventh worry and **set this** whole **matter** of inner complexity and hidden machinery **in a yet clearer light, I shall observe that what has been objected in Section 60 amounts in reality to no more than this: Ideas are not** impressed on us in just **any** order, **how**ever accidental some of them may seem to the ignorant: We do not see lightning preceding thunder on one occasion and organ music on the next; shoving a hand in flame is not followed by pain on one day and joy on another. Ideas arise in consistent **and** predictable patterns. They never occur **at random,** but are systematically **produced.** We thus experience lightning and thunder in sequence, **there being a certain order and connexion between them.** Proximity to flame is followed by pain—without exception. We have a natural, almost irresistible, tendency to **liken** such patterns **to** a binding relation—**that of cause and effect.** But as we shall see in Section 65, causality is the wrong relation. **There are also several combinations of** ideas—clusters within clusters of **them**—such as the parts inside of animals, or the microstructure of plants. These combinations are **made in a very regular and artificial manner, which** makes them **seem like so many** little machines—causally active tools and **instruments in the hand of nature.** They are configurations, or structures **that, being hid**den as it were **behind the scenes,** apparently **have an** unseen role—a **secret operation—in producing** the phenomena—**those appearances which are seen on the theatre of the world.** In other words, according to the objection, those parts within parts of plants, animals and all sensible things, **being themselves discernible only to the curious eye of the** natural **philosopher** who performs dissections, suggest some causal story about how they produce appearances. For why should all those hidden parts be there, if not to *do* something? And why should a malfunction in the visible parts of a sensible object be connected with some breakdown in the internal parts, if not because the internal parts cause the visible parts? **But since one idea cannot be the cause of another,** according to my principles, **to what purpose is that connexion** established? To what purpose

are the internal parts even there? **And since those instruments,** or parts, are causally inert—**being,** on my system, ***barely inefficacious* perceptions in the mind**—they do nothing at all, and so it is hard to make sense of their presence. Since they **are not subservient to the production of** any **natural effects,** since they don't serve that purpose which everyone imagines them to serve (namely, producing the phenomena), **it is demanded** by my opponents that I explain **why they are made** in the first place. I must account for the presence of so much dead machinery under the surfaces of things **or, in other words,** say **what reason can be assigned why God should make us, upon a close inspection into his works,** find so many layers of parts that do nothing. Explain why we **behold so great a variety of ideas** beneath the surface, the critic challenges me, **so** many structures **artfully laid together, and so much according to** strict **rules; it not being** at all **credible** that the creator would be so wasteful in his works, **that he would be at the expense (if one may so speak) of all that art and** skill, that he would install so many parts inside of parts with such perfect **regularity to no purpose** whatsoever. Why should he do all that?

The reformulated eleventh objection misconstrues the nature of the relation that ideas bear to one another: That two ideas are constantly conjoined in our experience hardly proves that one is the cause of the other. But one can serve as a sign of the other. The laws coordinating sensations are steady and coherent for the sake of expediency: Their constancy and comprehensibility allow God to convey much information about the natural world to us simply and effectively. The same goes for the intricate arrangement of structures within structures that we observe in natural machines.

---

65. To all of which my answer is, first, that the *orderliness* and *intricacy* of ideas is no evidence of their *causal connectivity*. Ideas occur in discernible patterns and are thus connected in experience by association. The **connexion of ideas** by association, however, **does not imply the relation of** *cause* and *effect,* **but only** the relation of *designation,* by which **a mark or *sign* is** correlated **with the thing *signified.* The fire which I see is not the cause of the pain I suffer upon my approaching it, but the mark that forewarns me of it.** I am alerted to the fact that I will suffer a burn at the sight of the flame that denotes it. The signifying relation between fire and pain is one of many useful things experience has taught me. **In like manner,** suppose I throw my book across the room or pitch my teapot over the railing: **the noise that I hear is not the effect of this or that motion or collision of the ambient bodies** (the book hitting the wall or the teapot shattering on a step), **but** merely **the sign thereof:** When my maid hears the clatter from the kitchen she is notified duly that something has broken. **Secondly, the reason why ideas are formed into** elaborate **machines, that is,** coordinated by God according to elegant laws and grouped together in **artificial and regular combinations,** is that it is simply a matter of expediency. This **is the same** sort of shrewd coordination we see **with** language—**that** is to say, the reason **for combining letters into words** is that it facilitates communication, especially if the number of letters is kept low. Try to imagine a language structured along different lines than ours. Suppose that English contained not 26 letters, but 20 000. Or say we assigned a unique number to every pebble, every horse and every tree—and let the number serve as a name. In the first case, communication would be difficult; in the latter, impossible. The system of language we have is the most expedient: Rules for combining a limited number of letters in seemingly endless ways maximize its expressive power. And nature is a language like ours—efficient and articulate. It is the language of God. Mastery of a few basic laws furnishes us with a wealth of knowledge at little cost. **That a few original ideas may be made to signify a great number of effects and actions,** requires an intelligible and accessible 'grammar'—elementary rules, easily learned and constant. For ideas to signify in the manner described—fire signalling pain, noise indicating motion—**it is necessary** that **they be variously combined together: and to** secure **the end** of simplicity, to ensure that **their use be permanent and universal, these combinations must be made by** settled *rules,* **and with** *wise planning and* **contrivance. By this means abundance of information is conveyed unto us** by God, **concerning what we are to expect from such and such actions, and what methods are proper to be taken** by us **for the exciting of such and such ideas; which** is, **in effect, a language. This is all that I conceive to be distinctly meant** by materialists **when it is said** in their books **that, by discerning the figure, texture, and mechanism of the inward, **'corpuscular' parts of bodies, whether natural or artificial, we may attain to** knowledge **of the several uses of** them **and** the various **properties depending thereon, or** even **the nature of the thing** itself. My system delivers the same results, but without the awkwardness of matter, which is, after all, impossible.

The relation obtaining between a 'cause' and an 'effect' is one of sign to signifier: Idea A alerts us that ideas B and C will follow. Science is the systematic study of natural signs. Material causes play no part in scientific explanation.

---

66. Hence it is evident that those connections of ideas—the fire and the pain, the throwing and the shattering—are **things, which** it is impossible to **under**stand in causal terms; **the notion of a** material **cause co-operating or**

concurring to the production of effects, or of a corpuscular microstructure altering the sensible qualities of things is, to my mind, unintelligible. These materialist dogmas **are altogether inexplicable and run us into great absurdities.** In contrast, the regular connections of ideas **may be very naturally explained and have a proper and obvious use assigned** to them, **when they are considered only as marks or signs** of what is to come. In their capacity as signs—rather than causes—they form the basis of **our** science by providing the **information** we need to make predictions. **And it is the** proper business of scientists to be continually **searching after, and endeavouring to understand those** regular connections and **signs instituted by God,** who is **the Author of** all the order in **nature,** and the true cause of that sublime coordination we find in things. Indeed, discovering such uniformities—**that** pain regularly attends fire or that planets always keep to their orbits—**ought to be the** chief **employment of the natural philosophers, and** the principal concern of science. Science does **not** require **the** doctrine of mind-independent material things—the predictions are the same whether matter exists or not—and is even hampered by the belief in it. This stubborn insistence on matter amongst the natural philosophers and the related folly of **pretending to explain things by** reference to **corporeal causes** is thus both useless and harmful; indeed, it is hard to imagine anything **which** has spawned more controversy and confusion than the postulating of corporeal causes. The materialist **doctrine seems to have too much estranged the** intellect, turning the **minds of men** away **from that** first **active principle** which directs the natural order. Far from being a weakness, therefore, the elimination of corporeal causes leads us back to **that supreme and wise spirit, 'in whom we live, move, and have our being'** (Acts 17: 8).

According to the twelfth objection, Berkeley has only ruled out the positive conception of matter. 'Matter' in some indefinite sense may still exist—an unperceiving substance existing outside the mind and 'occasioning' God to produce our sensations. 'Matter' in that indefinite sense may possibly exist. But this indefinite 'something or other' lacks properties and it's not clear that anything can exist without properties. Furthermore, even if the possession of properties were not a requirement for existence, indefinite matter would have no location.

---

67. In the twelfth place, it may perhaps be objected, that we have ruled out the possibility of matter in only one sense: **though it be clear from what**

has been said in the preceding sections, **that there can be no such thing as an inert, senseless, extended, solid, figured, moveable substance, existing without the mind, such as** I have portrayed matter to be above (observing the tendency of **philosophers to describe matter** in these terms): **Yet,** according to the objection, matter may still be possible when understood in some *other* sense. After all, my arguments only show that *ideas* cannot exist without the mind. Defining 'matter' by listing ideas, therefore—extension, figure, solidity and motion—guarantees its intra-mental existence and arguably begs the question. But the objector wants to try out a different conception: **if any man shall leave out of his idea of 'matter' these positive ideas of extension, figure, solidity, and motion, and say that he means only by that word an inert senseless substance, that exists without the mind, or unperceived, and which is the occasion of our ideas,** the trigger **or** cue **at the presence whereof God is pleased to excite ideas in us,** he may be able to push back a little: for **it does not appear,** that we have said anything against this conception of matter. The materialist could accept all of our previous arguments **but** still insist **that 'matter' taken in this** other **sense may possibly exist. In answer to which I say, first, that it seems no less absurd to suppose** that there is **a substance without** any properties or **accidents, than it is to suppose** that there are properties or **accidents without a substance.** Just as properties are always properties of *something,* so an alleged *something* without properties is a *nothing.* What 'substance' are materialists talking about if they won't ascribe any properties to it? And why call the lack of properties 'matter'? **But secondly,** leaving aside the apparent emptiness of the materialists' claim that a substance without properties exists, there is still the problem of its location: **though we should grant** that **this** naked and **unknown substance may possibly exist, yet where can it be supposed to be?** Either it exists in the mind or it exists in some place other than the mind. **That it exists not in the mind is agreed,** since anything in the mind is an idea and this alleged substance is not an idea; **and that it exists not in place is no less certain, since** all *places* are in space, **all** space is extension and **extension exists only in the mind.** This is beyond dispute, **as it has been already proved** by demonstration above (see Section 11). **It remains therefore that** 'matter' in this other sense has no location—**it exists no where at all.** And I feel no compulsion to disprove the existence of a nameless nothing that exists nowhere.

Matter on this latest conception lacks all properties but one—the 'supporting' of sensible qualities. But indefinite matter cannot support anything since it is wholly inert and has no positive characteristics. Materialists might want to cut their losses and say that matter is merely the occasion

for God to implant ideas: When matter is present, God will give us the
appropriate sensations. But if matter has no properties—if it is imper-
ceptible, inert and non-spatial—then it cannot be 'present' to anyone,
including God.

68. Let us examine a little further **the** latest **description that is here given**
to us of 'matter'. It is now described as something sorely lacking in positive
properties—it has no motion, no size, no shape, no colour, no anything. But
this is just to say that it **neither acts** on anything, **nor perceives** anything,
nor is perceived by any mind; **for this is all that is** implied—it's all that's
meant—by saying it is an inert, senseless, unknown substance. Material
substance, which is now explicated by **a definition** almost **entirely made up**
of negatives—motion*less*, sense*less*, size*less*, shape*less*—serves no discernible
purpose. In saying that the materialist's conception of matter is entirely made
up of negatives and that it serves no purpose, I am **excepting** the one positive
descriptor they offer: Matter 'supports' sensible qualities. This is, as I say, the
only property or function they accord to matter and it is a very curious task
indeed. The word 'matter' itself suggests no ideas to my mind, and **the relative**
notion of its 'standing under' or 'supporting' the sensible qualities of things
clarifies nothing. To say that matter 'supports' is, I admit, an attempt to characterize it. **But** the words are empty. For if matter is inert, it cannot act, and
if it cannot act, **then** it can hardly sustain or prop anything up. And what else
do we mean by 'support'? So if this is the proposed function of matter, then
it must be observed that it miscarries. Matter **'supports' nothing at all; and**
how nearly this comes to the description of a non-existent **non-entity, I**
desire may be considered by my readers. For my part, matter seems to have
nothing, to do nothing and to be nothing, which is all to say: it doesn't exist.
But, say you're so attached to matter, so disinclined to let it go, that you
invent yet another job for it to do and then pretend that the job is necessary.
Thus, like Malebranche, you insist that **it is the unknown 'occasion', at the**
presence of which ideas are excited in us by the will of God. Now that's
a strange commission, and **I would fain** have you tell me—or by any means
make it **known—how any thing** imperceptible, and lacking in properties
altogether, **can be present** either to God or **to us.** 'Matter', **which is** said to
be the 'occasion', is **neither perceivable by** the ordinary **senses nor** by inner
reflexion, nor is it **capable of producing any idea in our minds, nor is** it **at**
all extended, nor has it **any form.** It neither acts at any time, **nor exists in**
any place. How can a complete nothing *present* itself? To repeat, matter is said
to be the occasion *at the presence of which* God is supposed to implant ideas.
But *what* is present? **The words 'to be present', when thus applied** to matter,
must needs be a metaphor, or **taken in some abstract and strange meaning.**
These are words that have no resonance with me, **and which I am not able**
to comprehend.

The term 'occasion' occurs in the twelfth objection: Indefinite matter is the occasion for God to implant ideas. But what does 'occasion' mean here? Normally, it refers to an agent or to something observed to accompany an effect. But matter is passive, so it can't be an agent. And it is imperceptible, so it can't be observed to accompany anything. So its meaning is not apparent.

69. Again, let us examine what is meant by 'occasion' as it occurs in this objection. Where should we look to determine the meaning of a word other than to our actual linguistic practices? **So far as I can gather from the** meaning of 'occasion' in the **common use of language, that word signifies either the agent which produces any effect, or else something that is observed to accompany, or go before it, in the ordinary course of things**—an event beheld simultaneously with its effect or immediately before it. Sunshine occasions warmth, and blossoms occasion the spring. **But** this hardly clarifies 'occasion' as the materialist deploys the term, for **when it is applied to matter as above described, it can be taken in neither of those senses. For matter,** on the alternative definition being considered, **is said to be passive and inert:** 'an inert senseless substance, that exists without the mind, or unperceived'. An inert thing has no power, **and so cannot be an agent or efficient cause.** Matter is accordingly not an 'occasion' in the first sense. **It is also unperceivable, as** the proposed conception implies, and therefore unobservable: existing without the mind and **being devoid of all sensible qualities,** matter is not an object of perception. But when not construed as an agent, 'occasion' was understood as something *observed* to accompany its effect in the normal course of experience, **and so matter cannot be the occasion of our perceptions in the latter sense** either. Consider an example: **as when the burning of my finger**—something observed—**is said to be the 'occasion' of the pain that attends it.** I see my finger touch the flame and then I feel the pain. The burning 'occasioned' the pain. But matter can't 'occasion' like a flame, since it isn't *observed* to accompany anything. **What therefore can be meant by calling matter an 'occasion'? This term is either used in no sense at all, or else in some** unfamiliar **sense very distant from its received signification** in everyday discourse. What that distant signification could be, I have no idea—and neither, I take it, do you.

Another move for the materialist would be to say that God perceives matter, though we do not. Her reasoning would go something like this: Our sensations

are highly organized. The best way to account for that fact is in terms of mat-
ter. God perceives bits of matter as a person perceives road signs: They instruct
him what sensations to place in our minds. The orderliness of our sensations is
thus referred back to the orderliness of matter—the individual particles corre-
sponding to individual ideas.

70. You will perhaps respond by **saying that matter, though it be not perceived by us, is nevertheless perceived by God.** When the 'matter' of an
apple is before me, I do not see it. But God does, **to whom it is the occasion
of exciting ideas in our minds.** Upon perceiving the 'matter' of the apple in
front of me, he immediately implants the characteristic sensible qualities of
an apple—ideas of roundness, redness, etc.—in my mind. This 'occasionalist'
theory of matter strikes me as utterly absurd. But perhaps you disagree? Perhaps you even find it plausible. **For** our ideas occur in regular patterns—the
redness and roundness of an apple always occur in conjunction with tartness
and crunchiness. But, **say you** figure that, **since we observe our sensations to
be imprinted** on our minds **in** such **an orderly and constant manner, it is but
reasonable to suppose** that **there are certain constant and regular occasions
of their being produced.** After all, such perfect order can be no coincidence:
It must be occasioned by an external thing. **That is to say,** we may assume **that
there are certain permanent and distinct parcels of matter corresponding to
our ideas, which** 'occasion' a response from God. They are the ground of our
ideas, **though they do not** directly **excite them in our minds.** They do not
themselves impinge on our senses **or in any** other **ways immediately affect
us, as** they are totally inert, **being altogether passive and unperceivable to
us.** Even so, **they are nevertheless** of some use **to God, by whom they** can be
and always **are perceived.** Material things are signposts, **as it were,** that on **so
many occasions** serve **to remind him when and what ideas to imprint on our
minds;** the matter of the apple serves as a signal to God, **that** prompts him to
bring about the ideas of redness and roundness in the mind of anyone within
perceptual range. Thus, while not perceivable by us, matter exists **so** that the
things we do perceive **may go on in a constant uniform manner.**

*The materialist view is that material substances exist outside of minds. The
suggestion that certain ideas in God's mind may prompt or 'occasion' him to
produce sensations in us does nothing to support that thesis, for ideas are not
substances and they do not exist outside of minds. Idealism and occasionalism
are not in conflict.*

71. In answer to this I observe, that as the notion of matter is here stated—a thing perceived by God and functioning, somehow, as occasion for him to produce our sensations—it affords no advantage to materialism. For **the question is no longer** one **concerning the existence of a thing distinct from *spirits* and their *ideas*, from perceiving and being perceived,** since we're talking about God's *ideas*—the objects of his perception—and ideas exist in the mind: What good is that to the materialist? Matter was supposed to be a mind-independent substance. **But** that's not what we're getting on this interpretation—**whether there are not certain ideas, of I know not what sort, in the mind of God, which are so many marks or notes that direct him how to produce sensations in our minds in a constant and regular method** clearly has no bearing on the question at issue: whether there is matter *outside* of minds. I concede that there may possibly be ideas in God's mind which I neither perceive nor understand and that prompt him to create my sensations—**much after the same manner as a musician is directed by the notes of music to produce that harmonious train and composition of sound, which is called a 'tune'; though,** just as we are blind to the purported cues in God's mind, **they who hear the music do not perceive the notes, and may be entirely ignorant of them.** Sheets of music could, for all we know, be an apt metaphor for the master plan of nature. **But** I see no threat to idealism in all **this**. And the **notion of matter** put forth **seems too extravagant to deserve** serious consideration anyway or to warrant any attempt at **confutation. Besides, it is in effect no objection against what we have advanced** that there may be ideas in God's mind inscrutable to us, and unseen. Our system is quite able **to withstand** this latest materialist objection. Again, we assert **that there is no senseless, unperceived *substance*** distinct from spirit. This thesis remains untouched, for not even God's ideas are *substances* and they are hardly *distinct* from spirit.

The orderliness of our sensations points to the wisdom and goodness of God. It does not point to matter. The former hypothesis provides an adequate explanation for all the phenomena of nature. The latter explains nothing, and is not itself coherent.

---

72. Nevertheless, my critic was correct in insisting that the perfect harmony our ideas exhibit cannot have arisen by coincidence, and must therefore have some cause or other. **If,** however, **we follow the light of reason we**

shall not find our way to any material cause. Rather, **from the constant uni-formity** and **method**ical presentation **of our sensations,** we will discover an immaterial cause, and we can further **collect** from the beauty and orderliness of our ideas **the goodness and wisdom of the** *spirit* **who excites them in our minds. But this** sublime religious hypothesis **is all that I can see rea-sonably concluded from thence;** how impotent, stupid matter is supposed to figure I simply cannot see. **To me, I say, it is evident that** the existence of God—**the being of a** *spirit infinitely wise, good, and powerful*—is abun-dantly sufficient **to** account for the masterful coordination of our ideas and to **explain all the appearances of** order in **nature. But as for** *inert senseless matter,* once we have postulated God to do the work, of what use is it? As far as I can tell, it is of no use at all; **nothing that I perceive has any** evident dependence on matter or shows **the least** sign of standing in **connexion with it.** Nothing I see **or feel leads,** by any remotely plausible argument, **to the thoughts of it. And I would** be more than **faintly** surprised to **see any one** make use of matter to **explain any of the** simplest occurrences or throw any light on even the **meanest,** most basic *phenomenon* in nature. I'd be delighted to discover that we can account for anything **by it, or be shown** by **any manner of reason**ing that matter has some chance of existing. I won't set the bar very high: I'm not asking for demonstrative proof. I'd be astounded if there were even some probability that matter exists, **though** it be **in the lowest rank of probability.** I'd be astonished if the proponent of matter could show there to be one-hundredth of a chance that matter exists, and **that he can have** any reason at all **for** supposing **its existence;** indeed, I'd be quite impressed if he could just clarify what he means by saying that matter exists **or even make any tolerable sense or meaning of that suppo-sition. For as to its being an occasion, we have, I think, evidently shown** already **that with regard to us it is not** an **occasion,** since we don't perceive it. **It remains therefore that it must be, if** it is to serve any purpose **at all, the occasion** or signal **to God of** the appropriateness of **exciting** such and such **ideas in us** at such and such a time; **and what this amounts to, we have just now seen:** nothing.

Berkeley tries to remove the original motivation for positing matter. The ten-dency to regard sensible qualities as existing externally led people to suppose that some sort of 'substratum' or 'container' for them must exist externally as well. At some point they realized that the qualitative features of things are just ideas in the mind and then inferred that only the quantitative features exist outside. But that, too, was an error, since bulk, figure, motion and the like are merely ideas. So the theory needs further revision: Only the substra-tum exists externally, divested of every property. It was the need to house properties, however, that supported the original assumption. That support is now gone.

73. It is always **worth while,** when trying to counter a widespread but false belief, **to** consider *why* it is generally held to be true. Once the causes are identified—once it is clear what *motivates* men to make the supposition—it may then be possible to undermine confidence in the belief by simply removing the motivation. Belief in matter is particularly susceptible to this weakening technique. If we **reflect a little on the motives which** originally **induced men to suppose the existence of material substance,** we shall find **that** they are insufficient to sustain the belief in light of our earlier demonstrations. We'll scrutinize the original arguments for positing matter—the motives and reasons behind the supposition—so that, **having observed the gradual ceasing and expiration of those motives or reasons** under our scrutiny, **we may** then **proportionably withdraw the assent that was grounded on them**—belief will simply melt away. **First therefore, it was thought that colour, figure, motion, and the rest of the sensible qualities or accidents did really exist without the mind; and for this reason, it seemed needful to suppose some** repository for them—an **unthinking** *substratum* or *substance* **wherein they did exist, since they could not be conceived to exist by themselves.** This reasoning made sense, so long as it was assumed that the sensible qualities existed externally, for qualities or accidents are indeed inseparable from substance. **Afterwards,** however, **in the process of time,** the notion that sensible qualities exist outside the mind became doubtful; **men, being convinced** by arguments from perceptual relativity (see Section 14 above) **that colours, sounds, and the rest of the sensible secondary qualities had no existence without the mind,** rejected their mistaken assumption: **they stripped this** *substratum* or material **substance of those** secondary **qualities,** bringing colours, sounds, tastes and so on into the mind. Reluctant to abandon external existence all at one go, they stopped short of transporting the rest of the sensible world into the mind along with the secondary qualities, **leaving** behind **only the primary ones, figure, motion, and such like, which they still conceived to exist without the mind, and consequently to stand in need of a material support.** For again, qualities or accidents require a substance to accommodate them. **But it having been shown** in our treatise **that none, even of these** primary qualities, **can possibly exist otherwise than in a spirit or mind which perceives them,** since figure, motion, number and the like are only ideas, **it follows that we have no longer any reason to suppose the being of** *matter.* Why postulate a substratum, after all, if there are no qualities outside the mind in need of support? Nay, materialists must now admit **that it is utterly impossible** that **there should be any such thing** as matter, so long as that word is taken to denote an *unthinking substratum* **of qualities or accidents, wherein they exist without the mind,**

since we have shown it to involve a contradiction. The advocate of matter is thus in the awkward position of positing an absurdity for no reason whatsoever.

Though the original motivation for positing matter has been defeated, material-ists are still not ready to let it go. Their speculations are buoyed up by the word itself, the referent of which is increasingly obscure. No arguments are offered in support of 'matter'. But materialists are committed to it come what may, so deep-seated is the prejudice in its favour.

---

74. But even **though it** may be supposed that the original motivation is gone, even though it be **allowed by the *materialists* themselves, that matter was thought of** and postulated **only for the sake of supporting** qualities or **acci-dents** which, it turns out, need no such support, materialists still cling to their belief in matter; this is the height of irrationality. Usually when we believe something for a certain reason **and** it is subsequently shown that **the reason** is **entirely** void, **ceasing** to provide any evidence for the proposition in question, **one might expect the mind** to turn from the belief and give it up. For example, if we believe that it is four o'clock because the hour hand points to four, but then discover that the clock is broken and has been frozen at four for weeks, we **should naturally, and without any reluctance at all, quit the belief of what was solely grounded thereon:** We should admit that we don't know the time. **Yet the** commitment to matter is such a valued **prejudice, is riveted so deeply in our thoughts, that we can scarcely tell how to part with it, and** we cannot bring ourselves to shed it. We **are therefore inclined, since** belief in **the thing it self is indefensible, at least to retain the name** 'matter'; that is, we continue to use the word 'matter', **which we apply to an I-know-not-what,** a completely unknown and useless *something* behind our ideas. We mouth the word, as I say, while entertaining some **abstracted and indefinite notions of *being*, or *occasion*, though without any** evidence that there is such a thing or any **show of reason** whatever, **at least so far as I can see. For what** evidence do we have? What **is there on our part** that suggests mind-independence, **or what do we perceive amongst all the ideas, sensations, and notions, which are imprinted on our minds, either by** way of the **senses or** by introspective **reflexion, from whence may be** inferred **the existence of** matter, an inert, **thoughtless, unperceived occasion?** Quite simply, there is no evidence at all. **And on the other hand,** if you should resort to theological speculation, insist-ing that God would have created matter to guide him in coordinating our experiences, then I must ask **on the part of an *all-sufficient spirit*, what can**

there be that should make us believe, or even suspect, that **he is** indeed *directed* by an inert occasion to excite ideas in our minds? Nothing could induce me to believe that. Matter, being passive and inert, couldn't possibly 'help' anyone to do anything, and we can't suppose that God has any need of guidance in governing the world.

The affinity for matter is so strong in most people that they insist on the word and place their confidence in its mere possibility: Even after all the arguments in its favour have been undone, there is still a tendency to say, 'But at least it's possible!' It is difficult to see what possibility is being asserted here, however.

---

75. **It is a very extraordinary instance of the force of prejudice** that belief in matter persists even after the arguments for it collapse and the term is shown to be empty. Is it not surprising, **and much to be lamented, that the mind of man retains so great a fondness** for paradox that it petitions, **against all the evidence of reason, for a stupid** and **thoughtless** placeholder called 'material substance'—an unknown *somewhat* or something, **by the interposition whereof it would, as it were,** separate itself from God? There is no reason to postulate anything that can be sensibly classified as 'matter', and by stuffing 'occasions' between God and our ideas the mind only **screens it self from the** tender **providence of God, and removes** him **farther off from the affairs of the world.** We shall feel closer to our maker if we drop the 'occasions' and embrace the thought that he affects us directly. **But though** the grounds for positing matter have been removed, **we still do the utmost we can to secure the belief** in it. Habit dies hard and we are disinclined to rid ourselves **of** *matter,* just because we've used the word for so long. **Although** we thought we had good arguments for it, **when** the motives evaporate and **reason forsakes us, we endeavour to support our opinion on the bare possibility of the thing:** We tell ourselves it is enough if matter is merely *possible*. This is a tactical retreat revealing our desperation to retain a comforting prejudice, **and though we indulge our selves in the full scope of an imagination not regulated by reason,** though we let our minds run freely in trying **to make out that poor** *possibility* of matter, attaching any sense to the term that suggests itself, **yet** the best we can come up with is an account of matter in terms of 'occasions' directing God to cause our sensations. The **upshot of all** this talk of occasions **is that there are certain** *unknown ideas* in the mind of God. For this, if any **thing, is all that I can conceive to be meant by** the word 'occasion' **with regard to God. And this, at the** best and at **bottom, is** to give up matter and to be **no longer contending for the *thing*** itself, **but** merely **for the *name*.** If people want to toss around an empty term, that is of no consequence to me.

That certain ideas in the mind of God are called 'matter' by materialists is really beside the point: As ideas, they exist in the mind—if they exist at all. The bottom line is that 'matter' in the sense originally proposed by materialists is impossible: There can be no external, mindless support of sensible qualities.

76. Whether therefore there are such unknown **ideas in the mind of God, and whether they may** with any propriety **be called** 'occasions' or referred to **by the name 'matter', I shall not dispute.** I'm not going to be drawn into a verbal disagreement about the use of a term. **But if you stick to the notion of** matter proposed earlier—**an unthinking substance, or** hidden **support of extension, motion, and** the **other sensible qualities,** whether primary or secondary—**then to me it is most evidently impossible** that **there should be any such thing.** And this must be evident to my readers by now as well. **Since it is a plain repugnancy,** contrary to sound reason, **that those qualities,** which are in truth no more than ideas perceived in sensation, **should exist in, or be supported by, an unperceiving substance.** I can no more conceive of sensations existing in mindless matter than I can conceive of air existing in a void.

Grasping at straws now, the materialist might speculate on the possible existence of an unknown support, not of sensible qualities, but of unknown qualities that we would perceive if we had an organ of sense adapted to perceiving them. Berkeley's first response is that the existence of any such thing is irrelevant to human affairs.

77. But say you admit the force of my arguments against matter when conceived as the unperceiving substratum of colour, figure, extension, motion, hardness, softness, sound, smell, taste and so on. Such qualities are objects of perception and the objects of perception are ideas. As ideas they are incapable of existing outside of minds and hence you forfeit your previous claim that they reside in a mindless substance. But your prejudice is strong, we'll say, and in order to maintain it you seek another use for matter. You would have it support some *other* set of qualities, distinct from the ideas of sensation. And so you reason like this: **though it be granted that there is no thoughtless support of** colour, figure, **extension, and the other qualities or accidents which we perceive; yet there may, perhaps, be some inert unperceiving substance, or** *substratum* **of some other** set of **qualities, as incomprehensible to us as colours are to a man born blind.** Just as colours are nothing to the blind man, because he has no organ with which to detect them, so too these hypothesized qualities are nothing to us, **because we have not a sense adapted to** perceiving **them. But,** you will insist, **if we had a new sense,** some exotic organ designed specifically for perceiving qualities of this other sort, **we should possibly no more doubt of their existence than a blind man** who is **made to see does of the existence of light and colours.** Give him vision, and he will see red, yellow and blue. Give us a new sense, and we will perceive x, y and z—those unspecified qualities we are supposing require an unknown substratum. To this **I answer, first, if what you mean by the word 'matter' be only the unknown support of unknown qualities,** a mystery supporting a mystery, then **it is of no** consequence whatever. It does not **matter** in the least **whether there is such a thing or no, since it** in **no way concerns us; and I do not see the advantage there is in** asking any questions about it. What possible use is there in **disputing about we know not** *what,* **and we know not** *why?* I waste no words on nothing.

A *second response to the unknown support of unknown qualities hypothesis is that the qualities perceived by any new sense could only be ideas and—as ideas—could not exist outside of minds. The moral here is that all ideas—those that we do have and any we possibly could have—exist only so long as they are perceived by a mind.*

78. But besides the mysteriousness of the unknown qualities, there is, **secondly,** this problem: Even **if we had a new sense** capable of detecting them, **it could only furnish us with new ideas or sensations; and then we should have the** very **same reason against** supposing **their existing in an unperceiving,** material **substance,** as the reason we've advanced to show that the ideas of ordinary perception do not exist in a material substance. The line of reasoning **that has been already offered** to show that those qualities we are familiar **with**—I mean the argument we considered in **relation to figure, motion, colour, and the like**—would apply to any qualities we might learn about through the use of a new sense. **Qualities, as has been shown** in Section 7, **are nothing else but** *sensations* **or** *ideas***, which exist only in a** *mind* **perceiving them; and** our argument has established that **this is true not only of the** sensory **ideas we are acquainted with** from experience **at present, but likewise of all possible ideas whatsoever**, including any as yet undiscovered ideas that an exotic organ of perception could possibly introduce.

With mounting desperation, the materialist may claim that her empty asser-
tion, 'Matter exists', is at least free of contradiction. Berkeley concedes that
the use of meaningless terms is a sure-fire way of avoiding contradiction. But
meaningless terms express nothing. 'Matter exists' has no content.

---

79. But you will insist, the case for matter is merely *weakened* by my responses, not *lost*. Your fondness for the word will not be overcome by rational argumentation. So **what if I have no reason to believe in the existence of matter,** you will say, so **what if I cannot assign any use to it, or explain any thing by it, or even conceive what is meant by that word?** Yet I can **still** *use* the word, can't I? For **it is no contradiction to say that matter exists,** or could exist, **and that this matter is** *in general a substance***, or an** *occasion of ideas***;** these words can still be uttered **though, indeed,** every reason there was for positing matter—every reason we *thought* we had—has been eliminated. Any attempt to explain what is *meant* by saying that matter is a substance or an occasion of our ideas may leave us speechless; any effort **to go about** clarifying things, **to unfold the meaning, or adhere to any particular explication of those words, may be** fruitless and **attended with** the greatest **difficulties.** None of this stops us from *saying* that matter is a substance that exists and an occasion for implanting ideas. To this pig-headed plea **I answer, when words are used without a meaning, you may put them together as you please, without danger of running into a contradiction:** terms without content can hardly conflict. **You may say, for example, that** *'twice two* **is equal to** *seven'***, so long as you declare that you do not take the words of that proposition in their** normal sense. There's no trouble with your claim if you do not mean by 'two' and 'seven' what the rest of us mean, if you do not employ them in the **usual acceptation, but** let them stand **for marks of you know not what**—which is just to say that you let them stand for nothing. **And by the same reason you may say,** with no fear of contradiction, that **there is an inert thoughtless**

substance without accidents, which is the occasion of our ideas. You may say this because in your mouth 'thoughtless', 'substance', 'accident' and 'inert' are sounds denoting nothing: They pick out no thoughts; they suggest to us no ideas. So go ahead and say that matter is an 'inert', 'thoughtless' 'substance' without 'accidents' that may possibly exist. And I'll say that a 'gollywop' is no bigger than a 'flollyflop'. **And we shall understand just as much by** the one **proposition as** by **the other.**

Reduced to the last extreme, the materialist resorts to negatives: Matter has no extension, no place, no motion, no thought, no anything. But how does this account of matter differ from an account of nothing? Berkeley finally has the materialist where he wants her: She admits that matter is nothing. And that's what he set out to prove.

---

80. In the last place, you will resort to desperate measures. You **will** try to save matter by **saying what it is not, rather than what it is.** You will ask: **What if we give up the** hopeless **cause of** defending **material substance,** defined in any of the above ways, **and** push for its existence on some negative construal? May we not **assert that 'matter' is** to be described as **an unknown *somewhat*,** a perfectly mysterious something-or-other—**neither a substance nor** an accident, neither a spirit nor an idea,** something **inert, thoughtless, indivisible, immoveable, unextended,** and **existing in no place? For,** say you, **whatever** objections **may be urged against** the existence of matter when characterized as a *substance* or an *occasion,* or in terms of **any other positive or relative notion,** are of limited scope: They render doubtful only the positive definitions of matter proposed above. But none **of** them touch **'matter'** when construed in wholly negative terms, when matter is conceived of as a mere negation. You can't say, 'Matter, on your account, is incapable of doing what it's supposed to do', if we don't suppose it to do anything. You can't say, 'Matter isn't what you say it is', if we don't ascribe to it any properties. Matter **has no place** in the world, you say, and has no purpose **at all?** That's fine, since we didn't assign it any. All we said was that matter *isn't* any of these other things. The whole dispute can thus be avoided, **so long as this** strictly ***negative* definition of matter is adhered to. I answer** this desperation tactic by accepting it. Go ahead, I say: **you may, if you so** desire, and if **it shall seem good** to you, **use the word 'matter' in** whatever way you want. This is a verbal point and it doesn't concern me. But bear in mind that you are now using the word 'matter' with the same meaning and in **the same sense that other men use** the word **'nothing'.**

Everything you have said about 'matter' can as easily be said about 'nothing'. Like 'matter', 'nothing' isn't anything and it doesn't do anything; **and so you make those terms** synonymous and **convertible in your** curious **style** of speaking. **For after all, this is what appears to me to be the** inevitable **result of that** wholly negative **definition** of 'matter' just given. When I reflect on **the parts whereof** the definition is constructed and try to comprehend them, I come up with nothing. That is to say, **when I consider with attention** what might be meant by any of the negative terms occurring in the definition—how I consider them, **either** altogether and **collectively, or** else **separate from each other** and distinct, doesn't matter—**I do not find that there is any kind of effect or impression made on my mind different from what is excited** there **by the term 'nothing'.** The terms 'matter' and 'nothing' both give rise to the same idea (or, rather, to no idea at all), and I am happy to grant you that matter is nothing and that nothing is matter. That is the principal thesis of this entire treatise.

Having inadvertently relinquished matter, the materialist will try to regain some ground: A negative account of matter differs from an account of nothing, she will say, since it includes the idea of essence—or of entity, or existence. Berkeley replies that the ideas of essence, entity and existence are beyond his comprehension. Should the materialist retort that beings with minds greater than our own might grasp them, Berkeley will say that no being comprehends a contradiction—and existence apart from perception is a contradiction.

---

81. **You will reply perhaps, that in the** aforesaid definition of 'matter' there **is included** at least some content, from which it follows that the concept is not purely negative after all. You will say that, **what**ever properties this latest version of matter lacks, the slender content it **does** possess **sufficiently distinguishes it from nothing.** Though it is neither substance nor accident, neither spirit nor idea, matter on the proposed definition at least contains **the positive, abstract idea of** an essence—what medieval thinkers called the **'quiddity'** or 'whatness' of a thing—or, perhaps, the idea of an *entity,* **or** simply of *existence.* **I own, indeed, that those** philosophers **who pretend to** have **the faculty of framing abstract general ideas do talk as if they had such an idea** of matter. It is just the thought of an entity existing outside the mind—a placeholder with no known properties, an 'x' lurking behind our ideas—**which is, say they, the most abstract and general notion of all** (and is perhaps the sole member of a fourth class of abstract ideas in addition to the three classes

mentioned in Introduction, Sections 7, 8 and 9). Given its generality and the absence of discernible features, however, **that** notion **is to me the most incomprehensible of all others.** But should my inability to understand something be the criterion for determining what is and is not possible in perception? Yes, in one important respect, it should. I can't deny that minds more powerful than mine may have ideas falling outside the range of my perceptions or exceeding my powers of comprehension. But I can deny that any mind perceives a contradiction. **That there are a great variety of** minds I am happy to admit. There may be **spirits of different orders and capacities, whose faculties** are greater than mine, **both in** terms of the **number** of their abilities **and the extent** of their powers. That their abilities, and their powers, **are** superlative **(far exceeding those the Author of my being has bestowed on me), I see no reason to deny. As** far as that goes, such minds may experience ideas that I can't even imagine. It is not **for me to pretend to determine by** reference to **my own few,** imperfect and **stinted** sensory organs, those **narrow inlets of** all **my perceptions, what ideas the inexhaustible power of the supreme spirit may** choose to **imprint upon them.** How could I possibly know that? It would be irrational, **were** I to take any definite stance on this, and would **certainly** reveal **the utmost folly and presumption** on my part. **Since there may be, for aught that I know** and anything I can say on the basis of my own experience, **innumerable sorts of ideas or sensations** in superior minds of which I haven't the faintest notion. Such ideas would be completely invisible to me, and **as different from one another, and from all** the ideas **that I have** ever **perceived, as colours are from sounds. But how ready soever I may be, to acknowledge the scantiness** and insufficiency **of my comprehension with regard to the endless variety of spirits and ideas that might possibly exist,** I can at least rule out one thing with certainty: contradiction. An incoherent combination of words corresponds to no idea. Higher spirits may perceive many fantastic ideas I can't begin to comprehend; **yet for any one to pretend to** have **a notion of entity or existence,** *abstracted* from *spirit* and *idea*, **from perceiving and being perceived, is, I suspect, a downright repugnancy and** a distinctively philosophical way of **trifling with words.** This completes our survey of materialist counterarguments. **It remains that we consider the objections** to our principles, **which may possibly be made on the part of religion.**

Religious arguments for matter may carry weight against idealism where philosophical arguments fail. The first religious argument invokes the authority of Scripture: Many passages make reference to bodies—rivers, mountains, stones, etc. So Christians must believe in matter. Berkeley brushes this worry aside: Christian doctrine is not committed to matter in the philosophical sense. Rivers, mountains and stones may be bodies, as the passages

suggest, but nothing is said about matter. The Bible takes no stance on the metaphysics of bodies.

82. Moving, then, from reason to revelation, let us consider some of the arguments for matter arising from religion. That consistency with Christian doctrine is imperative will be evident to every pious believer. **Some** believers will take these objections to idealism very seriously indeed; **there are** those **who think that,** although the philosophical **arguments** for matter are unsuccessful, scriptural arguments **for the real existence of bodies** outside the mind will succeed. In other words, while the philosophical arguments, **which are drawn from reason,** must be regarded as failures and **allowed not to amount to** the certainty of **demonstration, yet** there are better arguments to be made on the basis of **the Holy Scriptures.** Indeed, these arguments from orthodoxy **are** supposed to be **so clear** and compelling **in** establishing **the point, as will sufficiently convince every good Christian that bodies do really exist, and are something more than mere ideas.** Very simply, the scriptural argument appeals to the circumstance of **there being in** the **Holy Writ**ings reports of **innumerable facts related** to and implying the existence of matter. To take just a few examples, there are verses **which evidently suppose the reality of timber** (1 Kings 5: 18), **and stone** (Genesis 28: 11), **mountains** (Exodus 19: 2), **and rivers** (Exodus 7: 20), **and cities** (Numbers 35: 11), **and human bodies** (Nehemiah 9: 37). **To** the charge of unorthodoxy **which** is here propounded, **I answer, that no sort of writings whatever,** whether **sacred or profane,** imply the existence of matter as the philosopher understands it. There simply are no religious texts **which use those** words 'matter' **and** 'body' in the philosophical sense. And none of **the** texts which use the **like words in the vulgar acceptation, or** the everyday sense—**so as to have any meaning in them,** rather than an outright contradiction—**are in danger of having their truth called in question by our doctrine.** The biblical verses do truly imply the existence of timber, stone and other material things in the everyday sense of 'timber', 'stone' and 'material thing'. **That all those things do really exist, that there are bodies, even corporeal substances, when taken in the vulgar sense, has** already **been shown to be agreeable to our principles; and the difference betwixt** what might commonly be called **'things' and 'ideas', 'realities' and 'chimeras', has been distinctly explained** in Sections 29, 30, 33, 36 and 41. While there are no 'material' things in the *philosophical* sense—sensible things existing *outside* the mind—there are concrete, physical things in the ordinary sense, which are vivid, constant and independent of our will. **And I do not think that either what philosophers call 'matter', or the existence of objects without the mind, is any where mentioned in Scripture,** since Scripture contains no absurdities. You won't find references to 'substrata', 'occasions'

or 'unknown somewhats': Scripture mentions timber, stones, mountains and rivers—sensible things with sensible qualities.

Idealism does no violence to everyday language. Common words refer to the common objects of experience. Materialists are the ones who use words incorrectly.

83. Again, whether there are objects outside the mind or not, whether **there be, or be not external things,** either way our principles do no violence to everyday language. For **it is agreed on all hands that the proper use of words, is the marking of our conceptions, or** the denoting of **things only as they are known and perceived by us.** Objects seen and felt—these are the things we talk about, the proper referents of our words. Language is abused when made to describe hidden natures existing behind the objects of perception; **whence it plainly follows, that in the tenets we have laid down, there is nothing inconsistent with** the customary modes of expression, no divergence from **the right use and significancy of *language*.** Materialists speak of non-perceptible substances and occasions, whereas on our system the word 'red' applies, as it should, to the red thing we perceive, and the word 'apple' picks out the very fruit I am holding in my hand and sufficiently distinguishes it from an olive or a turnip. It is evident that the words of the common man retain their usual signification on idealist principles **and that discourse of what kind soever, so far as it is intelligible, remains undisturbed. But all this** has already been demonstrated and **seems so manifest, from what has been set forth in the premises** of our arguments, **that it is needless to insist any farther on it.** It is the materialist, not the idealist, who distorts language.

Idealism detracts from the wonder of miracles. This is the second religious objection. If the world is composed of ideas, then Moses didn't turn any rod into a snake, for instance. Certain ideas in his mind gave way to certain others—nothing extraordinary. This sounds more like an illusion than a wonder. Berkeley replies that Moses did have a real rod and that he turned it into a real snake. For a rod is just a certain cluster of ideas suitably arranged. Divine interventions are still miraculous—and they still astonish mortals—even if objects

are merely ideas. There is nothing to prevent God from effecting real changes in the natural order of sensations, according to Berkeley. Matter is not required.

84. But, it will now **be urged** by my critics, **that** my principles make miracles impossible, or at least make them far less momentous than they are commonly thought to be. For miracles are supposed to effect changes in matter contrary to the laws of physics, whereas on my principles there is no such thing as matter. Thus, I will be charged with removing the possibility of miraculous intervention in nature, since there is no matter—no 'nature'—to be changed. But even if my principles didn't imply that much, it would still be said that **miracles do, at least,** turn out to be less impressive, and to **lose much of their stress and** religious **import**ance, since the great events reported by witnesses to miracles are merely reports on changes to their own ideas. And so once again, Christian orthodoxy is apparently damaged **by our principles. What must we think of Moses's rod, was it not *really* turned into a serpent** (Exodus 4: 3), **or was there only a change of *ideas* in the minds of the spectators?** Scripture tells us that the rod was miraculously transformed into a snake. But if my principles are correct, there are no material things; and if there are no material things, there are no material rods; and if there are no material rods, there can be no unnatural changes in them. The 'rod' could not have been miraculously transformed, since there really was no rod: Moses witnessed ideas of a rod being replaced by ideas of a snake. Unusual, yes—but hardly miraculous. **And,** similarly, **can it be supposed that our Saviour did no more, at the marriage-feast in Cana, than impose** images **on the sight, and smell, and taste of the guests, so as to create in them the appearance or idea only of wine** (John 2: 1–11)? Did he just give them new ideas? So what? **The same may be said of all other miracles, which, in consequence of the foregoing principles, must be looked upon only as so many** parlour tricks—mere **cheats or illusions of fancy**—and not as astonishing changes in the natural order. **To this** objection **I reply, that** my principles negate neither the existence nor the significance of miracles. On the basis of scriptural authority, I maintain that **the rod was changed** on that historic day **into a real serpent, and the water** was changed **into real wine. That** these things truly happened, I believe. And **this does not, in the least, contradict what I have elsewhere said, as will be evident from Sections 34 and 35.** For on my principles a rod reduces to its qualities—the brownness we see, the hardness we feel. It is a cluster of characteristic sensations. Thus, a sudden replacement of the ideas composing a rod with the ideas composing a snake *is* a miraculous transformation. And this can be no optical illusion. Prior to the transformation, the ideas composing the rod were as constant and real as anything can be; subsequently, the same may be said of the snake. Could a human change it back? Of course not—the thing is a snake. **But** I've covered **this** ground before. This whole **business of** what makes for the difference between *real* and *imaginary* things has been already so plainly and fully explained, and so often referred to, and the difficulties about it are so easily answered from what has gone before, that it would be bothersome for me to repeat. It were surely an affront to the reader's understanding, a great insult to their intelligence, to resume again the explication of it in this place, everything being already so clear. I shall only observe that if, at the table, all who were present should see, and smell, and taste, and drink wine, and find the normal effects of it on their mood and manners to follow the drinking of it, I should say, without hesitation, that for me there could be no doubt of its reality. So that, at bottom, the scruple raised here concerning the reality of miracles has no bearing on idealism and places it at no disadvantage with respect to materialism. That there are all these scriptural references to God transforming sensible objects has no impact whatever on our principles, but only on the received *materialist* principles I have been arguing against. After all, mind-independent rods and water cannot be transformed into anything, since they don't exist. The centrality of miracles to Christian orthodoxy thus undermines the materialist philosophy, and consequently makes rather an argument *for,* than an argument *against,* what has been said in this treatise.

Berkeley turns to cataloguing the beneficial consequences of embracing idealism. The first advantage is that it invalidates certain questions that have long occupied philosophers and kept them from addressing real problems.

---

85. Many objections to idealism have been considered and overturned: that it demotes the sensible world to an illusion (Sections 34–40) and runs the real into the imaginary (Section 41); that it can't be reconciled with our perception of outness (Sections 42–44); that it makes sensible objects pop in and out of existence (Sections 45–48); that it turns the mind into something extended (Section 49); that it undermines the corpuscular philosophy and the principles of mechanism (Section 50); that it replaces material causes with mental causes (Sections 51–53); that common opinion disproves it (Sections 54–57); that it is inconsistent with several principles of mathematics and natural science (Sections 58 and 59); that it cannot explain the internal complexity of natural machines (Sections 60–66); that it doesn't rule out alternative conceptions of matter (Sections 67–81); that it clashes with religious doctrine (Sections 82–84). Having now done away with these objections, which I endeavoured to propose in the clearest possible light, and to treat even-handedly throughout—I gave them all the force and weight I could, in spite of their evident weakness—we

proceed in the next place to take a view of our tenets in light of their consequences. What are the principal benefits of idealism? Some of these will appear
at first sight, such as this very obvious advantage: that several difficult and
obscure questions which have baffled philosophers for too long, and on which
an abundance of time has been wasted and potentially useful speculation has
been thrown away, are entirely banished from philosophy. In vain philosophers have asked: Whether corporeal substance can think? Whether matter
be infinitely divisible? And how it operates on spirit? Though these and the
like inquiries have given infinite amusement to philosophers in all ages, they
haven't produced any results. But the questions evaporate on the idealist system; for, depending on the existence of *matter* as they do, they have no longer
any place in our principles. And that's not all: Many other advantages there
are, not merely negative. Ours is a positive philosophy of spirit as well, yielding
many benefits with regard to *religion* and the *sciences*, which it is easy for any
one to deduce from what has been premised in our arguments. But this will
appear more plainly when I spell it out next in the sequel.

---

*Idealism increases our knowledge of (1) ideas or unthinking things and (2)
minds or thinking things. These will be treated in turn. Starting with (1),
Berkeley notes that materialists divide the natural world into two realms:
There are ideas in the mind and their originals outside the mind. Drawing
this distinction results in scepticism. If real things exist outside the mind, we
can never know them. For knowledge requires correspondence, and it is not
possible to check ideas against originals that are inaccessible.*

---

86. From the principles we have laid down in this treatise, it follows that
there are two categories of things in the world, and hence that all the objects
of human knowledge may naturally be reduced to two headings: first, that
of *ideas*, and, second, that of *spirits*. Ideas are the things we perceive immediately: redness, hardness, roundness, and the apple constructed out of them.
Spirits are the perceivers: human minds, the minds of angels or of God—in
a word, all thinking things whatever. Of each of these things—ideas and
spirits—there is much to say. I shall treat them in order. And the first is the
category of ideas, which shall be covered from here until Section 134. The second is the category of spirits, which shall be covered in Sections 135 through
147. Now, as to the ideas or unthinking things, our knowledge of these has
been very badly distorted by popular philosophical blunders. These blunders
have much obscured what would otherwise have been clear, and they have

confounded our efforts to achieve lasting philosophical knowledge. Indeed, faulty reasoning from false principles has raised the spectres of scepticism and atheism, **and we have** thus **been led into very dangerous** doctrinal **errors**. However, all of these problems come down to one fundamental mistake: They all arise **by supposing a twofold** division in the sensible world. We imagine a sort of 'double **existence' of the objects of sense**, splitting them apart and assigning them to different locations. Thus, on **the one hand**, the immediate objects of perception have an existence in the mind alone; the medieval philosophers called such things '**intelligibles**', since they were taken to exist only 'intellectually' **or in the mind**. Then, on **the other** hand, external objects are taken to have a '**real**' existence outside the intellect. We infer them, **and** assume that they resemble our ideas, yet **without** being able to perceive them. What exists in **the mind**, then, are the ideas of redness, roundness, etc., which constitute the apple. Outside the mind, in the external world, are the real shape and surface of the apple, and whatever other qualities it 'really' has. This real existence, **whereby unthinking things are thought to have a natural subsistence of their own,** is supposed to be **distinct from** their **being perceived by spirits**, such that the real apple would still possess its real shape and surface, even if no one were ever to perceive the redness and roundness it is capable of producing in a mind. **This** view, **which, if I mistake not, has** now **been shown to be a most groundless and absurd notion, is**, as I say, **the very root** and basis **of** *scepticism*. **For so long as men thought that** the **real things** were out there in the external world and that they **subsisted without** being perceived by **the mind, and** further **that their knowledge was only** genuine to the extent that their ideas corresponded to the external objects, they could never have knowledge since they could never be certain that correspondence was achieved. In the entire history of philosophy, we have **so far** seen not a single good argument for establishing a correspondence between a mind-dependent and a mind-independent thing—and none are **forth**coming: *real* knowledge appears to be as unattainable now **as it** has been ever since the twofold division of nature **was** first introduced. Again, since the advocates of 'double existence' could not determine that their ideas were in fact **conformable** and truly corresponded to the *real things*, **it follows, that they could not be certain that they had any real knowledge at all. For how can it be known that the things** in the mind, **which are** ideas perceived, **are conformable to those** external things **which are not perceived, or exist without the mind?** You would have to perceive the correspondence between your ideas and the external things. But you can't, since external things are imperceptible.

If sensible qualities exist in the mind, there is no question as to our knowledge of them: They are grasped fully in perception. If sensible qualities are regarded as representations of external realities, then knowledge of the world eludes us: We see appearance but not reality.

87. Colour, figure, motion, extension and the like qualities are fully present in perception, their natures on open display for the understanding. This gives our tenets a clear advantage over materialism in defeating the sceptical position. There can be no dispute as to the existence of sensible objects for the idealist: **considered only as so many *sensations* in the mind, they are** completely accessible and **perfectly known, there being nothing in them which is not perceived. But if** we allow the twofold existence of objects mentioned above, distinguishing the external existence of *things* from the internal existence of *ideas*, we open a rift between mind and world that cannot be bridged by argument. When **they are looked on as notes or images** signifying material causes, as signs **referred to** physical *things or archetypes* **existing without the mind,** sensible qualities are highly fallible indicators. They do not *prove* the existence of 'real' objects behind them, since we cannot pull back the curtain of our own ideas to see what's there. This distinction, **then,** between things and ideas divides us from the world. It regards those objects alone as real whose existence is forever unknowable. And thus, having placed the real objects beyond the bounds of sense, materialists deprive us of certainty and we **are** left with no means of establishing their existence: **we are thereby involved in all** the absurdity of philosophy and forced **into** hopeless *scepticism*. **We see only the appearances,** according to the sceptic, **and not the real qualities of the things** that supposedly cause them. **What may be the extension, figure, or motion of any thing really and absolutely, or in it self, it is impossible for us to know,** if the real things themselves are inaccessible. We know not their true qualities **but only** their effects on us, **the proportion or the relation they bear to our senses. Things** outside the mind **remaining the same, our ideas** may **vary, and which of them** correspond to a true quality in the thing, **or even whether any of them at all represent the true quality really existing in the thing, it is** impossible to say and completely **out of our reach to determine.** Treating ideas as a barrier between us and the world renders any knowledge claims about the real objects in it purely speculative. **So that, for aught we know, all we see, hear, and feel, may be only** a **phantom and** illusion, a **vain chimera, and not at all agree with the real things, existing** outside the mind in the world as they are **in *rerum natura*,** or the nature of things. **All this scepticism follows from our supposing** that there is **a difference between *things* and *ideas*, and that** the things are the external causes of our sensations. If we consider **the former** alone to be real and assume that they **have a subsistence without the mind or unperceived,** we will never know them and our view will be limited to appearance. **It were easy** for us **to dilate** further **on this subject, and show how the arguments urged by *sceptics*** in all ages, depend

on the supposition of external objects. But rather than composing a history of scepticism, let us think a little more about the advantages of rejecting this twofold existence.

Materialists are mired in scepticism, for it is impossible to confirm the existence of cognitively inaccessible objects or to know anything about their nature. This realization has led philosophers to disparage the senses and to doubt the existence of their own bodies. Idealism is the antidote to scepticism. There are no hidden realities outside the mind and there are perceptual realities in it. Sensible objects are known as well as minds.

88. **So long as we attribute a real existence to unthinking** material **things,** an existence that is **distinct from their being perceived** by the mind, we fall into the pit of scepticism. If there are such things, **it is not only impossible for us to know** anything about them, but even to say **with** confidence that they exist, since we have no **evidence** either way. Whatever **the nature of any real unthinking being** may be, it is totally foreign to us and forever beyond our reach; **but,** as I say, our knowledge of the 'real' object behind our sensations is **even** more restricted than this, since we can never have the slightest reason to suppose **that it exists.** For, as we have seen, we do not observe such 'real' things and we can form no coherent thoughts about them. **Hence it is that we see philosophers distrusting their senses, and doubting of the existence of heaven and earth, of every thing they see or feel,** and **even** questioning the existence **of their own bodies.** Descartes, for example, was not satisfied with the certainty of his own ideas and tried to reason his way out from them to the external world. He began his famous meditations by doubting the existence of ordinary things such as candles, clothes and paper, which he previously held to be material objects existing behind his perceptions. Supposing ideas to be intermediaries between his mind and the world, he tried to get behind the curtain, as it were, and to demonstrate the existence of real objects outside him. But his arguments failed and it is generally agreed that he never managed to escape from the sceptical trap he had laid. So it is with all philosophers who try to prove that there are objects outside the mind. **And after all their labour** to overturn scepticism, **and** after all their **struggles of thought, they are forced to own** the hopelessness of this endeavour, **and** to admit that **we cannot** ever **attain to any self-evident or demonstrative knowledge of the existence of sensible things** outside us. **But all this doubtfulness, which so bewilders and confounds the mind, and makes *philosophy*** look **ridiculous**

in the eyes of the world, can be avoided completely if we just abandon the project and renounce the external world. The sceptical problem **vanishes if** the things we want to know—ordinary sensible objects—exist within the mind. Our perplexity would disappear at once, if **we** would just **annex a** clear **meaning to our words, and** understand that everyday speech and thought is not about external objects but the very things we see and touch. We will be free of scepticism so long as we **do not amuse our selves with the terms 'absolute', 'external', 'exist', and such like,** employing them outside their field of application—as **signifying** thoughtless matter, a **we-know-not-what** outside the mind. Descartes was confident of his own existence, but doubted the objects around him. **I,** on the other hand, who understand what it is for a sensible object to exist, **can as well doubt of my own being as** I can doubt **of the being of those things which I actually perceive by sense**—which is to say, I can have doubts about neither. My existence and the existence of what I see and feel can be asserted with equal confidence, **it being a manifest contradiction** to say **that any sensible object should be immediately perceived by sight or touch, and at the same time have no existence in nature.** For example, **since** the candle on my desk is a cluster of ideas, I can no more doubt the existence of the candle than I can doubt the existence of the ideas. And I can no more doubt the existence of ideas in the mind than I can doubt the existence of the mind itself. On my view, **the very existence of an unthinking being**—something other than a mind—**consists in its *being perceived*** by a mind. Since I can be sure of my own ideas, I can be sure of the beings those ideas compose. I therefore know that the candle exists. My opponents do not.

Getting clear on basic terms is a necessary preliminary to establishing a lasting philosophy. The term 'thing' has three distinct referents: ideas, minds and relations. These are the objects of human knowledge. Ideas are perceived. Minds are known through feeling and reflection—in our own case—or by inference—in the case of others. Minds and relations are not perceived, though we do have notions of them.

---

89. Idealism thus provides a complete system of the world and a stable account of human knowledge impervious to sceptical attack. A quick review of its basic principles in this and the following two sections will make the advantages of our theory even plainer. **Nothing seems of more importance towards erecting a firm system of sound and real knowledge,** than to overturn the metaphysics of materialism by showing that it perverts everyday language, offends against common sense and leads inevitably to scepticism. There is no better way to establish a true philosophy of nature, **which may be proof against the assaults of *scepticism*, than to lay** its foundation in common sense and to express it in everyday modes of discourse; **the beginning** of this return to ordinary thinking and plain language consists **in** offering **a distinct explication of what is meant by 'thing', 'reality', 'existence': For in vain shall we dispute** with anyone **concerning the real existence of things, or pretend to** have **any** certain **knowledge thereof, so long as we have not fixed** precisely **the meaning of those words. 'Thing' or 'being' is the most general name of all; it comprehends under it two kinds** of things, which are **entirely distinct** from each other **and heterogeneous, and which have nothing in common but the name** 'thing' or 'being'. The two kinds of things are**, to wit, *spirits* and *ideas*. The former**, spirits, **are *active, indivisible substances*,** as we have seen already; **the latter**, ideas, **are *inert, fleeting, dependent beings*, which subsist not by themselves but are supported by, or exist in, minds or spiritual substances.** For it is incoherent to maintain that ideas exist in non-mental substances. Otherwise I don't know what an 'idea' is. The mind we know first is our own. **We comprehend our own existence by inward feeling or reflexion.** This reflexive act of immediate self-comprehension is unique**, and** though we are all acquainted with it from our own experience, it cannot be described further. It must be admitted, moreover, **that** our knowledge **of other spirits** is not as direct and intuitive as is our knowledge of ourselves, but is acquired **by** analogical **reason**ing from our own case (see Sections 140 and 145 below). **We** encounter our own minds through feeling and infer other minds by analogy with this feeling, and we **may** thus **be said to have** not a picture or image of spirits, but rather **some knowledge or notion of** them. This knowledge of **our own minds, and of** other **spirits and active beings,** comes to us, I maintain, through reflection and reasoning. To the extent that this enables us to distinguish minds from sensible objects, we have *notions* of things, **whereof in a strict sense we have not ideas. In like manner we know and have a notion of** the various **relations** that obtain **between things or ideas** (such as being bigger or smaller than, to the left or the right of, and so on); **which relations are distinct from the ideas or things related, inasmuch as the latter may be perceived by us without our perceiving the former.** I can perceive two things, A and B, without perceiving that A is bigger than B, smoother than B, brighter than B, etc. Relations thus include an act of mind whereby two things are related and they are, by virtue of that, active. **To me it seems** plain **that** we are acquainted not just with **ideas,** but with **spirits, and relations** as well. They **are all in their respective kinds the objects of human knowledge and** together they comprise the possible **subjects of discourse.** This is another point on which I disagree with the illustrious Locke, who said that we 'can have *knowledge* no farther than we have *ideas*' (*Essay*, Book IV, Chapter 3, Section 9). Since, in addition to ideas, we can speak and think of minds **and** relations, it may be concluded **that** our knowledge reaches somewhat further than Locke would have it, and that **the term 'idea' would be improperly extended to signify every thing we** can **know or have any notion of.**

Ideas do not exist outside of minds, since the existence of an idea consists in being perceived. And ideas do not look like anything outside of minds, since ideas can resemble only other ideas. Though sensible objects are composed of ideas, they can still be called 'external' insofar as they are caused by another mind or exist in another mind.

---

90. **Ideas imprinted on the senses are real things, or,** when combined and appropriately coordinated with other ideas, real objects, and they **do really exist. This we do not deny, but** there are two important things regarding ideas that **we** *do* **deny.** First, we deny that they have any kind of independent existence, that **they can subsist without the minds which perceive them.** Secondly, we deny that they correspond—**or** even *can* correspond—to any mind-independent things, **that they are resemblances of any archetypes** or originals **existing without the mind.** We deny the first, **since the very being of a sensation or idea consists in its being perceived,** as explained in Sections 3 to 5; **and** we deny the second, since **an idea can be like nothing** else **but** another idea—as explained in Section 8. **Again,** though they lack independent existence and correspond to nothing outward, **the things perceived by** the **senses may** still **be termed 'external'** without any violence to language. They obviously cannot be 'external' in the sense of existing outside the mind. But they can be 'external' in two other senses. First**, they can be 'external' with regard to their origin, in** the sense **that they** are brought about by another substance, and **are not generated from** the imaginative powers **within us,** or produced **by the mind it self.** Of course, the substance that brings them about cannot itself be mind-independent, **but** must be another mind. The 'external' things are thus **imprinted** on the senses **by** God, another **spirit** who is **distinct from that** mind **which perceives them.** The apple I see is 'external' to the extent that the qualities composing it are impressed on my mind by another. This other we know to be God. **Sensible objects may likewise be said to be** 'external' and to exist **without the mind, in another,** second **sense, namely, when they exist in some other mind. Thus when I shut my eyes, the things I saw may still exist, but** since they cannot float about freely, **it must be** that they continue to exist **in another mind.** I see this apple. It exists in my mind. I shut my eyes. Does the apple cease to exist? No, for it may continue to exist

in your mind. And if you're not around, it continues to exist in the mind of God, who is everywhere.

The reality of bodies is not compromised by the denial of matter. It is true that idealism asserts the dependence of perceptual objects on substances: The sensible qualities composing an apple do not exist on their own. But even materialists admit this. Materialism is distinguished from idealism only in respect of the type of substance that does the supporting—mind versus matter. And minds are at least as real as matter—more real, in fact, since matter is impossible. So the location of sensible objects in minds implies no loss of reality. On the contrary: It is a necessary condition of their reality, since minds are the only place they could exist.

---

91. It were a mistake to think that idealism reduces the sensible world to a dream or illusion. Only those who misunderstand my principles could suppose that **what is here said** takes anything away from nature or **derogates in the least from the reality of things. It is acknowledged on the received principles that** colour, figure, **extension, motion, and in a word all sensible qualities** whatever, **have need of a** substance to bear them. For without this **support,** where would they be? What is a quality, if not the quality of something? This seems to be implied by the very notion of a quality. And it borders on incoherence to say that one quality is supported by another—red is not supported by purple, and square is not supported by smooth. What remains, therefore, is substance: **as not being able to subsist by themselves,** and never supporting each other, sensible qualities are tied to substances. **But the objects perceived by sense are allowed to be nothing but combinations of those** sensible **qualities** observed to accompany each other in our experience: an apple is a combination of a reddish colour, a tart taste, a characteristic shape **and** texture, etc. These qualities, **consequently,** which we signify by the name 'apple', **cannot subsist by themselves. Thus far it is agreed on all hands**—even materialists recognize the need for substance. **So that in denying the things perceived by sense**—the various sensible qualities—to have **an existence independent of a substance, or support wherein they may exist, we detract nothing from the received opinion of their *reality*.** All systems of philosophy assert the dependence of qualities on substances, **and** no one equates this with a lack of being; we **are** thus **guilty of no innovation in that respect** and no downgrading of sensible reality. **All the difference** there **is** between materialism and idealism, therefore, concerns the nature of the substance supporting the qualities. But it is simply not the case **that** reality becomes an illusion when you drop matter and replace it with mind. And it's not as if there were a choice to be made between two equally plausible theories: Matter is impossible, **according to us, and the unthinking beings perceived by sense** (apples, carriages and candles), **have no existence distinct from being perceived, and cannot therefore exist in any other substance, than** minds—those **unextended, indivisible substances, or spirits, which act, and think, and perceive them.** But they are no less real for existing in minds—it is the only place where sensible qualities *could* exist, after all. **Whereas philosophers vulgarly hold, that the sensible qualities exist in an inert, extended, unperceiving substance, which they call 'matter', to which** we have no cognitive access either by reason or by sense. To this purely hypothetical substance **they attribute a natural subsistence, exterior to all thinking beings, or distinct from being perceived by any mind whatsoever,** including **even** the mind of God. This seems to me the height of philosophical pretension, asserting the existence of something invisible to **the eternal mind of the Creator, wherein they suppose** there to be **only ideas of the corporeal substances created by him, if indeed they allow them**—the corporeal substances—**to be at all created.** Some materialists have denied this, regarding matter as uncreated; blind to their faulty assumption—that matter even exists—they have been led down the path to atheism.

Belief in matter goes hand in hand with atheism and other forms of religious dissent. For example, Aristotle believed in the existence of matter, and since he couldn't fathom matter being created from nothing, he surmised that it was uncreated and eternal. This conclusion is contrary to the traditional religious teaching that all was created by God. And atheism gets a huge boost from materialism—it wouldn't even be thinkable without it, according to Berkeley. Atheists need to make sense of the natural order, but they reject design from above. So they try to explain everything in terms of matter. That won't be possible, however, if matter doesn't exist. So if they want to make sense of the natural order, atheists will need to assume a designer and thus abandon their atheism.

---

92. For just **as we have shown the doctrine of matter or corporeal substance to have been the main pillar and support of *scepticism*** about the external world, **so likewise** it is the main support of atheism. Even a cursory glance at the history of philosophy reveals that **upon the** very **same foundation** as scepticism **have been raised all the impious schemes of *atheism* and irreligion. Nay,** the doctrine of matter has likewise tempted many honest believers into holding religiously objectionable views. Materialists all face the difficulty of explaining how matter came to be. And **so great a difficulty has**

it been thought to conceive of **matter** as having a beginning of existence, to imagine it being **produced out of nothing, that the most celebrated among the ancient philosophers** have regarded it as eternal. This unorthodox tenet is not restricted to atheists, however. For **even** the wisest **of these** Greeks, those **who** unquestionably **maintained the being of a God, have thought matter to be uncreated and coeternal with him.** This is the position of Aristotle, for instance, and Aristotle was hardly an atheist. Still, materialism has a special connection with atheism, for atheism is unthinkable without it. **How great a friend** the doctrine of **material substance has been to** *atheists* **in all ages**—a kindred spirit, as it **were**—I shudder to think. This pairing of atheism and materialism is so well known that it is **needless** for me **to relate** much more on that score. **All their monstrous** philosophical **systems have so visible and necessary a dependence on it, that when** the doctrine of materialism is repudiated, when **this corner-stone** of godlessness **is once removed, the whole fabric** of their unbelief **cannot choose but fall to the ground.** Atheists can make no sense of the natural order—they are baffled by the regularity of their experiences—without the supposition of matter: They need something stable to account for their perceptions. But since material things are impossible, we refer them instead to God; it is God's will that gives us ideas. And **insomuch** as the arguments **that** we have given against matter remove the entire motivation for adopting any form of atheism, **it is no longer worth while** to consider each version individually, or to waste time contemplating their intricacies. Since my principles negate them all at once, there is no need **to bestow a particular consideration on the absurdities of every wretched sect of** *atheists*.

Belief in matter supports the denial of immortality and human freedom, and leads one away from the governing spirit. This explains its attraction for atheists. Idealism appeals to the pious, religiously-minded person, since it arms her against the atheist: Understanding the contradiction involved in postulating matter, she will be able to kick the legs out from under the views that she (and Berkeley) find so appalling.

---

93. Opponents of religion have always used matter as a crutch. **That impious and profane persons should** endorse it is unsurprising. That philosophers with a secular bent should **readily fall in with those** materialist **systems which favour their inclinations** towards atheism and irreverence is only to be expected. For, **by deriding immaterial substance, and** putting matter in its place, nonbelievers validate their rejection of Christian doctrine. First, **supposing the soul to be divisible and** as **subject to corruption** and decay **as the body,** they deny immortality; second, doing away with spirits, **which** are the only conceivable originators of causal sequences, they **exclude all freedom** from the world; third, recognizing nothing but matter in motion, they remove all trace of **intelligence, and design from the formation of things, and instead thereof make a self-existent, stupid, unthinking substance** to be **the root and origin of all beings.** What room is there for religion in a world without salvation, freedom or a governing spirit? Atheists welcome these consequences; **that they should hearken** and defer **to** materialist philosophers is therefore natural. That they side with **those who deny a providence, or** the caring **inspection of a superior mind over the affairs of the world, attributing** instead **the whole series of events** we witness **either to blind chance or to fatal necessity, arising from the** random **impulse of one body on another** and the collision of atoms: **all this is,** I say, **very natural. And on the other hand,** righteous and devout people will be drawn to idealism. For **when** right thinking **men of better** judgement and sounder **principles observe the enemies of religion laying so great a stress on** *unthinking matter,* they will surely regard it with suspicion. When they see godless sceptics promoting matter above spirit **and** labouring **all of them** in the **use** of **so much industry,** sophistry **and artifice to reduce every thing** in the world **to it,** they will surely be ready to embrace a system that shows matter to be impossible. In fact, **methinks they should rejoice to see them deprived of** matter, **their grand support, and** to see them **driven from that** last stronghold of irreligion, the mechanistic philosophy inherited from Epicurus (341–270 BC) and maintained in our own day by Thomas Hobbes (1588–1679). Matter is the **only fortress** of atheists, **without which your** *Epicureans, Hobbists,* **and the like** nonbelievers are powerless to win adherents or to turn impressionable souls from God. Without material substance, they **haven't got a prayer, not even the shadow of a pretence,** to maintain their atheism, **but become** easy targets for those armed with idealist principles. Take matter from the doubters and defeating them will be **the most cheap and easy triumph in the world.** What better practical reason could there be for accepting idealism?

Materialism also encourages idolatry. Special powers are accorded to the sun, moon and stars because they are held to be colossal material entities in the sky. If idolaters only recognized that these astronomical objects are powerless clusters of ideas in their own minds, they would be less likely to treat them as worthy of worship.

---

94. **The** harmful effects of this faulty assumption don't stop there. Commitment to the **existence of matter, or bodies** that exist **unperceived, has not**

only been the main support of *atheists*, like Epicurus **and** Hobbes. Materialism has also been the main support of *fatalists,* or hard determinists, who maintain that every event is the effect of a necessitating cause and that this precludes free will. For if our actions have material causes, and if material causes necessitate their effects, then our actions are necessitated; **but,** if they are necessitated, they are not free. If that weren't bad enough, from a moral and religious point of view, consider that **on the same principles** *idolatry* **likewise in all its various forms depends.** After all, the idolatrous worshippers of the sun, moon and stars only accorded them any power because they thought them mighty and imposing material beings, totally independent of mortal man. **Did men** ever think fit to venerate and pray to mere ideas in their heads? Of course not; **but** then, had they just **consider**ed my principles they would have understood **that the sun, moon, and stars, and every other object of the senses, are only so many sensations** or ideas **in their minds, which have no other existence but barely by being perceived.** And**, doubtless, they would never** have **fallen down and worshipped their own** *ideas* had they only recognized them as such. They would have had no cause to worship the stars or the moon**, but** would **rather** have discerned the true power behind them, **address**ing **their homage** instead **to that eternal invisible mind which produces and sustains all things** in the world.

Materialism even causes trouble for Christians. If the body of Jesus is not its outer appearance, for example, but a material substance behind it, there will be an identity problem for the story of resurrection: The body of a person who died is presumably continuous with a body resurrected only in respect of its sensible qualities—its surface features or outward form. We can identify the resurrected man as Jesus because he looks, acts, feels like Jesus, and so on. But if our principle of identification is a hidden material substance, it's not clear how we could confirm that the man before us now is the very one who died.

95. The same absurd principle—that matter exists behind our ideas—spells trouble even for those who resist the snare of atheism. For**, by mingling it self with the articles of our faith,** belief in matter **has occasioned no small difficulties to** mainstream **Christians. For example, about the** *resurrection* of the body upon the return of Christ**, how many scruples and objections have been raised by** *Socinians* **and others?** These so-called 'Socinians'— the misguided followers of Fausto Sozzini (1539–1604)—deny the immortality of man and the resurrection of Jesus. Objections to this central tenet of Christianity have indeed been raised by many nonconformists. **But do not the most plausible of them depend on the supposition** that the body resurrected is *material?* The difficulty they perceive is this: A resurrected body can hardly be composed of the very same matter as the body of a person long since dead. How can a body resurrected be the very *same* as that possessed by the person who died if it is assumed **that a body is denominated the 'same', with regard not to the** visible **form or that which is perceived by sense, but** with respect to **the** invisible **material substance which remains the same under several** sensible **forms?** There is no conceivable principle of identity that would justify classifying a resurrected body as *one and the same* with the material substance which disintegrated and decayed after death. The problem vanishes, however, if bodies are collections of ideas: **Take away this *material substance*, about the identity whereof all the dispute is** carried on, **and mean by 'body' what every plain ordinary person means by that word,** and the Christian doctrine will be far less tricky **to** maintain. Identify the body with the outward form, with **that which is immediately seen and felt,** the body **which is only a combination of sensible qualities, or ideas, and then** you may confound the Socinians with ease: **their most unanswerable objections come to nothing.**

Scepticism and confusion, fatalism and atheism, idolatry and heresy—these harmful errors depend on materialism. If it falls, they fall. This gives us a practical reason for renouncing matter. Even if all of Berkeley's demonstrations proved unsound, readers sympathetic to religion would be wise to reject it.

---

96. Matter being once expelled out of nature, drags along **with it so many sceptical** doubts **and impious notions,** and **such an incredible number of disputes and puzzling questions,** that I should be glad to see it go. Refute materialism, and all the philosophical and theological difficulties **which** attend it disappear at once. These imaginary puzzles **have been thorns in the sides of** theologians and **divines, as well as** our eminent **philosophers, and** have **made so much fruitless** and empty theoretical **work for mankind** that the greatest minds have been diverted from the pursuit of more valuable undertakings. So many problems has materialism caused, **that** even **if the arguments we have produced against it are not** totally decisive or **found** to have a persuasive force **equal** to that of **demonstration (as to me they evidently seem** to have), **yet I am sure** that all who reject scepticism and atheism, **all who are friends to knowledge, peace, and religion, have** sufficient **reason to wish** that they

were. Even lacking a demonstrative proof against materialism, therefore, we should have ample cause to reject it.

The belief in abstract ideas is another great source of error and confusion. Ordinary people understand time, place and motion: They are woven into the fabric of their experiences. Metaphysicians try to extract these elements from experience and consider them on their own. Knowledge is lost in the process.

---

97. This is not the only doctrine that friends of knowledge should wish to see expelled from science and nature. **Besides** the belief in matter, which involves **the external existence of the objects of perception,** we must also abandon the ruinous view that our mind has a power of separating qualities from things, for this is **another great source of errors and difficulties,** especially **with regard to** our knowledge of time, place and motion—call it **'ideal knowledge',** if you like. This **is the** celebrated **doctrine of *abstract ideas,* such as it has been set forth,** and decisively refuted, **in the Introduction.** What sort of damage does this doctrine cause? Quite simply, it takes us from a state of understanding the things around us to a state of confusion and ignorance. **The plainest things in the world, those we are most intimately acquainted with and** which we **perfectly know, when they are considered in an abstract way, appear** to us **strangely difficult and incomprehensible.** An honest farmer or blacksmith, with no training in philosophy, has a firmer grip on the nature of things than a modern metaphysician. He understands because his mind has not been poisoned by the theory of abstraction. **Time, place, and motion**—for the man working the field, these are the hours until sundown, the hollow under the tree and a walk along the river. When **taken in particular or concrete** experiences, **they are what every body knows** and understands; **but having passed through the hands of a metaphysician, they become** totally incomprehensible, **too abstract and fine to be apprehended by men of ordinary sense.** Bid **your servant to meet you at such a** *time,* **in such a** *place,* **and he** will know exactly what you mean. He **shall never stay to deliberate on the meaning of those words** 'time' or 'place'; **in conceiving that particular time and place** that you mentioned ('Meet me by the church at noon'), **or the motion by which he is to get thither** ('I think I'll walk rather than ride'), **he finds not the least difficulty.** Time and place are nothing beyond their contents—the particular moments we experience and the concrete settings in which we live—and these are familiar to everyone. **But if 'time' be taken** abstractly, **exclusive of** our surroundings and divorced from **all those particular actions and ideas**

that diversify the day, we have no hope of understanding it. Let 'time' stand merely for the continuation of existence or duration in the abstract, and then you've got a riddle where you should have comprehension, and it will perhaps impress the learned—like defining the winding gravel path you take to church as the 'continuum of coexisting points'—and not even a philosopher will be able to comprehend it.

Time cannot be considered on its own, abstracted from the succession of ideas we experience: There is simply nothing there to be considered apart from the particular ideas constituting any perceptual sequence. Since there is no independent measure, the length of time in which a mind exists is to be calculated by reference to the number of ideas experienced in succession. If there is no time apart from the perceptions a mind undergoes, there is no time at which a mind has no perceptions. So minds are always thinking—always undergoing perceptions.

98. **Whenever I attempt to frame a simple idea of** *time* considered on its own, **abstracted from the succession of ideas in my mind,** I find myself at a loss. The train of perceptions **which** pass before me—seeing redness at one moment, tasting sweetness at the next—**flows uniformly and** uninterrupted. These are things I understand: Seeing an apple and tasting it, hearing a bird and smelling smoke. Sequences of perceptions such as these are familiar to everyone. No one is perplexed by the taste of bread or the sound of wind, since this sort of experience **is participated** in **by all** conscious **beings.** However, when I try to give selective attention to *time* considered apart from the surrounding ideas, **I am** completely bewildered. What am I supposed to be thinking? I find myself **lost** in a haze, stuck in intellectual knots **and embrangled in inextricable difficulties.** What is this thing, which my opponents call 'time', supposed to be? **I have no notion of it at all;** when they speak about 'time' I hear **only** words, unable to connect them with any thoughts. What **I hear others say** about time embarrasses me and makes them appear ridiculous. They assert, for example, that **it is infinitely divisible, and** this implies that any portion of time is composed of smaller portions, which are themselves composed of smaller portions. So an hour includes half an hour; half an hour includes 15 minutes; 15 minutes includes seven-and-a-half minutes; seven-and-a-half minutes includes…and so on forever. When my opponents **speak of it in such a manner,** time becomes mysterious and some very weird things seem to follow. In particular, the doctrine of time **as** infinitely divisible **leads**

me to entertain odd thoughts about the nature **of my existence:** First, consider that on the doctrine of time as infinitely divisible, there will be infinitely many points of time between any two consecutive ideas. For if time is infinitely divisible, there will be no simple, indivisible points of time. If so, there will be no point of time that is followed immediately by another point of time. If so, there will be no point of time at the end of one idea that is immediately followed by a point of time at the beginning of another. And if that is so, there will be a point of time between any two consecutive ideas. **Since** this point of time will itself be infinitely divisible—into an infinity of other points—there will be infinitely many points of time between any two consecutive ideas. Now either one exists throughout all the points of time between any two ideas or one does not. If one does, then one passes through an infinite number of points of time—and without thinking at all, since we're supposing **that** one has no ideas over the interval. Conversely, if one does not pass through all the intervening points, then one pops in and out of existence between any two perceptions. Thus, the **doctrine** of the infinite divisibility of time **lays one under an absolute necessity of thinking, either that he passes away innumerable ages without a thought, or else that he is annihilated every moment of his life: both** of which **seem equally absurd.** How could one pass through infinitely many points of time without so much as a thought? How could one pop in and out of existence between any two ideas? **Time, therefore,** cannot be infinitely divisible. Furthermore, time cannot be an independent **being** or an abstraction. After all, **nothing** can be **abstracted from the succession of ideas in our minds**—abstraction already having been shown to be impossible. Time, therefore, can be nothing over and above the succession of ideas itself. Aside from these general considerations about time, there is an interesting implication concerning the nature of minds. Since time does not exist apart from the series of ideas in minds, the length of the existence of a mind cannot be measured or determined by time apart from its perceptions. From this **it follows that the duration of any finite spirit**'s existence **must be** determined by reference to its perceptions, and **estimated by the number of ideas or actions succeeding each other in that same spirit or mind. Hence, it is a plain consequence that** throughout its existence **the soul** undergoes perceptions. Given that the soul's duration is measured by the number of its ideas, so long as it exists, it **always thinks; and in truth whoever shall go about** trying **to divide** his existence from the succession of ideas **in his thoughts, or abstract the *existence* of a spirit from its *cogitation*, will, I believe, find it no easy task.** If I am right, he will find it impossible.

Folk ontology has a firm grip on extension and motion: They are features of complex experiences. Try to abstract them from experience—as philosophers are in the habit of doing—and our understanding of them evaporates. There is no such thing as extension or motion in the abstract. There are concrete things, some of which are extended or in motion.

99. So, likewise, is the simple and certain knowledge of the common man lost **when we** depart too far from any other concrete experience. If, for example, after receiving some training in philosophy we **attempt to abstract extension and motion from all other** sensible **qualities** that accompany them in our perception, **and consider them all by themselves,** we are instantly stripped of whatever hold we had on them prior to the attempted abstraction. I think I knew what motion was when I was riding in the carriage watching the trees go by; I understood extension when I stretched out on my bed. We all start out this way. But then some of us turn to books. We study metaphysics, which teaches us to abstract, and we find extension and motion henceforth confusing—**we presently lose sight of them and run into great extravagancies** and contradictions. **All which** absurdities and inconsistencies **depend on a twofold** process of **abstraction: First, it is supposed that extension, for example, may be abstracted from all other sensible qualities,** such as colour and shape; **and secondly,** it is assumed **that the entity** itself—the very being **of extension—may be abstracted from its being perceived. But whoever shall reflect** on his experience **and take care to understand what he says, will, if I mistake not,** have to **acknowledge that all sensible qualities are alike *sensations*, and** that they are all **alike *real*; that where the extension is, there is the colour too,** for to conceive the one without the other is impossible. Both exist, therefore, **in his mind, and** he must admit **that** whatever he supposes to exist beyond the ideas of his mind—whatever he supposes **their archetypes** might be—**can exist only in some other *mind*;** as sensible qualities, extension and motion cannot be abstracted from experience and imagined to exist on their own. The plain man knows extension as he knows an open meadow; he knows motion as he rides his horse. These are the things he sees **and feels**—they are his sensations. And the reflective man knows **that the objects of sense are nothing but those sensations combined, blended, or (if one may so speak) concreted together, none of all which** sensations **can be supposed to exist unperceived.**

There are no abstract ideas in the moral sphere either: Ideas of happiness, goodness, justice, virtue and the like are known concretely in particular examples and experiences. We cannot consider happiness apart from particular

pleasurable sensations, for instance. The opposing view—that moral thinking employs abstractions—has complicated the study of value. This is more than an academic problem, since our moral evaluations have practical import.

100. Setting time, space and motion aside for the moment, let us turn our attention to the ideas of value and disvalue—things like happiness and sadness, goodness and badness, rightness and wrongness, virtue and vice. **What it is for a man to be happy, or** for **an object** to be **good, every one may** quite properly **think he knows** simply by reflecting on his own experience and his various assessments of comparative worth. The farmer is happy when he feels the sun on his face; a thriving field he considers good. **But my opponents want us to frame an abstract idea of 'happiness',** cut away or **prescinded from all** the **particular** ideas of **pleasure, or** an idea **of 'goodness'** apart **from every** particular **thing that is good.** I am certain, however, that **this is what few** of us **can** even **pretend to** do. Just try to frame an idea of happiness without thinking of a particular joyful moment, a particular beaming face or a particular pleasant sensation. Can you? I cannot. **So, likewise,** we are capable of knowing whether **a man may be just and virtuous, without having precise** abstract **ideas of 'justice' and 'virtue'.** Can an unschooled peasant identify a villain as bad? Of course he can. **The opinion that those** value words **and others like** them—**words** such as 'kind' or 'cruel', 'required' or 'forbidden'—**stand for general notions, abstracted from all** our ideas of **particular** kind or cruel **persons and** particular obligatory or forbidden **actions,** is false and misguided. Even **worse,** the assumption that there are such abstract ideas **seems to have rendered** the pursuit of **morality difficult, and the** philosophical **study thereof of less use to mankind.** After all, struggling to clarify abstract moral notions distracts philosophers—and their readers—from more pressing, real-life moral concerns. **And in effect, the doctrine of *abstraction* has** produced **not** just **a little** philosophical confusion, but, given the importance of moral knowledge, has **contributed towards spoiling the most useful** and practical **parts of knowledge**—so much so that we often see those with formal training in ethics behaving just as badly, or even worse, than those without.

The benefits of idealism extend to science and mathematics as well. Modern physics drives a wedge between the knower and the objects to be known: Our perceptions are like curtains drawn between us and the underlying reality. Scepticism is the result. Idealism solves this problem by treating perceptions themselves as realities and denying the existence of anything behind them. This

restores confidence in the senses and makes immediate perceptual knowledge of the world possible.

101. This completes our survey (running from Sections 86 to 100) of the general advantages our principles have for the knowledge of unthinking things or ideas. **The** next question is what advantages they bring to the **two great provinces of speculative science.** Both of these deal with ideas, the one being **conversant about the ideas received from** the **senses and** the other treating of **their relations.** The sciences I have in mind, of course, **are *natural philosophy*** (the science of nature, comprising physics, biology and the like) **and *mathematics*; with regard to each of these I shall make some observations**—the science of nature first (Sections 101–117), followed by mathematics (Sections 118–132). (Advantages pertaining to the knowledge of spirits come up at the end—Sections 135–156.) **And so, first, I shall say some** things about **what** benefits can be expected from our principles for the theories **of natural philosophy or science. On this subject it is** clear **that the** mechanistic scientists of our day—who are, in truth, thoroughgoing *sceptics*—**triumph** over common sense and take away our knowledge of things. All their speculations about 'corpuscles'—**that stock of arguments they produce** which aim **to depreciate our faculties, and make mankind appear ignorant and low**—are based on a fallacy, the mistaken supposition of a twofold existence. Their arguments **are drawn principally from this head,** the assumption that **to** get any information about the real objects **without** the mind we would have to somehow look behind our own ideas. In other words, the division between ideas and things implies **that we are under an invincible blindness as to the *true* and *real* nature of** sensible **things** because we are separated from them by sensations. **This** theme **they exaggerate** greatly, **and love to enlarge on. We are miserably bantered** by sensations, **say they,** teased **by our senses, and amused** by ideas, which present us **only with the outside** surfaces and superficial **show of things. The real essence, the internal qualities**—those microscopic particles that are supposed to cause the observable, macroscopic features of everyday objects—are totally out of reach. The substance **and** inner **constitution of every** thing, **the** core of even the **meanest,** lowliest **object, is hid**den forever **from our view; something** real is said to be behind our ideas that we shall never come to know. And so however far science may progress in its dissections of nature, however penetrating its analyses, **there is** always going to be **in every drop of water, in every grain of sand,** something essential **which it is beyond the power of human understanding to fathom or comprehend. But it is evident from what has been shown** so far in this treatise, **that all this complaint** about science **is groundless, and that we are influenced by false principles** if we submit to such hopeless scepticism. For we can only depart **to that degree** from common sense **as to mistrust our senses, and to think we**

know nothing of those things which we perfectly comprehend, if we suppose that ideas are phantoms instead of real things.

Materialists posit unobservable internal structures to account for the observable qualities of things. The real essence of an apple, for instance, is supposed to be some unseen corpuscular structure that causes the observable colour and flavour. This structure operates mechanically, the invisible particles of various shapes, sizes and trajectories impacting on our sense organs to produce ideas of colour and flavour in us. Berkeley finds this story incoherent, for shapes, magnitudes and motions are inert. Only minds can act. Any attempt to explain observable qualities mechanistically will be susceptible to this response.

---

102. **One great inducement to our pronouncing our selves ignorant of the** real **nature of things**—probably the greatest incentive—**is the currentl**y prevailing **opinion that every thing includes within it self** an internal structure or mechanism that is **the cause of its** external **properties, or,** in other words, **that there is in each object an inward,** hidden **essence, which is the source** from **whence its** visible, **discernible qualities flow and whereon they depend.** My opponents thus group the properties of things under two headings: the inner, real ones, which we cannot see, and the outer, apparent ones, which we can—the outer depending on the inner. For example, the apple has the outer properties of redness, roundness and sweetness, which we detect by sight, touch and taste. These superficial qualities of the apple are supposed to be produced by its inner nature. Don't be fooled: This inner nature is not the white fleshy part that supports the red and round surface—it's not the part holding the sweet, flavourful juice. Rather, it is said to be some internal constitution, a secret texture we cannot observe. The perceivable white core depends no less on the unperceivable machinery than does the red surface, according to these mechanistic thinkers. **Some** of the ancient and medieval philosophers **have pretended to account for** the **appearances**—the outward properties of things—**by 'occult qualities',** about which nothing whatever could be said, **but of late** philosophers and scientists claim to understand the inner workings of things. They claim to have identified the hidden springs of all that we see—of trees, mountains, apples and churches. On their principles, **they are mostly resolved into** particles of unseen matter that function as **mechanical causes** of the outward forms. This hypothesis is sufficient, they say, **to** account for all the phenomena of nature: **without** offering any explanation of the actual mechanism by which it happens, they just assert that **the figure, motion, weight, and such like**

qualities of insensible particles cause the visible appearances of things. Thus it is the motions and collisions of atoms in the apple that ultimately explain its redness, roundness and sweetness. My opponents insist on mechanical causes of this sort, **whereas in truth** we must reject them. As I made clear, **there is no other agent or efficient cause than** *spirit*, it being evident that motion, as well as all other *ideas*, is perfectly inert and incapable of producing anything. See Section 25. Hence, to endeavour to **explain the production of** observable properties—the **colours** we see **or the sounds** we hear—**by** postulating an inner nature—the **figure, motion, magnitude, and the like,** of unseen particles— **must** be time ill spent. Science has no **need** of mechanistic explanations, and any attempt to provide them will **be labour in vain. And accordingly, we see** clearly that **the** past **attempts of that kind are not at all satisfactory.** But it is not just that figure, motion and magnitude are causally inert and thus incapable of doing anything. Of all possible combinations of ideas, how many of them have causal powers? **Which** of them are capable of *acting*? None. Thus our negative verdict **may be said** to apply, **in general,** to every system of nature presupposing the causal efficacy of matter. All **of those instances** of mechanistic explanation, **wherein one idea or quality is assigned for the cause of another**, are fundamentally wrong. As for the superiority of our system, **I need not say how many** useless *hypotheses* **and speculations are left out** when you admit only ideas and spirits, **and how much the study of nature is** simplified and **abridged by this** idealist **doctrine** I have been defending.

Scientists who try to explain the observable qualities of things in terms of the impact of minute particles on our sense organs—by way of 'contact action', in other words—need some other story when it comes to explaining the apparent interactions of bodies placed at a distance from each other. What mechanical principle explains the falling of a stone or the rising of the tides? Modern physicists cite gravity or 'attraction': A body falls towards the earth because of attraction. But this explains nothing, according to Berkeley. It is equivalent to saying that a body falls towards the earth because it falls towards the earth. Similar reasoning applies to the coherence—or stable appearance—of hard bodies: A rod of steel retains its shape, we are told, because of 'attraction'. Again, Berkeley regards this as a non-explanation. 'The parts are attracted to each other' says no more than that the rod of steel retains its shape.

103. Unfortunately, natural scientists have failed to recognize the explanatory potential of spirit as a cause of ideas. **The** trend is rather to 'explain'

the phenomena by appeal to 'impulse'. That is to say, the collisions of hidden particles are supposed to cause, by some unknown mechanism, the various ideas we perceive. Where bodies are not in direct contact with one another, where we can't suppose the particles to actually be touching, the **great mechanical principle** of explanation, which it is **now in vogue** to cite, **is** gravity or ***attraction***. **That a stone falls to the earth, or** that **the sea swells towards the moon,** is a matter of 'attraction', we are told, and it **may to some appear** that the phenomena in question are **sufficiently explained thereby. But how are we enlightened by being told** that **this is done by attraction? Is it that that word signifies the manner of the tendency** by which **stones fall, and** seas swell? Are we being told about the direction of causation, **that it is by the mutual drawing of bodies, instead of their being impelled or protruded towards each other? But** I don't feel any better informed after hearing someone say, 'It's because of attraction', for **nothing is determined of the manner** by which the stone is drawn to the earth. And the mechanism **or action,** which causes the tides, is still completely mysterious to me. I am left in the dark on this theory, **and it may as truly (for aught we know) be termed 'impulse' or 'protrusion' as 'attraction',** for none of those words tell me anything. **Again, the parts of steel we see cohere firmly together, and this also** requires an explanation. This cohesion of parts—the firmness of steel—**is accounted for by attraction** as well; **but in this, as in the other instances,** the observed phenomena are simply restated. The parts of steel stick together because of their mutual attraction—in other words, because they stick together. **I do not perceive that any thing is signified** here **beside the effect itself**—the sticking together of parts. **For as to the manner of the action whereby it is produced, or the cause which produces it,** nothing is said. Indeed, **these** further details **are** left out of the account entirely, being, it seems, **not so much as aimed at in the explanation.**

Scientists account for various natural phenomena in terms of gravitational attraction—from the falling of stones to the rising of seas, from the cohesion of steel to the crystallization of minerals. That bodies tend towards the earth is something familiar to everyone from their own experience. That they also move upwards towards the moon will strike many people as strange, since this tendency is typically seen only in connection with the tides. But it won't faze a scientist, since she observes gravitational effects elsewhere—amongst the planets, for instance—and is always watching for patterns. This is an instance of science bringing diverse phenomena under a general rule—the only sort of 'explaining' that natural science can do.

---

104. Though modern scientists are fond of explaining the behaviour of bodies in terms of attraction, I don't find such 'explanations' particularly revealing or deep. That is not to deny that bodies do exhibit this tendency. **Indeed, if we take a** closer **view of the several** different *phenomena* supposedly 'explained' by attraction **and compare them together, we may observe** that there is **some** similarity or **likeness** in their character **and** a fair bit of **conformity between them.** **For example, in the falling of a stone to the ground, in the rising of the sea towards the moon, in** the **cohesion** of parts **and the crystallization of minerals, there is something alike** in their behaviour, **namely an union or mutual approach of** the **bodies** towards each other. **So** scientists have identified something real here—the propensity of bodies to approach each other—and this gives them a certain advantage over non-scientists, even though the term 'attraction' doesn't really explain anything. In fact, there are so many instances of bodies tending towards each other **that any one of these** examples I've given **(or** any **others like** them) are regarded by most scientists as routine *phenomena*. At the very least, they **may not seem** so **strange or surprising to a man who has** studied science **nicely** and has closely **observed and compared the effects of** bodies on each other in **nature. For** we think **that** a type of behaviour is strange **only** when it is unusual; an event **is thought** surprising only **so** long as it is something **which is uncommon, or** is **a** unique **thing** that stands out **by it self, and** which is **out of** keeping with **the ordinary course of** nature, or at odds with **our** own **observations. That bodies should tend** to fall **towards the centre of the earth is not thought strange, because it is what we perceive every moment of our lives. But that they should have a like gravitation**al inclination upwards, that they should tend **towards the centre of the moon, may seem odd and unaccountable to most men, because** they don't observe **it** in any other bodies. Natural motion upwards **is discerned** by most people **only in** connection with **the tides. But a** natural scientist or **philosopher, whose thoughts take in a larger** scope, and whose observations **encompass** much more **of nature,** will surely know better. The scientist, **having observed a certain similitude of appearances,** will find it unremarkable that bodies should also gravitate towards the moon. After observing mutual attraction everywhere—**as well in the heavens as on the earth**—the movement of the tides will hardly surprise, or confuse him. It is thus the pervasiveness of this tendency **that** habituates the scientist to otherwise curious phenomena like the tides and **argues** against their strangeness. He sees **innumerable bodies to have a mutual tendency towards each other,** and he classifies their motions by reference to a principle, **which he denotes by the general name 'attraction'.** This he takes to be a basic feature of the natural order, and **whatever** goings on **can be reduced to that** general rule, **he thinks justly accounted for** and adequately explained. **Thus he explains the tides by the attraction of the** earth (a **terraqueous globe) towards the moon** (a chunk of rock)**, which to**

him does not appear odd or anomalous, but only a particular example of a general rule or law of nature: universal gravitation.

Mechanistic materialism locates the causes of our perceptual experience in a mind-independent realm of particles that can never be accessed directly. Idealism, by contrast, rejects causal explanations in favour of systematic pattern recognition within the realm of ideas. The natural scientist formulates general rules based on observed regularities in sensation and then uses those rules to make predictions about the phenomena that will occur under such and such conditions. The scientist's knowledge is therefore broader and more methodical than the layperson's, but it is not different in kind.

---

105. Compare this model of scientific explanation with that put forward by Locke. According to Locke, attaining scientific knowledge of a material substance would require knowing its 'real essence'—its underlying corpuscular structure—and scientific explanation would involve showing how the observable qualities and powers of a thing flow from its hidden nature. But grasping the nature or essences of things is impossible, if reality is assumed to lie behind the phenomena. On the contrary, we have shown that the phenomena themselves are real and that scientific explanation consists in relating particular effects to general rules. **If therefore we consider the difference there is betwixt natural philosophers and other men with regard to their knowledge of the *phenomena*, we shall find** that the scientific man is simply better at recognizing patterns in nature than one who is ignorant of science. His view of nature is more systematic in that he is able to formulate rules covering a broader range of phenomena; **it consists, not in an exacter knowledge of the efficient** or moving **cause that produces them, for that can be no other than the *will of a spirit*, but only in a greater largeness of comprehension**—a more expansive vision rather than a deeper understanding of causation. His is an instrumental sort of knowledge **whereby analogies, harmonies, and agreements are discovered in the works of nature, and the particular effects explained, that is** to say, related or **reduced to general rules (see Section 62), which** he learns through observation. Such **rules are grounded on the analogy and uniformness observed in the production of natural effects,** and they **are most agreeable and sought after by the mind,** their agreeableness and value stemming from the increase in predictive power we gain by knowing them. Aside from discerning the wise ends embodied in the rules of nature (see Section 107), the aim of science is to learn and record them; **for that they**

extend our prospect, that they broaden our view **beyond what is present, and near to us** in sensation, **and enable us to make very probable conjectures,** touching on **things** remote from our immediate experience, things **that may have happened at very great distances of time and place, as well as to predict things to come,** is confirmed by the steady advance of science; **which sort of endeavour towards omniscience is** also **much** sought after and hardly **affected by** inherent limitations of **the mind.**

The observation of regularities in nature feeds a tendency to generalize beyond the range of the phenomena observed. We see many bodies inclining towards each other, for example, and we rashly conclude that all bodies incline towards each other without searching for possible exceptions. And yet there are exceptions: the fixity of the outermost stars, the upward growth of plants, the expansion of air. If gravitational attraction were an essential feature of bodies, then these bodies would incline towards other bodies as well. Since they (allegedly) don't, gravitational attraction is not an essential feature of bodies. Rather, the bodies that do exhibit gravitational attraction are determined to do so by the will of God.

106. But we should proceed warily and exercise cautious restraint **in such things.** We should not be too confident of our conclusions or just assume that the rules we discover have no exceptions, **for** then **we are apt to** make mistakes. Men are disposed to **lay too great a stress on analogies, and** to exaggerate the connections they observe between things. We tend **to see the** similarities and to overlook the differences. This is mere **prejudice** on our part and offers no guarantee **of** accuracy or **truth.** Indulging the natural tendency to see resemblances between things where none exist, philosophers and scientists often land in error; they **humour that eagerness of the mind whereby it is** eventually **carried to extend its knowledge into general theorems** and universal laws and they fail to notice the special cases where the laws don't apply. **For example, gravitation or mutual attraction, because it appears in** so **many instances,** is taken to govern the behaviour of all bodies without exception. After seeing countless objects incline towards each other, **some** scientists **are straight**away convinced that every object is so disposed as to seek out its neighbour. They see in those instances of attraction reason enough **for pronouncing** gravitation a strictly **'universal'** force; **and**, indeed, they make attraction a basic feature or intrinsic property, insisting **that to 'attract, and be attracted by every body, is an essential quality inherent in all bodies**

whatsoever'. Whereas, on the contrary, **it appears** that **the fixed stars have no such tendency** to move **towards each other; and so** attraction is not an essential quality of bodies and gravity is not a universal law—**far** from it! What we find if we look at things impartially **is that** bodies behave in a variety of ways; **gravitation** is so far **from being 'essential'** to the behaviour of **bodies that, in some instances, a quite contrary principle seems to show it self.** Thus, some things tend not to attract but to repel and move away from each other**, as in** the case of **the perpendicular growth of plants and the elasticity of the air.** If gravity were universal, plants would not reach up from the ground but should run along the surface or push down into it, since they would be powerfully attracted to the earth; similarly, air should not expand to fill a container as it does, but should always set a downward course, since air is no less a body than a rock is. **There is nothing necessary or essential in** the mutual attraction of bodies, as **these cases** illustrate**, but** there is something aside from gravity that governs universally: the decrees of God. Thus **it** is that what happens **depends entirely on the will of the *governing spirit*, who** determines how various bodies will move. There is gravitational attraction only because God **causes certain bodies to cleave together or tend towards each other according to various** natural **laws.** However, he can always decide otherwise; **whilst** God brings some bodies together, **he keeps others** (such as the outermost stars) **at a fixed distance** from each other**; and to some** others **he gives a quite contrary tendency to fly asunder** and resist the gravitational pull (as in the case of plants and the air)**, just as he sees** fit and **convenient** to do. The only necessity in nature, accordingly, is the necessity of God's will.

Berkeley draws a few conclusions regarding the scope and methods of natural science. First, no investigation of the sensible world will uncover efficient causes, so they are not within the purview of science. Second, natural 'philosophers'—which is to say, scientists—should sometimes think in terms of final causes, trying to identify the purposes and functions of things. Third, the natural world is still a fit object of scientific investigation, even though there is no penetrating to the inner essences of things or moving beyond the phenomena. Fourth, the identification of regularities in nature allows scientists to make reasonable predictions about what sensations will occur in various perceptual contexts.

107. After what has been premised in our arguments above, **I think we may lay down the following conclusions** as established. **First, it is plain** that scientific explanations in terms of the 'attraction' of bodies to one another or the 'cohesion' of their parts do not provide any insight into the efficient causes of the events they are meant to explain. Nor do 'explanations' of colour, sound and the like sensible qualities by reference to the collisions of unseen particles reveal anything. The point of scientific explanation is rather to recognize patterns in the phenomena and to subsume them under general rules. And so **philosophers** just **amuse themselves in vain, when they inquire** into corpuscular structures or look **for any natural**—that is to say, material—**efficient cause** of things. As we have shown, there is no cause **distinct from a *mind* or *spirit*. Secondly, considering** that **the whole of creation is the workmanship of a *wise and good agent*,** it **should seem** fitting for scientists **to become** familiar with the purposes God may have had in creating things. Indeed, natural **philosophers** ought **to employ their thoughts** in this way, and **(contrary to what some hold)** spend some time thinking **about the final causes**, or ultimate purposes, **of things: And I must confess** that, contrary to what Descartes says in his *Principles* (Part I, Section 28), **I see no reason why pointing out the various** purposes or **ends, to which natural things are adapted, and for which they were originally** and **with unspeakable wisdom contrived, should not be thought** scientifically valuable. It is certainly **one good way of accounting for them, and** is an undertaking **altogether worthy of a philosopher. Thirdly, from what has been premised** someone might infer that there is **no** good **reason** to study the natural world or to learn what follows what in the course of nature, since there are no causal mechanisms connecting the phenomena. But no such conclusion **can be drawn.** I do not see **why the** whole **history of nature should not still be studied, and** why scientific **observations and experiments** not still be **made.** For of the many systematic observations and experiments, **which** have already been made in the name of science, it can hardly be denied **that they are of** great **use to mankind, and** that they **enable us to draw many general conclusions,** both about what has happened in the past and about what is likely to happen in the future. And this **is not the result of any immutable habitudes or** permanent causal **relations** obtaining **between the things themselves,** since there are none, **but only of** the uniformity of the laws our creator has decreed. **God's goodness and kindness to men** is most evident **in the** constancy of events: there is steadiness and purpose in his **administration of the world. See Sections 30 and 31. Fourthly, by a diligent observation of the *phenomena* within our view** and a propensity to watch for patterns, **we may** soon **discover the general laws of nature, and from them deduce** the sensations to follow. Once we know rules, we may predict **the other *phenomena*.** I do **not say** we may *demonstrate* with complete certainty that such and such an event will always be followed by such and such other event, **for all deductions of that kind depend** upon the immutably of the laws of nature—a very natural but unprovable **supposition.** For **that the Author of nature always operates uniformly, and in a constant observance of those rules we take for**

principles, is something **which we cannot evidently know** without knowing God's overall plan.

A successful scientific investigation may result in the articulation of a natural law. Such laws tell us nothing about causes; they tell us only what is likely to happen in such and such circumstances. For example, the law of universal gravitation does not tell us that a big body will cause a little body to move towards it; it just tells us that the little body will move, not why. Why does a stone fall when released? It's not the main business of science to say. Laws help us to predict what will happen to stones that are released—nothing more. But we must be cautious: Too strict an adherence to the 'rules' of nature can lead to mistaken predictions, just as too strict an adherence to the rules of grammar can lead to linguistic mistakes.

---

108. Those most perceptive **men** of science, such as Newton, **who** search for natural laws do not regard them as articulating fundamental features of the world or as providing any deep understanding of reality. Laws are nothing but useful instruments for making predictions about the behaviour of bodies, as I explained already in Section 66. The aim of science is to **frame general rules** governing bodies **from** a careful observation of **the** natural *phenomena,* **and afterwards** to use those rules to make predictions and **derive the** *phenomena* that are likely to occur in the future. For example, we may first observe that bodies tend to fall towards the earth: This we have seen a thousand times. Taking note of our observations we then formulate a rule to the effect that all bodies are inclined to fall. Finally, **from those rules** thus formulated we make a prediction concerning the future course of some particular body: It will tend towards the earth as well. Nothing has been said in all this of the power or force of bodies, and indeed scientists do **seem to consider** natural laws as **signs** of things to come **rather than** as real **causes** of them. It is worth noting, however, that formulating rules is not always necessary for making accurate predictions. Just as a native speaker can master English without understanding its grammar, a mindless rustic can master the language of nature. **A man** with no training in science **may well understand natural signs**—he may antici-pate that a stone will fall, that a strip of metal will expand or that a partic-ular crop will grow—**without knowing** the laws his predictions presuppose. He can extrapolate from specific cases familiar to him without grasping **their** general form, without seeing the **analogy** they bear to similar cases, **or being able to say by what rule a thing is so or so. And,** at the other extreme, just

as it is very possible to write improperly by focusing too much on grammatical rules, it is possible to make faulty predictions by applying laws too widely. For example, we read in the grammar books that apostrophes are used to indicate possession. Upon learning this rule, some grammatical extremists will want us to write 'the 1690s' rather than the '1690's', since this is not a genitive construction—the decade is not in possession of anything. Carried away by the rule, they fail to notice that apostrophes are also used to indicate the omission of letters, as in 'don't' and 'won't', as well as to separate numerals from letters, as in 'The 2's and 3's were missing from the deck'. Similarly, prior to observation, one might insist that the fixed stars tend towards each other, since all bodies tend towards each other. But as we saw in Section 106, this rule has exceptions. The important lesson here is that **through too strict an observance of general grammar-rules** we may end up writing incorrectly; and, just **so, in arguing from general rules of nature it is not impossible** that **we may extend the analogy** between cases **too far, and by that means run into mistakes** and make inaccurate predictions.

It is best to take a broad perspective when reading a book. Try to distil the central theme and the main idea the author wants to convey: This will lead to insight. Focusing too narrowly on the language in which it is written will only cloud the issues. Berkeley extends this point to the book of nature: Excessive fussing over the rules connecting phenomena may prevent one from getting the bigger picture.

---

109. Though the laws of nature are like the rules of grammar God uses to communicate with us (see again Sections 43, 44 and 65), we must not lose sight of nature by focusing too much on the rules. **As in reading other books, a wise man will choose to fix his thoughts on the sense** of the words **and apply** his mind to grasping the whole and **its** overall significance; he should try **to** understand the sentences as they were **used** by the author, **rather than** to **lay them** all **out** on his writing slate and parse their grammar **in** detail. A man will fail to understand the meaning of a literary work—he won't appreciate its beauty—if he gets caught up in compiling **grammatical remarks on the language** in which it is written; he must put his grammar aside and simply read it. Just **so, in perusing the volume of nature,** in reading the book of God, **it seems beneath the dignity of the mind to** obsess about the laws to the exclusion of the natural environment. One may **affect an exactness** of mind in studying nature. One may put on airs of precision **in reducing each particular**

phenomenon to general rules, or showing how it follows from them. But this dulls the spirit. **We should propose to our selves nobler** and more sweeping **views** of nature, **such as to recreate** a sense of wonder in ourselves. We should reinvigorate **and exalt the mind, with a prospect of the beauty, order, extent, and variety of natural things; and hence, by proper inferences, to enlarge our notions of** the world, to appreciate more fully **the grandeur, wisdom, and beneficence of the Creator; and lastly, to make the several parts of the Creation, so far as in us lies,** fulfil their natural purposes. The ultimate aim of science is not to dissect the things around us, but to make them **subservient to the ends they were designed for,** namely, **God's glory, and the** nourishing, **sustentation and comfort of our selves and** our **fellow-creatures.** This is the pragmatic dimension of science, which I regard as central.

The greatest work of natural science—Isaac Newton's Principia—contains some notable errors. In particular, he mistakenly supposed that space, time and motion exist outside the mind, and that space and time can be hived off from sensible objects completely.

---

110. **The best key for** understanding **the aforesaid analogy** between grammar and the laws of nature, **or** just for understanding the methods of **natural science** in general, **will be easily acknowledged to be a certain celebrated treatise on *mechanics*,** undoubtedly the finest 'grammar' of nature available. I am speaking, needless to say, of Newton's *Principia*. The extraordinary achievements of this man are not in question. I should simply like to note the several points on which our theories diverge. In the comments to his eighth definition, **in the entrance of** that book—**which** is otherwise a **justly admired treatise**—**time, space and motion, are** each **distinguished into** two types, variously called 'absolute' and 'relative', 'true' and 'apparent', 'mathematical' and 'vulgar' (Definition VIII, Scholium): **Which** is to say that there is absolute space and relative space, absolute time and relative time, absolute motion and relative motion. The **distinction** between absolute and relative, **as it is at large** and in considerable detail **explained by the author, supposes those quantities** of space, time and motion **to have an existence without the mind.** In other words, it is assumed that both absolute and relative time, absolute and relative space, absolute and relative motion all exist independently of our sensations, **and that they are** nonetheless identified, and **ordinarily conceived of, with relation to sensible things.** Bodies are the sensible measures of space, time and motion, according to Newton, but they are measures **to which the**

first and second of these quantities **nevertheless in their own nature** owe nothing. (Unlike space and time, absolute motion may require, even for Newton, at least *one* body moved.) Space and time would exist even if sensible things did not, he insists, and **they bear no relation**—neither of dependence nor resemblance—to sensible objects **at all.** These are opinions which I flatly reject, as may be apparent already from my comments above. I will now clarify Newton's thinking about absolute space, time and motion as best I can and endeavour to say exactly where he goes wrong. This will give me opportunity to lay out my own thoughts on the subject in somewhat greater detail.

Arguments against absolute time were considered above. Absolute space and absolute motion are targeted over the next several sections. Absolute space and motion contrast with relative space and motion. Newton's criteria for distinguishing true or absolute motions from apparent or relative motions are summarized.

111. **As for *time*, as it is there** in Newton's *Principia* understood—that is to say, as for time **taken in an absolute or abstracted sense,** standing **for the duration,** continuity **or perseverance of the existence of things,** but divorced from the succession of ideas that mark its passage—**I have nothing more to add concerning it.** There is no need to dwell on absolute time, **after what has been already said on that subject,** in **Sections 97 and 98,** where it was shown to be impossible. **For the** other two quantities—absolute space and absolute motion—a lengthier discussion is required (I devote the **rest** of this section, as well as Sections 112 to 117, to the unravelling of these confused notions). In the treatise just mentioned, **this celebrated author holds** that **there is an 'absolute space', which** is an entity in its own right and would still exist even if there were no objects in it. This absolute space, underlying our visual and tactile perceptions but **being unperceivable to sense, remains in it self** completely uniform throughout and **similar** in all its parts, each part having a distinct identity; it is unchanging **and immoveable,** perfectly indifferent to its contents. On the other hand, **relative space** is a moveable measure or region of absolute space, **to be** determined by our senses in relation to surrounding bodies. Since absolute space is imperceptible, relative space is for us **the measure thereof, which being moveable, and defined by its situation in respect of sensible bodies, is vulgarly taken for immoveable** or absolute **space.** To adopt one of Newton's examples (*Principia*, Definition VIII, Scholium): because the air in the heavens above us is fixed with respect to the earth, we normally suppose that its space is immoveable, though in fact the space occupied by the air moves through absolute space as the earth rotates. **'Place' he defines to be that part of space which is occupied by any body.** So the absolute place occupied by the moon right now is that part of absolute space in which it is currently sitting. **And according as the space is absolute or relative,** true or apparent, **so also is the place.** An absolute place corresponds to an absolute space and so is truly at rest, whereas the place occupied by my carriage is relative and will change when the horses get going. **'Absolute motion' is said to be the translation** or shifting **of a body from** one **absolute place to** another **absolute place, as relative motion is** the transferring of a body **from one relative place to another. And because the parts of absolute space do not fall under our senses** and are therefore inaccessible, **instead of** determining place and motion with respect to **them, we are obliged to use their sensible** analogues in experience. In the ordinary affairs of life, we use concrete **measures** of motion and place as points of reference, **and so define both place and motion with respect to** particular **bodies, which we regard as immoveable,** whether or not they really are. Thus, lying on the bunk of my cabin in a ship under sail, I consider myself and the bunk as at rest, while the mouse on the floor runs about. The ship moves as it crosses the sea, while the sea, we suppose, stands still. **But it is said** that **in philosophical matters,** where the only concern is truth, **we must abstract from our senses, since it may be that none of those bodies which seem to be quiescent** and stationary **are truly so.** The fixed stars may be shifting their positions relative to some body in the outer reaches that is absolutely at rest, **and the same thing which is moved relatively** here in our vicinity **may be really at rest** with respect to that distant object. **As likewise,** with a variable frame of reference, **one and the same body may be in relative rest and motion, or even moved with** two or more **contrary relative motions at the same time, according** to the point of view; **as its place is variously defined, so is its motion. All which ambiguity** of reference **is to be found in the apparent** or relative **motions, but not at all in the true or absolute, which should therefore be alone regarded in philosophy. And the true** motions, **we are told** (Definition VIII, Scholium), **are distinguished from apparent or relative motions by the following properties. First, in true or absolute motion, all parts which preserve the same position with respect to the whole,** all contained bodies in fixed alignment with their containers, **partake of the motions of the whole.** So, if the crust of a planet is truly in orbit, then so is the core—even though the core fails to transfer out of the vicinity of the immediately surrounding body, as the Cartesian theory of motion would require for the core to be considered in motion. **Secondly, the place being moved, that which is placed therein is also moved: so that a body moving in a place which is in motion, does participate in the motion of its place.** Were it possible for the place where the sun is to move absolutely, then, should that place move, so would the sun. (But the absolute places that constitute absolute space are, according to Newton, absolutely immoveable, and so the absolute motion of a body cannot be defined independently of absolutely immoveable places.) **Thirdly, true motion is never generated or changed, otherwise than by force impressed on the body it self,** whereas relative motion can be generated or changed by a force impressed on *other* bodies. If my carriage is at rest relative to yours and then your horse starts pulling your carriage, then my carriage acquires motion *relative* to yours, though no force was impressed on mine. **Fourthly, true motion is always changed by a force impressed on the body moved,** while a relative motion may not be. If a salmon is chasing a minnow upstream and a sudden swell hurls them back whilst preserving their relative positions, they might continue swimming upstream with the same relative motion. **Fifthly,** absolute circular motions have real effects, whereas relative circular motions do not. For example, with the ini**tial circular motion** of water in a spinning bucket—when the water has **barely** had a chance to catch up with the bucket—the **relative** motion, between bucket and water, is greatest and **there is no centrifugal force.** But then the water accelerates, **which** minimizes the relative motion, and its surface becomes concave. Water may have great relative circular motion, therefore, with no centrifugal effects; **nevertheless, in that** water **which is** exhibiting **true** motion, **or** which is spinning **absolutely,** the force **is proportional to the quantity of motion.**

There is no such thing as the motion of a body without reference to another. We can conceive a body moving only with respect to another body or background. But motion towards, away from, across another body and so on, is relative. Since conceivability is a criterion of possibility for Berkeley, non-relative motion is impossible.

112. But notwithstanding what has been said by Newton about absolute motion, **it does not appear to me that there can** in fact **be any motion other than** the *relative* sort we have been discussing; **so that** for me **to conceive of motion, there must be at least** conceived **two bodies, whereof the distance** between them changes, **or their position in regard to each other is varied. Hence, if there was one** body **only,** with no other **body of any kind in being, it could not possibly be moved.** Try this for yourself: Imagine a single thing moving without referring it to any other thing whatever—not even a backdrop. Try to picture a carriage moving away, not from a castle or a church, but from…nothing at all. **This** seems to me **evidently** impossible, **in that the idea I have of motion necessarily includes** the idea of one body moving in **relation**

to another body. The statement 'x moves' is incomplete; 'x moves relative to y' is not. Absolute motion is therefore a fiction.

Some philosophers relativize motion too far. They accept both of the following claims: (1) To conceive of some body, A, as in motion, we must relate it to some other body, B, by reference to which A moves; (2) Either body in a relative motion may be regarded as the one moving. Berkeley accepts (1) but not (2). The moving body is the one receiving the force that initiates the change in relative distance. Berkeley is certainly aware that in some relative motions a force is impressed on both bodies. In such cases, both A and B are moving. His point is that sometimes it is correct to say that A moves relative to B, but incorrect to say that B moves relative to A. B's 'motion' is only apparent.

---

113. But though we reject Newton's conception of absolute motion as unintelligible, this does not mean that we must abandon the everyday distinction between true and apparent motion. We needn't allow, in other words, that whenever two bodies can be conceived as undergoing relative motion with respect to one another that each of them has an equally valid claim to being the one in motion. Look at it this way: though **in every motion it be necessary to conceive more bodies than one, yet it may be that one** body **only is moved, namely that on which the force causing the change of distance is impressed, or in other words, that** body **to which the action is applied.** If I throw my hat in the air, what's moving: the hat or the earth? Clearly it's the hat, for the hat received the impulse. **For however some** philosophers **may define relative motion, so as to term that body 'moved' which changes its distance from some other body, whether the force or action causing that change were applied to it or not; yet** this relativizes motion too far, **as if** *either* body in a **relative motion is** with equal propriety said to be moving. All I say is that conceiving of motion requires conceiving of two or more bodies. Absolute motion, therefore, is inconceivable, and even Newton admits it is imperceptible. So we leave pure motion aside and focus on **that which is perceived by sense, and regarded in the ordinary affairs of life,** viz., relative motion. Considering its familiarity, **it should seem that every man of common sense knows what it is, as well as the best philosopher. Now I ask any one, whether in his** everyday **sense of motion as he walks along the streets, the stones he passes over may be said to *move*, because they change distance with his feet?** Isn't it rather the man who moves, the one exerting the force? Rambling along in a carriage, he sees houses and trees whipping past. Do you expect him to say that the *houses* are in motion? No, the carriage is moving, since it is on the carriage that the force causing the change is impressed. **To me it seems that though motion** always **includes a relation of one thing to another, yet it is not necessary that** in every relative motion **each term of the relation be** moved. In other words, just as the relation 'x thinks of y' can be asymmetrical, so can the relation 'x moves relative to y'. Suppose the thing **denominated** by 'x' moves away **from** the thing denominated by 'y': **it** doesn't follow that y is also in motion. **As a man may think of some** inanimate object—**what**ever it may be—**which does not** in turn **think** of him, just **so, a body may be moved towards** or away **from another body, which is not therefore itself in motion**—motion towards or away being, of course, relative.

Frame of reference plays a large part in determining which body is in relative motion with respect to which other body. From an everyday point of view, the earth is the ultimate frame of reference for motion. From an astronomical point of view, the outer walls of the universe are ultimate. But this is just a matter of perspective. The frame of reference can always be changed, so absolute motion is illusory. Berkeley attributes an error regarding circular relative motion to Newton. This error invalidates the conclusion Newton wants to draw from his experiment with a spinning bucket of water. In short, Berkeley is denying that Newton can distinguish absolute from relative motion by appeal to centrifugal force, since the relatively 'moving' body Newton identifies as lacking centrifugal force isn't moving at all—not even relative to the bucket.

---

114. As the place we use for our point of reference **happens to be variously defined, the motion which is related to it varies** as well. **A man** sitting at a table **in a ship may be said to be** stationary relative to one object and moving relative to another. Since he is sitting at the table rather than walking around inside the ship, he is **quiescent**—he doesn't move at all—**with relation to the sides of the vessel.** You must admit that the man sitting at the table bears a different relation to the mast, **and** the walls, of the ship, than a dog running up and down the deck does. The dog moves back and forth relative to the mast, towards one wall and then away from it. The man is motionless with respect to both. And **yet** you can't deny that he **moves with relation to the land**—for the ship is travelling along the coast and carrying the man with it. **Or** suppose the bow of the moving ship is pointing east, and **the** man, tired of sitting, gets up and decides to walk westwards towards the stern. In that case we **may** say that the man **moves eastward in respect of the one** object—the land—since the boat is still heading that way, **and westward in respect of the other**—the table he was sitting at. **In the common affairs of life, men never go beyond the earth to define the place of any body;** the earth serves as a fixed frame of reference for any object on it, **and whatever is quiescent in respect of that,** whatever sits motionless on its surface, **is accounted *absolutely* to be so. But philosophers, who have a greater extent of thought, and** look at things from a wider perspective, generally acquire **juster notions of the system of things,** and far more accurate beliefs. They **discover even the earth it self to be moved,** along with all of the planets. **In order therefore to fix their notions** of what moves relative to what, and what moves absolutely, they look for an ultimate frame of reference by which to define the latter. And so **they seem to conceive the corporeal world as a finite expanse, and the utmost unmoved walls or shell thereof to be** perfectly at rest. The outer boundary of the universe, therefore, which is delimited by these walls, is **the place, whereby they estimate true motions.** Whatever moves relative to *that* is *really* in motion, they say. **If we** test the **soundness of our own conceptions,** however, **I believe we may find all the absolute motion we can frame an idea of, to be at bottom no other than relative motion thus** conceived—**defined** by relation to the boundary. So even where we think we are conceiving absolute motion, we are implicitly relying on a frame of reference involving another body—the unmoved rim of the universe. In other words, we are implicitly adverting to a relative conception of motion. **For as has been already observed, absolute motion exclusive of all external relation is** completely **incomprehensible; and to this kind of relative motion, all the above-mentioned properties, causes, and effects ascribed to absolute motion** in Section 111, **will, if I mistake not, be found to** apply and **agree. As to what is said of the centrifugal force, that it does not at all belong to circular relative motion, I do not see how this follows from the experiment which is brought** by Newton **to prove it. See *Philosophia Naturalis Principia Mathematica, in Schol. Def. VIII*. For the water in the vessel, at that time wherein it is said to have the greatest relative circular motion** (and no recessionary force), **has, I think, no motion at all.** When a bucket suspended from a twisted rope is released and first begins to unwind, Newton supposes that the water it contains enjoys a degree of circular motion relative to the bucket. But since the surface of the water is flat, he rightly observes that it doesn't recede from the axis of rotation and thus exhibits no centrifugal force. His error was to suppose that the water is at that moment in motion, **as is plain from the foregoing section** and will be explained more fully in the next.

A body can meaningfully be described as moving only if: (1) its distance or orientation relative to some other body changes, and (2) the efficient cause

*of the motion is impressed on it. We can thus be mistaken about which body
is moving, if we are mistaken about which body the moving force applies to.*

115. For to properly **denominate a body 'moved' it is requisite, first, that
it change its distance or situation with regard to some other body; and
secondly, that the force or action occasioning that change** of distance or
situation **be applied to it** rather than the other body. **If either of these** conditions fails, if either **be** found **wanting,** then the body didn't move. Indeed, **I
do not think that agreeably to the** common **sense of mankind, or** in keeping
with **the propriety of language,** such **a body can be said to be in motion.**
Now when the bucket initially starts to spin, the water in it meets the first
condition for motion but not the second. Since the bucket twists away, the
water does change its situation with respect to it—that satisfies condition 1.
But in that first instant the force from the unwinding cord is applied only to
the bucket, not the water. So it doesn't satisfy condition 2. Since no force is
impressed on the water, it receives no motion. And hence we don't have a
case of relative circular motion lacking centrifugal force—for the water isn't
in motion at all. **I grant indeed, that it is possible for us to think a body, y,
which we see change its distance from some other** body, x, **to be moved,
though it—y—have no force applied to it (in which sense there may be
merely apparent motion in y); but then it is, because the force causing the
change of distance is imagined by us to be applied or impressed on that
body, y, which we thought to be moved.** As soon as we discover that the moving force was applied to x rather than y, we correct our mistake and surrender
the belief that y was in motion. Suppose I'm standing on a dock gazing at a
ship close by. Suddenly it appears that the dock is moving. But then I notice
her sails have caught the wind and I realize that the ship has moved rather
than the dock. This sort of experience is common: **Which indeed shows that
we are capable of mistaking a thing**—such as a dock—**to be in motion which**
really **is not, and that is all** that the apparent motion of an unaffected body
amounts to—a mistaken point of view.

---

*Perhaps the existence of absolute motion would imply the existence of absolute
space as the ultimate frame of reference. But the relative conception of motion
just presented implies no such thing. Indeed, absolute space—a great container, ontologically prior to its contents—cannot even be conceived. When
we try to picture empty space, the best we can do is to imagine ourselves free
to move our limbs in all directions without meeting any resistance. But that is*

not pure empty space, for our limbs are bodies too. Remove our bodies from the scene and the scene itself will vanish.

116. **From what has been said** in the last four sections, **it follows that the true philosophical consideration of motion does not imply the being of** space as Newton conceives it—**an *absolute space*, distinct from that which is perceived by sense, and related to bodies** as container is to contained. Here again we find that seemingly independent beings are essentially tied to perception: Space, like body, is something **which** cannot exist otherwise than in a mind perceiving it. In fact, **that it cannot exist without the mind, is clear** for the same reasons and **upon the** very **same principles that demonstrate** the intra-mental existence of apples, carriages and **the like.** They cannot exist outside **of** perception and neither can space. My principles thus apply equally to space, apples, carriages and **all other objects of sense. And perhaps, if we inquire** a little more **narrowly** and think about it carefully, **we shall find** that **we cannot even frame an idea of *pure empty space***—that is to say, space emptied of its occupants and **exclusive of all body. This I must confess seems impossible** to me; **as** I reflect on the idea of empty space containing no other **being** whatever, it seems **a most** hollow and **abstract idea.** So do we have no conception of empty space? Do we never speak intelligibly about it? On the contrary, I think we do, but the space so conceived is considered only relative to some body and some motion. It is not *pure* empty space. **When I excite a motion in some part of my body,** by flapping an arm, for instance, **if it be free or without resistance, I say** that **there is space: But if I find** that I encounter **any resistance** to my flapping, **then I say** that **there is** a *body* blocking me; **and** when there is total resistance— say I flap my arm against a wall—then I say that the space is completely occupied. But if I flap my arm into a fern rather than a wall, the resistance is less pronounced and I regard the space where the fern is situated as partially occupied. Thus, the emptiness of space is gauged **in** direct **proportion** to the resistance we encounter **as** we move about. According as **the resistance to motion is lesser or greater, I say** that **the *space* is more or less *pure*. So that when I speak** loosely **of pure or empty space, it is not to be supposed that the word 'space' stands for an idea distinct from, or conceivable without, body and motion.** Quite the reverse: Emptiness is understood in terms of the absence of bodies impeding my motion. **Though indeed we are apt to think** that **every noun** or **substantive** term **stands for a distinct idea that may be separated from all others,** this is decidedly not the case. We suppose that the word 'space'—just like 'apple' or 'bonnet'—stands for something that can be pictured all on its own, without our conceiving the existence of anything else in the world alongside it. But this is an instance of the error I warned against earlier—focusing on names rather than the

ideas they are meant to stand for (Introduction, Section 21), and hence supposing that every name immediately signifies some determinate, abstract idea (Introduction, Section 18). And it is a mistake **which has occasioned infinite**ly many other **mistakes in turn. When therefore** I imagine myself alone in the universe, **supposing all the world to be annihilated besides my own body, I** can **say** that **there still remains** *pure space*: But I do not mean to say that I **thereby** conceive of space independently of all bodies. Rather, **nothing else is meant, but only that I conceive it possible** in that lonely universe, **for the limbs of my body to be moved on all sides** and to flap about **without** encountering **the least resistance** from anything else. **But if** the situation were such **that** my body **too were annihilated, then there could be no motion, and consequently no space**; in emptying the universe of contents, we whisk the universe away as well. **Some perhaps may think** they come to know space in some other way. They may insist that **the sense of seeing does furnish them with the idea of pure space; but** that is not how the mind works. For **it is plain from what we have elsewhere shown, that the ideas of space and distance are not obtained by that sense,** but by relating ideas of sight, which are one thing, to ideas of touch, which are another. Judging an object of sight to be at any distance from us is thus a matter of experience rather than vision. Space is not something seen. **See the** *Essay concerning Vision*, Section 126.

If absolute space is impossible, then the controversies surrounding it may be safely ignored. Particularly significant here is the debate about how absolute space relates to God: Are they the same thing? Similar things? Two eternal and infinite things? These difficult questions can be shelved, if absolute space does not exist. (The non-existence of God would settle those issues as well, but that's a non-starter for Berkeley.)

---

117. **What is here laid down** about the relativity of spatial determinations **seems to put an end to all those disputes and difficulties, which have sprung up amongst the learned concerning the nature of** *pure space*. If every characterization of space makes reference to body and if the very conception of space is therefore relative, then there is no motive whatever for disputing about absolute space. For why dispute about nothing? **But the chief advantage arising from it is that we are freed from** the sole inducement to a particularly strange heresy. I refer to **that dangerous** *dilemma,* **to which several** philosophers have recently been driven by their speculations on absolute space. For

those **who have employed their thoughts on this subject imagine themselves** forced into a view on which God is **reduced,** or likened, **to** space. Space, without relation to body, is abstract and pure—an unlimited and ideal being. On this way **of thinking,** therefore, you must **either** hold **that real space is God, or else that there is something** else **beside God which is eternal, uncreated, infinite, indivisible,** and **immutable. Both which may justly be thought** as **pernicious and** irreligious, as they are **absurd notions. It is certain that not a few** of our **divine** clergymen and priests, **as well as** several **philosophers of great note, have,** reasoning **from the difficulty they found in conceiving either** outer **limits** to expansion **or** the total **annihilation of space, concluded** that **it must be** *divine.* Locke, for example, calls space and time 'infinite abysses' and 'boundless oceans of eternity and immensity', which, 'in their full extent, belong only to the deity' (*Essay,* Book II, Chapter 15); Newton even declares that God 'constitutes duration and space' (*Principia,* III, General Scholium). **And some** philosophers **of late,** such as Joseph Raphson (c. 1648–1715), **have set themselves particularly to show, that the** unfathomable and **incommunicable attributes of God**—his impassivity, indivisibility, etc.—are to be found in space (*De Spatio Reali*). Others, such as my friend Samuel Johnson (1696–1772), think that his immensity and eternity are understood only by analogy with the notions of space and duration (*Correspondence,* Letter 2). This analogical view is common, and I believe that Newton would **agree to it** as well (see again the General Scholium). **Which doctrine**—that God is, or is very much like, space—**how unworthy soever it may seem to the Divine Nature,** however unflattering, has taken hold of several prominent minds; **yet I do not see how we can get clear of it, so long as we adhere to the received opinions** concerning space.

Mathematics, the clearest and strictest of the sciences, might be considered above reproach and incapable of lasting error. In respect of purely quantitative matters, that is partly true. But there is reason to be cautious: Though mathematical demonstrations are themselves impeccable, there are hidden assumptions that need to be weighed. In fact, it will emerge that mathematics is badly infected with the non-mathematical doctrines of abstractionism and materialism.

---

118. **Hitherto,** from Sections 101 to 117, we have been concerned with the advantages our principles may bring to the knowledge **of** ideas in **natural philosophy,** which deals with sensations: **We come now,** in Sections 118 to

132, **to make some inquiry concerning** the improvements they may confer on **that other great branch of speculative knowledge,** which to repeat, deals with relations between ideas. I refer, of course, to the great speculative science of *mathematics*. These mathematical investigations, **how celebrated soever they may be,** are not immune from error; **for all their clearness and** for all the **certainty of** their **demonstrations,** mathematicians still make mistakes. Their precision, **which is** greater than that attained in any of the natural sciences and is **hardly any where else to be found, cannot** place them above criticism. I do not pretend to uncover any particular inaccuracies in mathematical reasoning; **nevertheless** mathematicians cannot **be supposed** to be **altogether free from mistakes, if in their** philosophical **principles there lurks some secret error, which is common to** all mathematical and scientific pursuits. That is, indeed, what I hope to show here—that there is an error **the professors of those sciences** share **with the rest of mankind. Mathematicians, though they deduce their theorems from a great height** on the basis **of** powerful **evidence,** and are therefore quite certain of them, **yet their first principles are limited by the consideration of quantity.** The sole concern in mathematical demonstrations, in other words, is quantity or number. But though the demonstrations pertain exclusively to number, they surely presuppose certain general principles that are not themselves quantitative in nature; any examination of those presuppositions will thus fall outside the scope of mathematics. Mathematicians simply calculate—they crank out numerical proofs—**and they do not ascend into any inquiry concerning** their non-quantitative assumptions—**those transcendental maxims,** or highest principles, **which** nearly everyone accepts. Being so common, these principles **influence all the particular sciences, each part whereof** assumes their truth—and, as I say, **mathematics is not excepted** from this. The science of number, **consequently, participates** in any **of the errors involved in them. That the** strictly mathematical **principles laid down by mathematicians are true,** we do not presume to question, **and** that **their way of deduction from those principles is clear and incontestable, we do not deny.** But we hold, that **there may be certain erroneous maxims of** much **greater extent and** broader application **than** mathematical principles proper. Though **the object of mathematics** is number, mathematicians can make conceptual errors that are not specifically numerical, **and for that reason** they may **not** be explicit or **expressly mentioned** in mathematics itself, **though** to be sure they may be implicit. Indeed, I will show that certain errors are **tacitly supposed throughout the whole progress of that science; and that the ill effects of those secret unexamined errors** have infected mathematics, and **are** thus **diffused through all the branches thereof,** including arithmetic and geometry. **To be plain, we suspect** that **the mathematicians are, as well as other men,** susceptible to precisely those errors our Introduction was **concerned** to expose. In particular, we think they are entangled **in the errors arising from the doctrine of abstract general ideas,** and in the error we have dealt with subsequently—supposing **the existence of objects without the mind.** I turn now to the task of pinpointing these errors in the practice of arithmetic (Sections 119–122) and geometry (Sections 123–132).

The assumption has always been that arithmetic investigates pure, abstract quantities. This has lent a certain charm to the science, especially for those with lofty thoughts and mystical tendencies. Reverence for abstractions is misplaced, however, and we should disdain any reflections on number that serve no practical purpose.

---

119. Arithmetic has been thought to have for its object abstract ideas of number, of which mathematicians seek **to understand the properties and mutual habitudes** or relations. This activity **is supposed** to be central to science and therefore worthy of pursuit—**no mean part of speculative philosophy. The opinion of** many philosophers is that **the pure and intellectual nature of numbers, in** contrast with the mixed and material nature of sensible things, implies that mathematics trades solely in **abstractions. This has made them** seem theoretically significant and brought them to be held **in esteem with those philosophers** in particular, **who** turn their minds away from the senses, and who **seem to** possess—or at least to **have affected** to possess—**an uncommon fineness and elevation of thought. It has** rendered mathematics attractive and **set a high price on the most trifling of numerical speculations, which in practice** are of no use, **but** which **serve only for amusement; and it has therefore so far infected the minds of some** thinkers, **that they have dreamt of mighty *mysteries* involved in numbers,** and virtually enthused over them. I refer to such thinkers as Nicholas of Cusa (1401–1464), who sees a deep parallel between the unfolding of mathematical concepts in the human mind and God's unfolding of creation, or Galileo and Johannes Kepler (1571–1630), who each affirm in their own way that the book of nature is written in mathematical characters. These worshippers of numbers suppose that arithmetical and geometrical relations are woven into the very fabric of the universe **and** they have thus **attempted the explication of** all **natural things by** means of **them. But if we inquire into our own thoughts, and consider what has been premised** by these mystics, **we may perhaps** come to **entertain a low opinion of those high flights** of imagination **and** the mathematical **abstractions** they purportedly involve, **and look on all inquiries about numbers** that don't serve some practical purpose, **only as so many *difficiles nugae*—**laborious trifles—to be avoided in our thinking. Mathematical speculations, **so far as they are not subservient to** actual

practice and do not **promote the benefit of life**, should be regarded with suspicion, as distracting men from their more useful occupations. Divide your field into acres and calculate the number of crops you may plant in x number of rows—your time is well spent; work out the square root of 1 000 003— you've wasted an hour.

The idea of any particular number depends on the idea of unity, for numbers are composed of units. If there is no abstract idea of unity, therefore, it will follow that there is no abstract idea of any particular number. And we have seen already that there is no abstract idea of unity. So there are no abstract ideas of numbers. If arithmetic deals with anything, then, it must be the names of numbers, particular things numbered and practical applications.

---

120. Unity is the central idea **in** mathematics, for every number is composed of units. But the **abstract** idea of unity is something **we have** seen **before.** Locke's belief that unity is a simple idea suggested by all other ideas and accompanying them into the mind was **considered** and rejected **in Section 13.** Now, **from** the premise that unity is abstract, **which** is what Locke certainly supposed, **and** from **what has been said in the Introduction** about the impossibility of abstract ideas, **it plainly follows** that **there is not any such idea** as unity. **But** from this we may likewise deduce that there are no abstract ideas of numbers. Since any given **number** is **being defined** as a **'collection of units', we may conclude that** the idea of a number is just as abstract as the idea of a unit. After all, a collection of abstract ideas must itself be abstract. Think of it this way: If all numbers are built up out of units, and **if there** can **be no such thing as** an idea of **unity or** a **unit in** the **abstract,** then there can be no idea of a number. And so we infer that **there are not** any **ideas of numbers in** the abstract and, for the same reason, that there is nothing abstract **denoted by the numeral names and figures.** For example, the numerals '7', '3' and '123' do not pick out any abstract ideas. In short, there are no numbers—only things numbered. **The theories therefore in arithmetic,** insofar as they depend on abstract ideas of numbers, are fundamentally confused. Such theories, **if they are abstracted from the names and figures, as likewise from all use and practice, as well as from the particular things numbered**—say, the number of acres or the number of crops—**can be supposed** empty of content and **to have nothing at all for their object.** Hence we may see how entirely arithmetic—**the science of numbers**—**is subordinate to** and dependent on our practical affairs and everyday **practices, and how jejune and trifling** it is—how irrelevant and silly it all **becomes—when considered as a matter of mere speculation** divorced from concrete applications.

There is something gratifying in the thought that one is able to prove things about pure, abstract objects so far removed from the senses. Berkeley tries to counteract the vanity of this abstractionist conception of arithmetic by considering its lowly origins. Reflection on the likely history of arithmetic suggests that it arose as a matter of convenience, and was gradually transformed into a purely nominalistic science, calculating sums in symbols—without considering their referents—and then projecting the outputs back onto the things signified.

---

121. **However, since there may be some** mathematicians **who,** after proving many theorems, become **deluded by** their success and then suppose that **their specious** and hollow **show of discovering abstract** truths discloses a realm of pure concepts, it is tempting to think of arithmetic as an abstract science. Captivated by the 'speculative **verities'** revealed by their proofs, these mathematicians **waste** more of **their time in** solving **arithmetical theorems and problems, which have not any** practical application or real-world **use.** Given its prevalence, **it will not be amiss, if we more fully consider and expose the vanity of that pretence**—the opinion that arithmetic deals in abstractions rather than concrete particulars. The attempt to uncover abstract mathematical truths is vain and futile, since there are none; **and this will** most **plainly appear** if we proceed historically, **by taking a view of arithmetic** as we imagine it looked **in its infancy,** trying to picture the context in which it first emerged **and observing what it was that originally put men** in need of it. We should speculate **on** the circumstances that may have initially led men to **the study of that science, and** try to determine **what** the **scope** of the problems to which **they directed it was. It is natural to think that at first, men, for ease of memory and to help** them add, subtract and perform all kinds **of** basic **computations, made use of** pebbles, shells or twigs as **counters, or** introduced some other placeholder, such as the **writing of single strokes, points or the like.** These were just markers, **each whereof was** understood to be a sign—every pebble or stroke **made to signify an unit, that is, some one thing of whatever kind they** wanted to count or **had occasion to** include in their mathematical **reckonings. Afterwards they found out** methods for improving **the** notation—**more** compact and **compendious ways of making one character stand in place of several strokes, or points:** say a square stood

for 10 units and a triangle stood for 20. **And lastly, the notation of the *Arabians* or *Indians* came into use, wherein by the repetition of a few characters or figures, and by varying the signification of each figure according to the place it obtains** in a sequence of numerals, **all numbers may be most aptly expressed:** This is a useful convention, **which** greatly shortens proofs, and **seems to have been done in imitation of** natural **language, so that an exact analogy is observed** to hold **betwixt the notation by figures** in math **and** the notation by **names** in language: Just as the position of a word in a sentence is partly determinant of the meaning of the sentence, so the position of a figure, or digit, in a sequence is partly determinant of the meaning of the sequence as a whole. This method of varying meaning by varying position in a sequence is seen both with the Arabic numerals (1, 2, 3...), as well as with the number words (one, two, three...), **the nine simple figures answering to the nine first numeral names**—'1' corresponds to 'one', '2' to 'two'—**and places in the former, corresponding to denominations in the latter**—the '7' in '97' is the counterpart of the 'seven' in 'ninety-seven'. **And** certain conditions, or rules, are attached to various positions in a sequence of figures or digits. Let's say that a complex number with two digits has two 'places', one with three digits has three, etc. The sequence '97', for instance, has two places. The 'simple' or 'local' value of the digit in the first place is 9; the local value of the figure in the second place is 7. Now for a rule: In a sequence with two places, the local value in the first place is multiplied by 10, while the local value in the second place is multiplied by 1. So, **agreeably to those conditions of the simple and local value of figures, were contrived methods of** calculating the value of the whole sequence—that is to say, methods of **finding from the given figures or marks of the parts, what figures and how placed, are properly** used **to denote the** value of the **whole, or *vice versa*.** To illustrate: In the sequence '97', you get the total value—the number of units signified—by multiplying the local value '9' by 10, multiplying the local value '7' by 1, and then adding the results together. The total value is thus 97 units. **And having found the sought figures,** the same thing can be done in words. Thus, **the same rule or analogy being observed throughout, it is easy to** drop the digits and **read them** back **into words; and so the number** of units—ninety-seven—**becomes perfectly known. For then the number of any particular things** signified— say the number of trees on a lot, or the number of people in a town—**is said to be known, when we know the name or figures (with their due arrangement** in the sequence preserved) **that, according to the standing** rule or **analogy for** determining value, **belong to them.** Then, by performing operations on the numerical values—by manipulating the signs rather than the things signi- fied—we can do calculations that would be practically impossible otherwise. **For these signs being known, we can by the** established procedures and **operations of arithmetic, know the signs of any part of the particular sums signified by them** without having to consult the particular things signified; **and thus computing in signs (because of the connexion established betwixt them and the distinct multitudes of things** such as trees or people, **whereof** each **one is taken for an unit), we may be able rightly to sum up, divide, and proportion the things themselves that we intend to number.** Arithmetic is not, therefore, a science of abstract concepts, but a system of symbols and rules that abbreviates any computations we want to make concerning particulars.

Focusing on symbols alone can simplify calculations, but it is useful only inasmuch as the results apply to particular objects symbolized. To do calculations for their own sake would be as silly as learning grammar with no intention of ever using it. Much worse is that it encourages a serious error: Since the objects can be left out of account altogether, there is a temptation to suppose that the symbols stand for abstract ideas of numbers.

---

122. In *arithmetic,* **therefore, we** pay no **regard** to the things we were originally counting, such as the acres or the crops. It is **not these** sensible *things* we think about while doing calculations, **but the** numerals and mathematical **signs.** As far as working out the right answer goes, **it** is only the signs **which** matter; **nevertheless, they are not regarded for their own sake.** They have no intrinsic value**, but** prove their usefulness through everyday applications, **because they direct us how to act with relation to** the real **things** they stand for **and to dispose rightly of them** in our undertakings. We are fully justified in concentrating on the rules and symbols when solving a problem in arithmetic, but only so that we do not get distracted by the non-mathematical features of the things represented by the numbers. If we want to know how many acres we need in order to plant 2 000 apple trees, and we know that each acre can accommodate 85 trees, we pull out our feather and our ink, just as we were taught in school: We manipulate the symbols '2 000' and '85' according to the rules of division and produce the figure '23.5'. And then we simply read the result off the symbols: We need twenty-three and a half acres. **Now** this fits quite **agreeably into what we have before observed, of words in general**—that not every word stands for an idea **(Section 19** of the **Introduction).** Failure to recognize this has led many philosophers to suppose that when a word does not stand for a particular idea, it must stand for an abstract idea instead. Similarly, **it happens here likewise that** since the numerals are not related to particular ideas during the calculation, they are assumed to stand for abstract ideas; thus **abstract ideas are thought to be signified by numeral names or characters, while they do not suggest ideas of particular things to our minds.** Since I've already dealt with this mistake in the Introduction, **I shall not at present enter into a more particular** discussion or give another lengthy **dissertation on this subject**. Read Section 19 again if you want more convincing, **but I need only observe that it is evident from what has been said** there, that **those things which pass** amongst philosophers **for** the **abstract truths** of arithmetic **and** the various **theorems concerning numbers are** all of them, **in reality,** related to particular objects and the symbols we use for counting. Anyone **conversant** with the actual practice of arithmetic knows that when doing sums one rarely stops to think **about** apples, trees or whatever items are being counted, and even when one does there is never any *abstract* idea of number featuring in the calculation—**no objects distinct from** the **particular numerable things** even come into it. There is, I believe, no **exception** to this rule: When doing arithmetic, we either consider the particular things counted—though we do so infrequently—or else we consider **only** the **names and characters** that denote them; these are just marks on a page ('7' and '9', for instance), or words spoken ('seven' and 'nine'). They are designations agreed upon by convention, **which originally came to be considered, on no other account but** for **their being *signs*, or** figures **capable of** pointing beyond themselves to other things, and thus able **to represent** the acres and crops **aptly, or whatever particular things men had need to compute. Whence it** plainly **follows that** for a mathematician **to** focus on signs and numerals—**study**ing **them for their own sake** rather than their uses—**would be just as wise, and** contribute **to as good a purpose, as if a man** were to immerse himself in grammar with no thought of communication, evoking emotion or whatever, and to study words for their own sake. In **neglecting the true use** of grammar **or** the **original intention** of spelling, **and** forgetting the **subserviency of language** to practice, he would be squandering intellectual resources that **should** be better employed in service to the common good. Only a fool would **spend his time in** making pedantic, **impertinent criticisms upon words, or reasonings and controversies** which are **purely verbal**, asking himself whether a man is 'stoic' or 'stoical', has 'brothers' or 'brethren', and that sort of nonsense. But that is exactly what mathematicians do when they divorce mathematics from its practical applications.

Geometers take it as given that finite extension is infinitely divisible and that their science depends on it being so. Yet this supposition is known to give rise to paradox and it complicates the study of geometry considerably. So if Berkeley can show that the infinite divisibility of finite extension is impossible—and also inessential to the proofs—he will have done a great service to geometry.

---

123. From numbers we proceed now to speak of *extension*, that which has figure or shape—anything with dimensions in space. This thing, or quality, **considered as relative** to perception, **is the object of geometry. The** *infinite* **divisibility of** *finite* **extension, though it is not expressly laid down, either as an axiom or theorem in the elements of that science, yet** it is **throughout** always assumed. Though it has not **the same** evidence as other geometrical notions, it is **every where supposed, and thought to have so inseparable and essential a connexion with the principles and demonstrations in geometry, that mathematicians never** even consider that it might be false, but simply **admit it** without question. At no time do they call this principle **into doubt, or make the least question** regarding the justification **of it. And as** anyone familiar with Greek philosophy will notice, **this notion is the source from whence do spring all those amusing geometrical paradoxes, which** were first discovered by Zeno of Elea (c. 490 BC–c. 430 BC)—such as the argument that motion is impossible since getting from point A to point B requires reaching the halfway point between A and B, plus getting halfway to the halfway point, plus getting halfway to that halfway point, and so on to infinity, so that, in the end you'd have to cover an infinite number of finite distances in order to get anywhere. This, and Zeno's other conclusions, **have such a direct repugnancy to the plain common sense of mankind, and are admitted with so much reluctance into a mind not yet** poisoned and **debauched by learning,** that they are rightly ridiculed by the unschooled. But the philosopher must locate the error. And **so we ask: is it** more likely that motion is impossible or that the opinion of infinite divisibility is false? The reluctance of mathematicians to part with infinite divisibility, despite its absurd consequences, is **the principal occasion of all that** pointless intricacy in geometrical proofs and speculations that would otherwise be **nice and** easy, all that **extreme subtlety, which renders the study of** *mathematics* **so difficult and tedious. We** are more inclined to side with common sense, however, and dismiss the doctrine of infinite divisibility as a needless confusion. **Hence if we can make it appear** more plainly that the key assumption of geometers is false, if we can show **that no finite extension contains innumerable parts, or is infinitely divisible, it follows that we shall at once clear the science of geometry from a great number of difficulties and contradictions, which have ever** plagued and **been** rightly **esteemed** an argument against it. That paradox lies at the heart of mathematics is a **reproach to human reason, and** yet, **with**out the hypothesis of infinite divisibility, they **all** disappear at once. By dropping this groundless assumption, therefore, we remove a great obstacle to geometrical knowledge and **make the attainment thereof a business of much less time and pains than it hitherto has been.** Four sorts of considerations count against the infinite divisibility of finite extension: (1) it conflicts with the transparency thesis of Section 25 (Section 124); (2) it presupposes either the doctrine of abstract ideas or else the mind-independence of sensible things (Section 125); (3) it involves an unjustified transfer of properties from the thing signified to the sign (Sections 126–128); (4) it has absurd consequences (Section 129).

Extension is a quality and qualities are ideas in the mind. So every extended thing is an idea in the mind. Every idea, and every part of an idea, is perceived. So every extended thing, and every part of an extended thing, is perceived. If there were an infinite number of parts in any finite extended thing, therefore, they would also be perceived. But an infinite number of parts are not perceived. It follows that no finitely extended thing contains an infinite number of parts. Indeed, it is obviously impossible for something finite to have an infinite number of parts. But conditioning can bring people to believe even the obviously impossible.

---

124. Every particular bit of **finite extension** we may conceive, every shaped or figured thing **which may possibly be the object of our thought, is an *idea* existing only in the mind.** Extension is just like any other quality insofar as it is an idea in the mind. And every idea in the mind must be perceived. This holds for the idea of extension too; we can hardly think of an invisible square or a breadthless line. Indeed, the contents of our ideas are 'transparent' to the mind. I mean that every part of every idea must be perceived, **and consequently** when we contemplate any idea of extension **each part thereof must** also **be perceived. If therefore I cannot perceive** infinitely many, **innumerable parts in any finite** bit of **extension that I consider, it is certain** that **they are not contained in it. But it is evident that I cannot distinguish** infinitely many, **innumerable parts in any particular line, surface, or solid, which I either perceive by sense, or** else conjure up in my imagination. Any **figure** I present **to my self in my mind** has only so many discernible parts; I can divide it over and over again—but not infinitely. In short, every part of an idea must be perceived—their contents are on display—and I do not perceive infinitely many parts in any idea I have of extension, **wherefore I conclude** that **they are not contained in it. Nothing can be plainer** and more obvious **to me than that the extensions I have in view are no other than my own ideas, and it is no less plain that I cannot** break down or **resolve any one of my ideas into an infinite number of other ideas, that is** to say, it is obvious **that they are not infinitely divisible.** Though my opponents must admit that they are incapable of dividing any given segment of finite extension into an infinite number of parts, they will also want to insist on another kind of extension that is neither perceived nor imagined—extension in the abstract—and this, they believe, can be so divided. But who understands these words? **If by a 'finite extension' be meant something distinct from a finite idea, I declare** sincerely **I do not know what that is, and so cannot affirm or deny any thing of it.** There simply is no extension beyond what can be perceived or imagined. **But if the terms 'extension', 'parts', and the like, are taken in any sense** that is **conceivable** to me, **that is** to say, if they are taken **for ideas; then** the limits on the number of their parts are open for inspection. And **to say that a finite quantity or extension consists of parts** that are **infinite in number is so manifest a contradiction, that every one at first sight acknowledges it to be so.** How can a finite thing be resolved into an infinite number of parts? Try chopping something up—how long will you go on? Isn't it rather the case that anything with an infinite number of parts must itself be infinitely large? Every schoolboy understands this. **And it is impossible** that intelligent people could suppose a finite thing to have an infinite number of components, unless they had been conditioned to believe it; it could never—**it should never—gain the assent of any reasonable creature who is not brought to it by gentle** propaganda **and in slow degrees, as a converted Gentile** is brought **to** accept **the beliefs** of Catholicism—say, for instance, the principle **of *transubstantiation*,** according to which the Communion bread is actually transformed into the body of Christ. **Ancient and rooted prejudices,** however ridiculous they may be, **do often pass into principles** and turn into dogmas; **and those propositions, which** are taken to be principles, will not be questioned or disputed by anyone. Indeed, **once** they have **obtained** all **the force and credit of a *principle*, they are not only themselves** thought indisputable, **but likewise whatever is deducible from them** is placed above criticism as well. Mere prejudices, and everything that follows from them, are thus **thought** to have a **privileged** status and to be exempt **from all** critical **examination. And there is no absurdity so gross** or outrageous, **which by this means the mind of man may not be prepared to swallow** hook, line and sinker—whether it be the pitiful doctrine of abstract ideas, the groundless belief in matter or the infinite divisibility of finite extension.

Geometers might agree that sensible things have only finitely many parts, but, if they believe in abstraction, they could argue that abstract things are not subject to the same limitation. A geometer who is also a materialist might agree that ideas of things have finitely many parts, but then insist that the material things behind them contain infinitely many. These counters won't hold up, of course, since abstractionism and materialism have been defeated already.

Berkeley's concern now is just to explain why geometers are so attached to the infinite divisibility of finite extension.

125. He who has studied philosophy and the other speculative sciences— he **whose understanding is** therefore drawn to and **prepossessed with the doctrine of abstract general ideas**—may imagine that an abstract thing, at least, can have an unlimited number of parts. In other words, he **may be persuaded, that (whatever be thought of the ideas of sense**—whether they exist within the mind or without—for instance**), extension in the *abstract* is infinitely divisible. And**, on the other hand, **one who thinks** that **the objects of sense exist without the mind,** may attribute to them an infinity of parts. He admits that *ideas* have only so many elements as may be distinguished by sight or touch, but in addition to ideas he postulates material things *behind* them, and so, having this belief, he **will perhaps in virtue thereof be brought to admit that a line but an inch long**—by which he means a two-dimensional *material* line of such a length—**may contain innumerable parts really existing, though** they are **too small to be discerned** by human eyes. **These errors**—supposing that there are abstract ideas and supposing that the objects of sense exist outside the mind—are widespread and firmly maintained. They **are grafted as well in the minds of *geometricians*, as of other men, and have a like influence on their reasonings; and it were no difficult thing to show how the arguments from geometry made use of to support the infinite divisibility of extension, are** at bottom **grounded on them.** And so, the geometrical arguments for infinite divisibility depending on these false suppositions, our earlier demonstrations of their falsity may be taken as defeating the geometrical arguments as well. **At present we shall** not pursue this matter any further, but shall **only observe in general, whence it is that the mathematicians** come to believe in infinite divisibility, why they **are all so fond** of it **and** why they stick so **tenacious**ly to a principle as little capable **of** proof as **this** one. Isolating the cause of their error should ease geometers away from a **doctrine** they have always regarded as central to their art.

In one sense, geometry deals in universals: A theorem pertaining to right-angled triangles, for instance, holds of all right-angled triangles. It is 'universally true' of right-angled triangles. But we can make sense of that claim without committing ourselves to an ontology of abstract, universal concepts.

Geometrical proofs employ selective attention: We focus on the common features of right-angled triangles, without taking any notice of the size or colour of the particular right-angled triangle on our paper. If the particular size and colour were left out of the proof, then we can be sure the theorem applies to every right-angled triangle regardless of size or colour. Using particular ideas as 'universal' symbols in geometrical proofs can spell trouble, however, since there is always the risk of attributing properties peculiar to the ideas signified to the ideas doing the signifying.

126. It has been observed in another place, that the theorems and demonstrations put forward **in geometry** are meant to have broad significance. Those who **are** even minimally **conversant** with the field know that geometry is **about universal ideas** (see **Section 15** of the **Introduction**). **Wherever** I speak of 'universal ideas', however, I am far from committing myself to abstractions. My true meaning should be clear already from the Introduction; **it is** there **explained in what sense** ideas can properly be called 'universal'. But to prevent any misunderstanding, I shall explain once again how **this** 'universality' of ideas **ought to be understood** in connection with geometry. I can take some particular right-angled triangle I am thinking of, or which I have drawn on my paper, **to** have universal significance **wit**hout supposing that the triangle, or its sides, are anything more than I perceive them to be, namely, concrete individuals of a definite size and shape. In calling them 'universal', I just mean **that the particular lines and figures included in the diagram, are supposed to stand for innumerable other** lines and figures **of different sizes**—and possibly different shapes (if, say, the right angle played no part in the proof, in which case my diagram can stand for isosceles triangles as well). When I say that the ideas employed in geometrical proofs are 'universal', then, all I mean is that what we say of a particular line or figure holds for any other lines or figures that are relevantly similar: **or in other words,** the lines and figures featuring in geometrical proofs are of 'general significance' insofar as **the geometer considers them** in their representative capacity, **abstracting from their** particular lengths or **magnitudes**, and supposing them to stand for all relevantly similar lines and figures: **which does not imply that the** geometrician **forms an abstract idea** of a line or a figure, **but only that he cares not** about any of the individuating properties of the idea he has in mind; for example, he does not care **what the particular** length or **magnitude** of the line or figure **is, whether** it is **great or small, but looks on that** particular magnitude **as a thing** totally irrelevant to what he hopes to prove of other lines and as **indifferent to the demonstration. Hence, it follows that a** geometrician may with good reason speak of some particular line which figures in his proof as if it actually possessed the properties belonging to various other lines it is meant to represent. Take some inch-long **line** appearing **in the** diagram or **scheme** being used: Though very small, it can represent lines that are very long. Of course, since the line is **but an inch long,** it cannot contain 10 000 parts: As I explained in Section 124, it has only so many parts as may be discerned in it. But the lines it stands for—these may contain 10 000 parts. And insofar as the geometrician wants to use this inch-line to establish things about all lines—including very long ones—it **must be spoken of as though it** really **contained ten thousand parts, since it is regarded not in itself but** only in its representative capacity. The particular line is considered **as if it is** a pattern for all lines **universally; and it is** a pattern for all lines **universally only in** what we take to be **its signification, whereby it represents innumerable lines greater than it self, in which may be distinguished ten thousand parts or more, though there may not be** anything **above an inch's** length **in** the particular stroke as **it** appears on the paper. **After this manner the properties of the lines signified are** read back onto the inch-line **(by a very** dubious inference, which is **usually** spontaneous and, I **figure,** unnoticed). The properties signified are **transferred to the sign,** in other words, **and thence through mistake thought to appertain to it considered in its own nature,** rather than in its role as signifier. It is precisely this process—of transferring properties possessed by the things signified back onto the signifier—that will ultimately explain why we tend to regard lines of finite length as containing infinitely many parts. This will be spelled out in Section 128 below.

An inch-long line on a sheet of paper can be made to stand for a line of any length whatever—one foot, one yard, one mile, one light-year and so on. Lines of greater length contain more parts than lines of lesser length, according to the idealist. But since the inch-long line denotes them, it is regarded— for purposes of the proof—as containing more parts than can be specified. It is easy to forget that the inch-long line contains these innumerable parts only for purposes of the proof—only by stipulation—and to suppose that it really does contain 10 000 parts, 100 000 parts, etc. This is clearly a mistake.

---

127. I should first like to explain the general point more fully: **Because the** inch-long stroke in my diagram can be taken to represent any line whatsoever, and because **there is no number of parts** in any one of those other lines **so great** that I cannot imagine a longer line containing even more, the inch-line is a signifier of unlimited scope. Though the line before me is but an inch long, because **it is** always **possible there may be a line contain-ing more parts, the inch-line** itself **is said to contain parts more than any assignable number,** and so to be potentially infinite; but this is an ambig-uous statement, **which is true, not of the inch taken absolutely**—not of the mark on the paper, the particular line that I drew—**but only for the things signified by it**—the various lines it's meant to represent. **But men not retaining that distinction** between sign and signified **in their thoughts,** easily **slide into a belief that the small particular line described on the paper**—the sign—**contains in it self** all of the properties possessed by the long lines signified, and thus that the sign too has **parts innumerable.** Look at it this way: **There is no such thing as the ten-thousandth part of an inch.** There are no parts in a thing beyond what is perceived, and I certainly perceive less than 10 000 parts in an inch; **but there is** a ten-thousandth part **of a *mile* or *diameter of the earth*,** since I could make out at least that many parts with my eyes. Both of **which** things—a mile or diameter—you will agree **may be signified by that inch. When therefore I delineate a triangle on paper, and take one side not above an inch, for example, in** length to be the *radius* of a circle whose centre is one of the triangle's ver-tices: **This** radius **I consider as divided into ten thousand or an hundred thousand parts or more.** I must consider it so, since the radius is going to signify for me lines with that many parts. **For though the ten-thousandth part of that** inch-long **line, considered in it self** as a mark on the paper, **is nothing at all—and** shouldn't be regarded as *really* existing—it simplifies our proofs to treat it as such. The fact of its non-existence, **consequently, may** be safely **neglected without any error or inconveniency** for the purposes of the proof; **yet these described lines**—the ones on the paper—**being only marks standing for greater quantities** (a mile or diameter of the earth), **whereof it may be that the ten-thousandth part is very considerable, it fol-lows, that to prevent notable errors in practice, the *radius* must be taken** to be **of ten thousand parts, or more.** Consider the circumference of the moon: its ten-thousandth part *is* a significant quantity. Since the inch-long mark in my diagram represents it, I must pretend that the inch has 10 000 parts. The accuracy of my proof requires it.

The foregoing account makes plain why geometers are apt to insist on the infinite divisibility of finite extension. The finite line used in a geometrical proof can represent a line of infinite length, containing infinitely many parts. The geometer treats the mark on her paper as if it contained the infinitely many parts that the infinitely long line it represents contains, and then falls into thinking that it really does contain them. But the universal validity of geometrical proofs requires only that we treat finite lengths as infinitely long

and as containing infinitely many parts. They needn't actually be as great as the lines they represent.

128. From what has been said in the last two sections **the reason is plain why** we must think and speak as if the particular line in our diagram contained an infinity of parts. After all, what we want **to do in the end** is to use that inch-long stroke to stand for other lines of **any** given length. For a geometrical **theorem** concerning lines **may become universal in its use**—it may be applied indifferently to any line not considered in the proof—only if what it says holds true of all lines whatsoever. And to show that the theorem holds even of lines containing thousands of parts, **it is necessary** that **we speak of the** little **lines described** in the imagination or drawn **on the paper, as though they** also **contained** thousands of **parts—which really they do not. In so doing**, however, we must not let ourselves be fooled into thinking that a line **of** one inch in length really does contain a thousand parts or more. This is something **which** our transparency thesis quite evidently precludes (Sections 25 and 124). For, **if we examine the matter thoroughly, we shall perhaps discover that we cannot** even **conceive an inch**-long line **it self as consisting of, or being divisible into, a thousand parts, but** that we can visibly discern maybe 50 or 60 parts **only**, and not much more. And since there is nothing in ideas but what is perceived—their contents being transparent—an inch-long line contains well under a thousand parts. However, this does not mean that we are unable to conceive of **some other**, much longer **line** consisting of a thousand parts—for example, a mile-long line, **which is far greater than an inch and** which can nevertheless be **represented by it. And that when we say a line is 'infinitely divisible', we must mean a line which is 'infinitely great'**, since it is impossible that any mind could discern an infinite number of distinct parts in any finite segment. **What we have here observed seems to be the chief cause,** and the best explanation, of **why** some philosophers have come **to suppose the infinite divisibility of finite extension** to be vital: It **has been thought necessary** for ensuring the generality of the principles advanced **in geometry.** Yet this is an error. In order to secure the universal applicability of geometrical principles, the inch-long line need not be infinitely divisible; we need only speak and think *as if* it were—we merely *pretend* that it is. Nothing more is needed for the purposes of geometry.

Absurd consequences follow from supposing that a finite bit of extension can be divided infinitely. That a view has absurd implications normally tells

against it. But mathematicians are largely unmoved by arguments from consequences.

129. Allowing the infinite divisibility of finite extension means allowing that half an inch contains as many parts as a whole inch, since they will each contain an infinity; it means allowing that a ladybug fills the entire world, since the ladybug and the world will each have an infinite number of parts, each part of the ladybug corresponding to a part of the world and thus filling it; it means smelling a rose from an infinite distance, since I may smell it from a foot and a foot contains an infinity. **These, and several** other **absurdities and contradictions which flowed from this false principle** of infinite divisibility **might, one would think, have been esteemed so many** *a posteriori* **demonstrations against it**—where an *a posteriori* argument is understood as one that draws out the unwelcome consequences of a principle, rather than arguing against it directly (see Section 21)**. But, by I know not what** *logic,* **it is** generally **held** by mathematicians that **proofs** *a posteriori* **are not to be admitted** as telling **against propositions relating to infinity.** Such logic is faulty—**as though it were not impossible even for an infinite mind to reconcile contradictions, or as if any thing absurd and repugnant** such as a ladybug filling the whole world **could have a necessary connexion with truth, or flow from it** as a result. **But whoever considers the weakness of this pretence** that arguments from consequences don't count in mathematics, **will** have good reason to **think it was contrived on purpose to humour the laziness of the mind** and give us an excuse for not thinking our way out of difficulties. But there's no cure for the lazy mind**, which had rather** admit defeat—would rather tolerate absurdities in mathematics and so **acquiesce in an indolent scepticism—than be at the pains to go through with a severe examination of those principles it** is accustomed to assuming and **has ever embraced for true.**

Absurdities concerning infinitesimals accumulate. Some mathematicians postulate infinitesimals beyond the first order—what we might call 'higher order infinitesimals': They propose that each of the infinite number of infinitely small parts in a finite length itself contains an infinite number of parts, and that each of these infinitely small subparts contains an infinite number of parts, and so on forever. Other mathematicians will countenance only one order of infinitesimals, rejecting all higher orders as fictional. They emphasize the bizarre properties that higher order infinitesimals would have: It would turn

out, for instance, that an infinite number of parts wouldn't even be big enough to qualify as infinitely small. But these more cautious mathematicians fail to recognize that their first order infinitesimals are every bit as strange as those of a higher order. The most sensible attitude is disbelief: There are no infinitesimals of any order.

130. Often we find that one absurdity is followed by another. And so it is with errors concerning infinity. If the above mentioned paradoxes didn't confuse things sufficiently, just consider that **lately the speculations about infinities have run so high,** have gotten so out of control **and** have **grown to** embrace **such strange notions, as have occasioned** many doubts—these are **no small scruples** either—**and** they have engendered numerous **disputes among the geometers of the present age,** which give no sign of reaching a conclusion. **Some there are of great note** and fame, such as Leibniz and the Marquis de l'Hôpital (1661–1704), **who** are **not content with holding that finite lines may be divided into an infinite number of parts.** No, they don't see any reason to stop at infinitesimal parts—as if those weren't strange enough: They go **yet farther, maintain**ing **that each of those infinitesimals is it self subdivisible into an infinity of other parts, or,** as we may call them, **infinitesimals of a 'second order'.** And each of these infinitesimals can itself be subdivided into an infinity of other parts so that we have infinitesimals of a third order, a fourth order**, and so on** *ad infinitum.* **These** mathematicians, **I say, assert that there are** infinitely small parts of infinitely small parts—**infinitesimals of infinitesimals of infinitesimals, without ever coming to an end. So that according to them an inch does not** contain just an infinity of parts—that **barely** scratches the surface. To be sure, it *does* **contain an infinite number of parts, but** it also contains **an infinity of an infinity of an infinity** *ad infinitum* **of parts.** What that means is beyond me. **Others there be,** such as Bernard Nieuwentijdt (1654–1718), **who** oppose Leibniz and the Marquis on this point. Nieuwentijdt agrees that things can be divided into an infinite number of parts, but he denies that these infinitesimal parts can in turn be divided infinitely. These mathematicians maintain that there are no second or third orders of infinitesimals. Indeed, they **hold all orders of infinitesimals below the** original **first** order **to be nothing at all, thinking it** an outrageous speculation to assume them, and **with good reason.** After all, if you multiplied a third order infinitesimal part of some random line infinitely many times it would still never amount to an infinitesimal part of the line. But this is **absurd:** I find it exceedingly difficult **to imagine that there is any positive quantity or part of extension, which, though** it be **multiplied infinitely, can never equal the smallest given** segment **of extension. And yet, on the other hand,** these mathematicians are themselves involved in absurdities by virtue of accepting the original, first order of infinitesimal parts. For **it seems no less absurd to**

think that **the square, cube, or other power of a positive real root, should it self be nothing at all; which they who hold infinitesimals of the first order** to exist, **denying** existence to **all of the subsequent orders, are obliged to maintain**—there being nothing below the first order, in their view, and so nothing smaller than an infinitely small part.

One argument against dropping infinitesimals from our ontology is that it would undermine much of the work done by geometers, since a good deal of it is concerned with the infinitely small. Berkeley's reply is that only the high-flown and useless parts of geometry will be lost. There is nothing of any practical value in geometry that depends on the existence of infinitely small parts.

---

131. Those who accept higher-order infinitesimals must recognize parts of extension so small that even multiplication to infinity yields no discernible quantity; those who allow infinities of the first order only to be real are forced to concede that the square, cube or other power of the first-order infinitesimal—which they treat as a real positive quantity greater than zero though less than one—has no magnitude whatever, since any quantity smaller than an infinitesimal is nothing, according to them. Both outcomes are absurd. **Have we not therefore reason to conclude that they are *both* in the wrong,** that neither first- nor higher-order infinitesimals exist? Should we not cast off infinities altogether **and** grant **that there is in effect no such thing as parts infinitely small, or an infinite number of parts contained in any finite quantity? But you will say, that if this doctrine obtains,** if there are no infinitely small magnitudes, **it will follow** that **the very foundations of geometry are destroyed, and** much important work in mathematics will be lost. Reject infinitesimals and in effect you'll be saying that our best geometers are confused, that **those great men who have** through painstaking effort **raised that science to so astonishing an height** and made it appear so grand, **have been all the while** blowing smoke and **building a castle in the air. To this** worry **it may be replied** with some confidence, **that whatever is useful in geometry,** whatever serves our practical purposes **and promotes the benefit of human life, does still remain firm and unshaken on our principles.** Geometry is not crippled when confined to perceivable extension: **That science, considered as practical, will rather receive advantage than any** harm or **prejudice from what has been said. But to set this** matter **in a due light** and show that geometry **may be** profitably pursued without supposing the infinite divisibility of finite extension is **the subject of a distinct inquiry** and exceeds our present concerns. **For the rest, though it**

should follow from dropping infinitesimals **that some of the more intricate and subtle parts of** *speculative mathematics* will have to go, these **may be pared off**—you may safely cut them loose—**without any prejudice to truth.** This implies a loss in content, of course, **yet I do not see what damage will be thence derived to mankind**—I don't see at all that it hurts them. **On the contrary, it were highly to be wished that** these **men of great abilities,** who now waste time on infinitesimals and their imagined properties, would honestly **and obstinately** apply their intellects to live problems with real-world **application.** These learned scholars **would** do well to **draw off their thoughts from those** pointless mathematical **amusements, and employ them in the study of such things as lie nearer to the concerns of life,** such as finding a universal remedy or founding a national bank, **or** apply them instead to things which **have a more direct influence on the manners,** such as setting up a Christian college—planting arts and learning—in the less civilized parts of the world.

Exponents of the infinitely small might appeal to mathematical practice: If infinitesimals play a crucial role in the demonstration of certain mathematical theorems, then they must exist. But a closer look at these demonstrations will show that infinitesimals do not play any such role, according to Berkeley. How could they, if they are impossible?

---

132. If it be said that several mathematical **theorems,** which are **undoubtedly true, are discovered** and proven **by** employing **methods in which infinitesimals are** brought in and **made use of,** I will simply deny that they were really essential to the proofs. Advocates of infinitesimals will presumably insist that there are certain mathematical truths which depend on there being infinitely small parts, and **which could never have been** established, **if their existence included a contradiction in it.** Since infinitesimals are presupposed and relied on in the proofs, they must exist; and if they exist, there can be no contradiction in supposing them. But **I** reject the premise—that the proofs require them. My **answer,** then, is **that upon a** more careful and **thorough examination it will not be found,** that in any instance of a mathematical proof or theorem **it is necessary to make use of or conceive infinitesimal parts of finite lines, or even quantities less than the** smallest that can be registered by the senses (the *minimum sensibile*): **Nay,** upon reflection **it will be evident that this is never done, it being impossible** to conceive of the infinitely small. Mathematicians doing calculus seem to have a different view, just taking it for granted that the little, almost insensible quantities they work with are infinitely small. But calling them 'infinitesimals' doesn't make them so. The solution of their problems can hardly depend on something impossible.

Every argument is on the side of idealism. Every consideration—practical, moral, theoretical—favours discarding matter and embracing mind. The benefits of idealism are so pronounced that we would do well to accept it even without argument.

---

133. By what we have premised above, **it is plain that** the prevailing philosophical and mathematical systems contain **very numerous and important errors.** Most of the errors are caused by faulty assumptions. Specifically, they **have taken their rise from those false principles, which were** challenged or otherwise **impugned in the foregoing parts of this treatise. And the opposites of those erroneous tenets**—the propositions I defend—**at the same time appear to be most fruitful principles, from whence do flow innumerable consequences** that are **highly advantageous to true philosophy as well as to** the Christian **religion. Particularly** the doctrine of *matter,* or belief in **the absolute,** mind-independent **existence of corporeal objects,** has caused much harm and confusion. For this doctrine **has been shown to be that wherein the most avowed and pernicious** sceptics, the most committed and destructive **enemies of all knowledge, whether** of **human or divine** things, **have ever placed their chief strength and confidence,** finding ample support for their sceptical conclusions in the imagined existence of material objects behind our sensations. **And surely, if by distinguishing the real existence of unthinking things from their being perceived,** as materialists do, **and allowing them a subsistence of their own** outside and completely independent **of the minds of spirits, no one thing is explained in nature, but on the contrary a great many inexplicable difficulties arise** in metaphysics, mathematics and science, then we shouldn't draw such a distinction: **If the supposition of matter is barely** better than a guess, if it is an unwarranted and **precarious** supposition, **as not being grounded on so much as one single** argument or **reason,** then we shouldn't make it; **if its consequences cannot endure the light of examination and free inquiry, but** prove to be absurd, **screening themselves under the dark and general pretence of** *infinites being incomprehensible* to finite minds and entangling them in difficulties (see Locke's *Essay,* Book II, Chapter 17, Section 21), then we shouldn't cling to it; **if, with all** the trouble it causes, we are forced to reject it, and if **the removal of this** *matter* be uncomplicated and **not attended with the least evil consequence, if it be not even missed in the**

world, but every thing be as well, nay much easier, conceived and explained without it, then we should be glad to see it go; if lastly, both *sceptics* and *atheists* are for ever silenced upon supposing only spirits and ideas in the world, and if this immaterialist scheme of things is perfectly agreeable both to *reason* and *religion*, then we should adopt it without hesitation; indeed, methinks we may reasonably expect it should be admitted as true and firmly embraced by everyone, though it were supposed only as an *hypothesis*, unsupported by any arguments or demonstration. Of course, the idealist ontology of minds and ideas is much more than an hypothesis, for the existence of matter is not even possible. Still, the benefits of idealism alone would be enough to recommend it, had our arguments not already established that minds and ideas are the only realities, and had the existence of matter been allowed so much as possible, which yet I think we have evidently demonstrated that it is not.

Many vexed philosophical questions are reduced to nothing, and the arguments on either side become insignificant, if the principles of idealism are accepted. Seeing all their hard work go up in smoke, philosophers who have devoted their time to these issues will resist the force of Berkeley's demonstrations with prejudice. But those with nothing invested in the debates will see it as an advantage that idealism does away with so many philosophical problems.

134. True it is that acceptance of idealism would, in one sense, amount to a philosophical loss. For in consequence of the foregoing principles, several philosophical disputes about objects that don't really exist will appear rather silly, and some metaphysical speculations, which are highly esteemed in the schools, will be reduced to nothing. What I mean to say is that more than a few parts of learning, which are currently regarded as cutting edge philosophy, are going to be rejected as useless by anyone who converts to my system. The 'puzzles' to which many philosophers have devoted so much of their time, and which they take so seriously, concern non-entities like abstract ideas, infinitely small parts and material substances. Seeing their efforts go to waste when confronted with my principles, these philosophers will want to dig in their heels and resist them. But so be it: how great a prejudice soever there may be against our notions, one must be guided by reason and truth—this is the very essence of philosophy. The force of my arguments may at least give pause to some of those thinkers who have already been deeply engaged in materialist metaphysics, and made large advances in studies of that nature: And yet it may turn out that our principles will even be embraced by others

who are more open-minded and better able to set prejudice aside. Most of all, **we hope it will not be thought any just** argument against idealism, or a proper **ground of dislike,** that it is new and sounds strange **to** learned ears. I think it is a virtue and a strength of **the principles and tenets herein laid down, that they** wipe out trivial pursuits, that they **abridge the labour of study,** that they redirect the mind **and make human sciences more clear** and comprehensible, more compact and **compendious,** more open **and attainable, than** ever **they were before.**

If a lack of ideas implies a lack of knowledge, then we have no knowledge of minds, since we have no ideas of minds. This might be considered a limitation on human knowledge. But no one complains that they can't smell colours or hear odours. So no one should complain that they can't perceive minds, since perceiving, or having an idea of, an active thing is categorically impossible—it would be like tasting a sound.

---

135. Having dispatched with all those useless speculations concerning infinity, numbers in the abstract, pure space, pure motion, gravitational attraction, real essences, invisible particles and the like, and with an eye to brevity having said **what we intended to say concerning the knowledge of *ideas*, the method we proposed** in Section 101 **leads us, in the next place, to treat of** our knowledge of ***spirits*; with regard to which** some philosophers have expressed scepticism. Locke, for instance, thinks that a man who would proceed beyond his own ideas to the inner nature of mental substance falls inevitably into darkness and obscurity (*Essay,* Book II, Chapter 23, Section 32). But **perhaps human knowledge is not so deficient** with respect to minds **as** philosophers seem to think or as **is vulgarly imagined. The great reason that is assigned** for this deficiency, the cause that is normally cited **for our being thought ignorant of the nature of spirits, is our not having an idea of it.** Some would consider this a cognitive defect—a flaw in our mental machinery. **But** such a negative assessment is hasty. If I had no idea of blue, or of sweetness, it would **surely** be considered a defect of my faculties and a curious perceptual gap—a blind spot for me where others have perception and understanding. Yet **it ought not to be looked on as a defect in a human understanding that it does not perceive the idea of** a mind or ***spirit*, if it is manifestly impossible that there should be any such idea.** Lacking an idea of mind entails ignorance of minds only if having an idea of mind is possible in the first place. **And** the absolute impossibility of **this** kind of perception, **if I mistake not, has been demonstrated** already in

Section 27; to which I shall here add that a spirit has been shown to be the only substance or support, wherein the unthinking beings or ideas we do have **can exist** and so we know that spiritual substances are real without our having to—or even being able to—perceive them: **But that this *substance* which supports or perceives ideas should it self be an *idea*, or like an *idea*, is evidently absurd**: for an active thing that supports cannot at the same time be a passive thing supported. My failure to perceive minds implies, therefore, neither ignorance nor cognitive limitation.

It's not a deficiency to lack what can't be had. Ideas of mind cannot be had. So lacking them is not a deficiency. To this argument from the previous section someone might reply: We could have an idea of mind. If only we had a new sense adapted to perceiving minds, we could acquire ideas of them. As seeing furnishes ideas of sight and hearing furnishes ideas of sound, this new sense—whatever you want to call it—would furnish ideas of mind. But this response is confused, for a new sense could only furnish new ideas, and a mind is neither an idea nor representable by an idea. Does anyone have the idea of a friendless friend or an unknown celebrity? Clearly not. But that doesn't make us cognitively deficient; to be incapable of the impossible is no limitation. So being unable to represent the unrepresentable—being unable to perceive a mind—is not a shortcoming either.

---

136. It will perhaps be said, that, on the contrary, **we** could have an idea of the soul, though it would require the procuring of a new sensory modality beyond sight, touch, hearing, taste and smell. An idea of soul is possible, in other words, though anyone who **wants** to perceive it would need **a sixth sense** in order to do so **(as some have imagined** is possible**).** Employing this new organ would be the only **proper** way of coming **to know** mental **substances** through direct perception, and **with** it we would be able to acquire an idea *of* the soul in addition to **all** the ideas we have from the other senses of what occurs *in* the soul. Of course, no one has any such sense, and it cannot be obtained by any natural process; the point is only that *in principle* God could miraculously afford us a new sense, **which, if we had it,** would provide us with new ideas. Thus, in theory **we might** be able to **know our own soul, as we do a triangle.** If God so desired, he could by this means furnish us with an idea of soul just as he has furnished us with an idea of triangles. But this does not seem to me a real possibility. **To this** argument from a new sense, **I** provide the same **answer** that I gave to a similar argument made in Section 77 concerning matter. Specifically, I will say again **that in case we had a new**

sense bestowed upon us, we could only receive thereby some new sensations or ideas of sense, not something that isn't an idea. Like the senses we possess, a new sense could deliver nothing but ideas—ideas of a new kind, to be sure, but ideas nonetheless. **But I believe no body will say, that what he means by the terms 'soul', 'spirit' and 'mental substance', is only some particular sort of idea or sensation.** Thus, whatever ideas we could acquire through a new sense, none of them could be the idea of a soul, since the soul is not, and cannot possibly be, represented by an idea—it's the wrong sort of thing. **We may therefore infer, that all things duly considered, it is not more reasonable to think our** cognitive **faculties defective, in that they do not furnish us with an idea of** a soul or **spirit or active thinking substance, than it would be if we should blame them for not being able to comprehend a 'round square'.** In fact, it would be wholly *unreasonable* to do so: Our faculties are no more at fault for supplying no idea of a mind or soul than they are at fault for supplying no idea of a 'round square' or 'female uncle'. And they could no more be augmented to provide us with an idea of mind or soul than they could be augmented to provide us with the idea of a 'round square' or 'female uncle'—all three are impossible. Admittedly, the ideas of a round square or female uncle are impossible because nothing can be both round and square or female and uncle. And it is certainly not the case that nothing can be a soul. It is only the *idea* of a soul that is impossible, because souls and ideas are nothing alike.

The belief that knowing minds requires having ideas of minds has led to scepticism about their nature and existence. One way to stem the scepticism is to reflect on the meanings of the terms 'idea' and 'agency'. We'll see that an idea (a passive thing) cannot resemble—and so cannot represent—an agent (or active thing). So we shouldn't expect to have ideas of them. One possible counter would be to say that an idea can resemble a mind not by reference to its active properties, but by reference to some other (presumably non-active) properties. In that case, representing minds would be possible and so the noticeable absence of ideas could still encourage scepticism.

---

137. From the opinion that spirits are to be known after the same **manner** as we know the objects of sense—that is to say, that we grasp spirits by means **of an idea or sensation—have risen many absurd**ities. Irreligious **and heterodox tenets,** the most unhealthy **and** unchristian views, crop up as soon as you suppose that knowing a mind requires having an idea of the mind, for this supposition leads to **much scepticism about the nature of the soul.** The reasoning goes something like this: 'To know my own mind I must perceive it. But I don't perceive it. So I don't know it'. **It is even probable, that this opinion** about ideas being requisite for knowledge **may have produced a doubt in some,** as to **whether they had any soul** or mind **at all distinct from their body.** Such doubt is hardly surprising in those who from the start expected to perceive their own soul, **since upon inquiry they could not find** that **they had any idea of it.** But this line of reasoning proceeds from a false assumption: It assumes that perceiving a mind—that having an idea of mind—is possible. The argument of Section 27 showed this to be an error. **That an *idea* which is inactive, and the existence whereof consists in being perceived, should be the image or likeness of** something so different from an idea, that it could be the image or likeness of **an agency subsisting by it self, seems to need no other refutation than barely attending to** and reflecting upon **what is meant by those words** 'idea' and 'agency'. **But perhaps you will say that, though an *idea* cannot resemble a *spirit*, in its thinking, acting, or subsisting by it self, yet it may** resemble it **in some other respects, and** hence represent it. For **it is not necessary that an idea or image be in all respects like the original** it represents. I can draw a barn with feather and ink, thereby representing the real barn in my field even though the real barn is red and the drawn barn is not. Representation does not require perfect similarity.

Since minds have none but active properties, there is no room for even partial similarity between a mind and an idea. So there is no room for representation. For if a mind is nothing more than a thing that thinks, wills and perceives—if it is a thing without a trace of passivity—then it cannot be represented by a thing incapable of representing activity. What is there to represent once all the active properties have been excluded? Nothing remaining, there is nothing to resemble.

---

138. I answer that your general claim, though true enough, does not apply here. Representation in an idea or image does not require perfect similarity—I'll give you that. But it does require *some* similarity. There must be *something* in common between an idea or image and the thing it represents. Otherwise it's not an idea *of* that thing. I just don't see how that's going to help you when it comes to spirits, however. For, if you claim to have an idea of a spirit or mind, but that **it does not** resemble a spirit or mind **in** any of **those** ways **mentioned** above, then **it is impossible** that **it should** resemble or **represent it in any other** way either. For there is no**thing** to spirits beyond acting and thinking. **Do but leave out the power of willing, thinking, and perceiving ideas, and there remains nothing else wherein the idea** you claim to have **can be like a spirit**—the two will have *nothing* in common. **For by the word 'spirit' we mean only that** thing **which thinks, wills, and perceives; this, and this alone, constitutes the** entire **signification of that term.** An idea of spirit minus the powers of thinking, willing and perceiving is like an idea of a barn minus colour, shape and size—rubbish! Such a thing, whatever it is, cannot in any respect resemble a barn; and so it cannot represent it. **If therefore it is impossible that any degree of those powers** of willing, thinking and perceiving **should be represented in an idea,** then **it is evident** that **there can be no idea of a spirit.** And since it is moreover impossible for willing, thinking and perceiving to be represented in an idea, there can indeed be no idea of spirit.

If mental terms such as 'soul', 'spirit' and 'mind' do not stand for ideas, then it might seem to follow that they mean nothing. Berkeley denies the inference: 'soul', 'spirit' and similar terms mean something insofar as they signify something—a thinking, perceiving, active being. But then one could argue from considerations of consistency that if mental terms signify, they must signify ideas. Since the things picked out by other terms are generally called 'ideas'—the word 'horse' signifies the idea of a horse—we should expect the same here: 'soul' should pick out the idea of a soul. Berkeley replies that the fundamental disparity of minds and ideas counterbalances considerations of consistency.

---

139. But it will be objected by the sceptic who limits knowledge to ideas, **that if there is no idea signified by the terms 'soul', 'spirit', and 'substance',** then **they** are empty and reveal nothing about the nature of minds. For, if the terms **are wholly insignificant, or have no meaning in them,** then we're not really saying or referring to anything when we use them. **I answer** that, on the contrary, **those words do** have a sufficiently clear **mean**ing or sense attached to them and so it is not the case that every meaningful term is associated with an idea. The words 'soul' or 'spirit' **signify a real thing, which is neither an idea nor** anything **like an idea, but** rather **that which perceives ideas and wills, and reasons about them. What I am my self, that which I denote by the term 'I', is the same** as the being I designate **with** the term 'mind'. **It is what is meant by** the words **'soul' or 'spiritual substance'. If it be said that this** whole disagreement with the sceptic **is only** a matter of **quarrelling** about language, that we are **at** odds over the meaning of **a word** rather than any legitimate question regarding knowledge, **and that** we would do better to focus on things rather than language; if we be urged to extend our use of 'idea' to include every nature of which we are aware so that 'knowing x' and 'having an idea of x' are equated, then, in this very broad sense of 'idea', we do have an 'idea' of mind, **since** minds are natures that we know. To put the objection differently: Since I allow the term 'spirit' or 'soul' to signify my mind, and since **the immediate significations of other names are by** the **common consent** of men **called 'ideas'**—as, I admit, they are—then **no** good **reason can be assigned, why that which is signified by the name 'spirit' or 'soul' may not partake in the same appellation** and be classified as an 'idea'. Why not call my mind an 'idea', in other words, since ideas are the things immediately signified by names? **I answer, that all the unthinking objects of the mind** are alike in one crucial respect and possession of this common property is what distinguishes them from minds. In short, all ideas **agree, in that they are entirely passive, and** hence **their existence consists only in being perceived: Whereas a soul or spirit is an active being, whose existence consists not in being perceived, but in perceiving ideas and thinking.** Two natures more opposed are never to be found: ideas and minds are completely diverse. **It is therefore necessary, in order to prevent** any **equivocation and the confounding** of two **natures perfectly disagreeing and** totally **unlike** each other**, that we distinguish** clearly between **'spirit' and 'idea'.** See Section 27 for more on this distinction.

We may use the word 'idea' strictly or loosely. In a loose sense, 'idea' refers to any object of knowledge. Since we do know minds, the relaxed usage allows that we have 'ideas' of them. But this is imprecise. In the strict and proper sense, an 'idea' is an object perceived with one or more of the senses. Since minds are not perceived in this way, we do not, strictly speaking, have ideas of them. It is not through ordinary sense perception that we know minds. Rather, everyone knows their own mind through inner reflection and other minds by way of inference.

---

140. I'd like to avoid verbal disputes, if possible. So if you press me on this, I'll just admit that we can use the word 'idea' in a loose and general sense to mean anything that is an object of knowledge. **In a large** and broad **sense indeed, we may** thus **be said to have an 'idea'** of spirit, meaning only that we know of spirit. However, my preference is to use the word 'idea' more narrowly, as referring only to passive **or** perceived objects, and the word 'notion' to cover active or perceiving subjects, as I explained in Section 89. Strictly speaking, then, we have **rather a 'notion' of** *spirit*. But the terminology doesn't really matter. If we know how to use 'spirit' in the appropriate contexts, if we know how to apply it, **that is,** no doubt, because **we understand the meaning of the word; for otherwise we could not affirm or deny any thing of it.** We could say nothing about minds or spirits, if we didn't understand the words; since we make plenty of meaningful claims about them, we do understand. **Moreover,** we come to know of other minds—the minds of our friends, for instance—in the same way we come to know of their ideas—by analogy with our own. Just **as we conceive the ideas that are in the minds of other spirits by means of** analogical reasoning from **our own ideas, which we suppose to be** similar to their ideas and fairly accurate **resemblances of them, so too we know of other spirits by means of our own soul.** On the basis of observed similarities between ourselves and other people we infer that they have ideas and souls similar to ours. This is explained more fully in Section 145. My soul, with **which** I am intimately familiar, provides me with a model for understanding other souls and their perceptions. And so, **in that** loose **sense** my soul **is the** 'image' of other souls **or** provides me with an **'idea' of them.** Knowing my own mind as I do, and observing countless parallels between my outward behaviour and the outward behaviour of others, I am in little doubt of **its having a** close **like**ness to other minds. In **respect** of its nature and fundamental features, in other words, I can be confident that my mind or spirit is similar **to other** minds or **spirits,** just as I am confident **that** an idea of **blueness or heat** as it is **by me perceived has** much similarity **to those ideas** as they are **perceived by another** soul in similar circumstances.

The soul is naturally immortal. It cannot be destroyed by any natural process. This is consistent with the soul being destructible in principle, should God wish to extinguish it. Those who liken the soul to a material being, such as a flame, feed the immorality of degenerates. For if the soul is material, it is mortal, and if it is mortal, there is no fear of retribution for misdeeds in the afterlife. This view is mistaken, however, since material things are ideas, and ideas differ from souls in every conceivable way.

---

141. That my own soul is a real, active, indivisible thing which perceives ideas without itself being perceived is evident to me through inward feeling; that other men have souls resembling mine in these respects is evident to me by inference (see Sections 89, 140 and 145). **It must not be supposed,** however, **that they who,** like us, **assert the natural immortality of the soul are of the opinion, that it is absolutely incapable of annihilation even by the infinite power of the Creator who first gave it being,** for surely God could snuff a soul out of existence just

204 Of the Principles of Human Knowledge

as easily as he brought it in. We do not say that the soul is absolutely immortal, therefore, **but only that it is not liable to be broken or dissolved by** anything operating in accordance with **the ordinary laws of nature or motion.** Here we find ourselves in agreement with Leibniz, who rightly observes that because souls are unextended and indivisible, 'they can begin only by creation and end only by annihilation' (*A New System of Nature*). It is the incorporeality of the soul, in our view, which renders it indivisible and thus naturally indestructible, for there can be no dissolution—no scattering of parts—where no parts are to be found. **They indeed, who hold the soul of man to be only a thin vital flame, or system of animal spirits,** cannot simultaneously uphold its immortality. By assigning the soul a location within the human frame, they **make it as perishing and corruptible as the body, since there is nothing more easily** broken up and **dissipated than such a being, which it is naturally impossible should survive the ruin of the tabernacle**—the destruction of the 'box'—**wherein it is enclosed.** This appears to be the view of Hobbes, who regards the soul as a body, 'however rarefied and imperceptible' (*Leviathan*, Part I, Chapter XII, Section 7). **And this notion** of a material soul **has been greedily embraced and cherished by the worst part of mankind,** who welcome any opinion that would free them from obligation. For why be good and pious if there is no afterlife in which to be punished? Such is their crude manner of thinking. Belief in the soul's mortality thus encourages sin and depravity—it acts, indeed, **as the most effectual antidote against all impressions of virtue and** goodness, effectively undermining the lessons of **religion. But it has been made evident** in our treatise **that** the soul is nothing like a body. All **bodies—of what frame or texture soever** they may be—**are** composed entirely of sensible qualities. And it **barely** needs repeating that sensible qualities are **passive ideas in the mind,** or soul, **which** perceives them. The soul **is** thus **more distant** from bodies, more different **and heterogeneous from them than light is from darkness. We have shown that the soul is** by its nature **indivisible, incorporeal,** and **unextended, and it is consequently incorruptible. Nothing can be plainer than that the motions, changes, decays, and dissolutions which we hourly see befall** the **natural bodies** around us **(and which is what we mean by the 'course of nature') cannot possibly affect an active, simple, uncompounded** mental **substance.** How could the falling of a branch, the crumbling of a bridge, the rotting of a fish—in short, the shifting of ideas in a mind—have any deleterious effect on a perceiver? The mechanism of such influence is perfectly inconceivable. **Such a being** as a mind **therefore is** untouchable by other finite beings and wholly **indissoluble by the forces of nature, that is to say, *the soul of man is naturally immortal.*** Materialist philosophers should weigh this conclusion carefully.

Minds and ideas diverging so radically—their natures differing at such a fundamental level—it is not even thinkable that we could grasp the one by means of the other. Perceiving a mind is a conceptual impossibility. So again, it makes more sense to say that we have a 'notion' of mind rather than an 'idea' of it. 'Notion' should be extended to cover relations between things as well, such as A's being brighter than B, or smoother than B. For the relating of things is an act of mind and we have 'notions' rather than 'ideas' of that which is active.

142. **After what has been said** in Sections 89 and 140, **it is I suppose plain that souls are not to be known in the same manner as** we know **senseless inactive objects, or by way of** perceiving *ideas*. **Spirits** and *ideas* **are things so wholly different that, when we say 'they exist', 'they are known', or the like,** the words 'exist' and 'known' do not have the same meaning in each case; when said of ideas and when said of spirits **these words must not be thought to signify any thing common to both** their **natures.** The kind of existence proper to ideas is profoundly different from that of spirits, as is our way of knowing them. **There is nothing** at all **alike or common in them; and** so **to expect that by any** miraculous **multiplication** of our powers of discernment, **or** any other **enlargement of our** cognitive **faculties, we may** acquire a new idea of a spirit, and **be enabled to know a spirit** by way of this idea, just **as we do a triangle, seems as absurd as if we should hope to** *see a sound.* **This is** a point that bears repeating: It must be instilled and **inculcated** in my reader **because I imagine it may be of moment**ous significance. Understanding why we may not acquire an idea of spirit will help us move **towards** a better ontology, **clearing** up **several important** metaphysical **questions, and preventing some very dangerous** theological **errors concerning the nature of the soul. We may not I think strictly be said to have an 'idea' of an active being, or of an action, although we may be said to have a 'notion' of them.** Even without the help of an idea, I still **have some knowledge or notion of my** soul or **mind, and of its acts, and about** how it produces **ideas,** and operates on them—at least **inasmuch as I** have some **knowledge or understand**ing **of what is meant by those words,** as explained above in Section 140. **Whatev**er **I know, that I have some notion of.** This seems perfectly plain. But I'm not going to hang anything on a verbal dispute. **I will not say, that the terms 'idea' and 'notion' may** absolutely **not be used** interchangeably, that in no context may they be employed **convertibly** as referring to both ideas and notions, **if the world will have it so:** If people prefer to speak with a little looseness in the ordinary course of things, that is fine by me. **But yet it** is **conducive to precision,** and helps us **to attain more clearness and propriety** in our thoughts, **that we distinguish things** that are **very different by** using **different** words or **names** to stand for them. Thus, ideas and notions differing so radically, it is preferable that we mark the distinction linguistically. One final point presents itself: I have been focusing on our knowledge of minds and ideas, and considering the propriety of using a different term for each. But I haven't said much about the *relations* between things and whether we know them by way of 'idea' or 'notion' (I mean such things as being brighter than, smoother than, etc.). **It is** probably best to consider them **also**, if we want to get clear on our terminology. The first thing **to be remarked** is **that** we do have some knowledge of relations: We recognize that things are related, or better, that *we* can so relate them. And *relating* being a mental act, we lack ideas of **all relations**—for nothing *active* may be represented by something *passive*. Relations, in other words, are not so much *things* as they are *acts* whereby a mind relates one idea to another. That relations are distinct from the things related, and that they include an act of mind, was indicated already in Section 89 where I observed that we may perceive two ideas, A and B, without perceiving their relation. And since nothing **including an act of the mind** in its very nature is wholly passive, relations are not to be classed with ideas. Strictly speaking, therefore, **we cannot so properly be said to have an 'idea'** of the relations that two ideas bear to one another, **but** it is **rather** more accurate to say that we have a **'notion' of the relations or habitudes between** such **things. But if in the modern** and relaxed **way** of speaking **the** meaning of the **word 'idea' is extended to** include **spirits, and relations and acts,** I make no objection: **this is after all an affair of** merely **verbal concern**, and very little turns on the use of a word.

Past philosophers thought they understood acts of mind in the abstract. They pretended to have an abstract concept of willing, for instance, apart from the object willed, and apart from the mind willing. This belief has contributed much to the obscurity of metaphysics and morality.

---

143. It will not be amiss to add that the doctrine of *abstract ideas* has had no small share in rendering those sciences intricate and obscure, which are particularly psychological in orientation and **conversant about spiritual things.** Locke, for instance, supposed that by reflecting on the operations of the mind a man could obtain the ideas of *believing, doubting, willing* and so on. These he called 'ideas of reflection' (*Essay*, Book II, Chapter 1, Section 4). That *believing, doubting* and *willing* are ideas, I deny outright. They are *acts of the mind*, and ideas, being wholly passive, can never represent that which is active—representation occurring only by way of resemblance (see Section 25). **Men** who are ready to acknowledge this point **have** sometimes **imagined they could frame**, if not **abstract** ideas or images, then at least abstract **notions of these powers and acts of the mind, and consider them** in isolation. Believing, doubting and willing are cut off or **prescinded,** they say, **as well from the mind or spirit it self** that acts **as from their respective objects and effects**—the things believed, doubted or willed. In contrast, I admit that I do indeed have a notion—that is to say, a reflective understanding—of willing, doubting, etc., but not apart from my mind in the abstract. As explained in Section 27, we know the active powers of the mind in the exercise of them. I understand believing in the act of believing, doubting in the act of doubting, willing in the act of willing. But I have no notion of willing or doubting on its own. **Hence a great number of dark and ambiguous terms,** mistakenly **presumed to stand for abstract notions, have been introduced into metaphysics and morality, and from these have grown infinite distractions and** endless **disputes amongst the learned.** Rejecting abstract notions allows us to bypass these disputes altogether.

We are apt to speak of the mind in metaphorical terms, describing it variously as 'dark' or 'light', 'cluttered' or 'empty'. Taking metaphors too seriously can foster philosophical misunderstanding. For example, the mind is sometimes described in mechanical terms, as undergoing certain 'motions'. It's a small step from here to the 'mind as machine' view of human agency, which explains our behaviour deterministically. This leads to a denial of freedom and finally to the renouncing of all moral responsibility. The mechanical metaphors thus land us in a perilous moral vacuum. All this can be avoided easily by taking greater care with our metaphors.

---

144. But nothing seems more to have contributed towards engaging men in controversies and disposing them to **mistaken views with regard to the nature and operations of the mind, than their being used to speak**ing **of those things in** metaphorical **terms.** I refer, in particular, to their habit of accounting for them in language **borrowed from** our descriptions of **sensible** objects and **ideas,** like when we say that someone has 'dark' thoughts or 'lightness' of mind. The use of such metaphors can have serious repercussions. **For example, the will is** sometimes **termed the 'motion' of the soul: This** view of the soul as 'movable' can be attributed to Epicurus and Lucretius (c. 99 BC–c. 55 BC), for instance, who seem to take a bad metaphor quite literally (see *De rerum natura*, 4.877–91). The comparison with motion **infuses** us with thoughts of machines and rotating parts, and it may encourage **a belief that the mind of man is as** dead as a clock, and that its acts of will are no more free than **a ball** is once it is set **in motion.** Misled by this image of a moving soul, philosophers come to think of the mind in the same way they think of a ball, as a thing **impelled** one way or the other without thought or decision, **and** as completely **determined** in its behaviour **by the objects of sense.** In the end, they deny that the mind has any freedom or power of choice at all. Its operations are governed by its physical environment **as necessarily as** the motions of a ball or the workings of a clock are governed by theirs; **that is** to say, philosophers deriving their terms from a sensory context tend to take the operations of the mind to be as fixed by external forces as the motion of a ball is fixed **by the stroke of a racket**, or the ticking of a clock is fixed by its cogs and springs. **Hence arise endless scruples** about free will **and** moral responsibility—significant doubts resulting in **errors of** the most **dangerous** kind, and having dreadful **consequences in** the sphere of **morality. All** of this is so much confusion and perplexity, **which, I doubt not, may be** easily avoided and **cleared** away if philosophers would just be more careful with their words**, and** consider more closely what their terms imply. The **truth** regarding the nature of the mind and its acts would then **appear plain, uniform, and consistent.** If only we could get them to be more mindful of the way they speak; for **could but philosophers be prevailed** upon **to retire into themselves** in self-reflection, **and attentively consider their own meaning,** the whole problem would disappear.

Though we do not perceive other minds, we can know them by inference. Observing various analogies between our own behaviour and the behaviour of others, we infer that actions similar to our own are attended by mental acts like our own, and that there are thus minds behind the ideas constituting other people's bodies. It is not a matter of sensation, therefore, but a very natural inference from sensation.

---

145. **From what has been said** in the last few sections, **it is plain that** our knowledge of other minds is inferential rather than perceptual. For **we cannot know the existence of other spirits, otherwise than by** observing **their operations** and then reasoning by analogy from our own experience. We deduce, **or** infer, their existence from **the ideas by them excited in us. I perceive several** varying combinations of ideas, such as the raising of a hand or the closing of a door. Such **motions, changes, and combinations of ideas** as these are similar to ones **that** I myself can produce at will. And thus by a natural inference I postulate a cause of these ideas similar in kind to me. After this fashion ideas, which I perceive, **inform me** that **there are certain particular agents like my self,** which I do not perceive, but **which accompany them and concur** with God **in their production**—the laws established by God ensuring that such and such acts of will are attended with such and such ideas. **Hence the knowledge I have of other spirits is not immediate, as is the knowledge of my** own **ideas, but** indirect, **depending** as it does **on the intervention of** characteristic combinations of **ideas,** which are **by me referred to** their causes. I attribute them, in other words, to **agents or spirits distinct from myself, as**

effects of their wills **or**, what amounts to the same thing, **concomitant signs** of their presence.

While some of what we see is caused by other human minds, most of it—the natural world around us—is not. So the natural world is either caused by a non-human mind or else it is uncaused. Since nothing is uncaused, we may infer a non-human mind. And when we consider the magnitude of order and beauty in the world, we must conclude that its cause is an all powerful, all knowing and all good being—viz., God. Berkeley can conceive of no competing explanation for order and beauty on such a massive scale.

146. But **even though there** may **be some things which convince us** that other finite spirits like ourselves inhabit the world, such beings cannot be thought responsible for bringing about most of what we perceive. With respect to some ideas, certainly, we may infer by analogy that other **human agents are concerned in producing them; yet** these ideas make up only a very small portion of what we actually see, hear, smell, touch and taste. For **it is evident to every one that those things which are called the works of nature, that is, the far greater part of the ideas or sensations perceived by us, are not produced by** finite creatures, **or** in any way **dependent on the** feeble **wills of men.** When I see shapes resembling my own body and hear sounds resembling my own voice, I conclude with some confidence that those shapes and sounds are the bodies and voices of my friends. But I cannot conclude that the stars and seasons, the mountains and plains, the sand, rocks and trees are caused by any human being. **There is therefore some other spirit that causes them.** They cannot be uncaused, of course, **since it is repugnant** to reason **that they should** come into the world and **subsist all by themselves. (See Section 29.)** So a non-human spirit must exist. **But** the works of nature cannot be caused by any mind weaker or less intelligent than a human. For **if we attentively consider the constant regularity,** the astounding **order, and** the intricate piecing together or **concatenation of all natural things,** we must deduce that the spirit who produces them is much wiser and more powerful than a man. There is also **the surprising magnificence, beauty, and perfection of the larger** parts of creation to consider, such as the clockwork precision of the solar system, **and the exquisite contrivance,** nay, the supreme ingenuity, **of the smaller parts of the creation** as displayed most vividly in the inner workings of plants. This, taken **together with the exact harmony and correspondence of the whole** machine, must astonish anyone who ponders it. These marks of intelligence and power point most visibly to an infinite creator, **but** the clearest indicators, **above all** others, are the delicate operations occurring within animate beings: What better evidence than **the never enough admired laws of pain and pleasure,** which function like signposts to guide us safely on our way, **and the instincts or natural inclinations,** the **appetites, and passions of** the **animals,** whose survival depends entirely thereon? The great orchestrator of it all is truly immense, in both power and goodness; indeed, **I say** that **if we** carefully **consider all these things, and at the same time attend to the meaning and import of the** traditional divine **attributes,** we will agree that the governing spirit possesses them to the highest degree and that God most surely exists. For a being who is **one, eternal, infinitely wise, good, and perfect** is none other than God. If we open our eyes to the wonder of nature, **we shall clearly perceive that** these attributes are everywhere present, that **they belong to the aforesaid spirit,** and that there is indeed a God **'who works all in all'** (I Corinthians 12: 6), **and 'by whom all things consist'** (Colossians 1: 17). But most of this was made plain in Sections 29 to 32.

Properly speaking, we do not perceive God. But as we become more adept at interpreting the signs of him in nature, it starts to feel that way. The inference to God's existence becomes so quick and smooth that 'seeing' him in nature—inferring him from nature—is almost like actually seeing him. This 'vision of God' is comparable to the sensing of other people's emotions: I don't actually see your jealousy or anger, but I infer them from your manner and expression so easily and naturally that one could say I 'see' them in some extended and loose sense.

---

147. When you read the words, 'I went to church on Sunday', you grasp my meaning at once and you are confident that you have understood me correctly. Strictly speaking, there is a movement in thought by which you deduce the sense from my words, but this is never noticed. So it is when you learn to 'read' God in nature. Though an inference occurs, it becomes so natural and smooth over time that you cease to notice it and eventually see God in his works as you see a man's enjoyment in his face. **Hence it is evident, that God is known as certainly and immediately** as you know your own sister or mother—indeed, we who understand nature are as well acquainted with our maker **as we are** with **any other mind or spirit whatsoever, distinct from our selves. We may even assert that the existence of God is far more evidently perceived than** is **the existence of** other **men, because the effects of nature are infinitely more numerous,** so much more obvious **and considerable, than those** that are **ascribed to human agents. There is not any one mark that denotes the**

presence of **a man, or** an **effect produced by him, which does not** even **more strongly** provide evidence for **the being of that spirit who is the** *Author of* **nature.** For **it is evident that in affecting other persons, the will of man** depends on the interconnections of things and **has no** manner of operating directly. He affects an**other** mind by moving **objects** and can do no better **than barely** to hope that the laws of nature will remain constant and that corresponding ideas will be produced in it, since he has basic voluntary control only over **the motion of the limbs of his** own **body.** Suppose we're standing by the churchyard. You will to move your hand and unlock the gate; **but that such a motion** should cause me to have ideas of your hand moving, the latch clicking, the gate swinging open—that it **should be attended by, or excite any idea in the mind of another** being agreeing to your own—is an astonishing feat of coordination, **and depends wholly on the will of the Creator** and the regularities he establishes. **He alone it is who 'upholding all things by the word of his power'** (Hebrews I: 3), **maintains that** lawful **intercourse between spirits, whereby they are able to perceive the existence of each other** through their actions. **And yet this** great sustainer of the natural order, this **pure and clear light which enlightens every one, is it self invisible,** since vision proper requires ideas and we have no ideas of God. All the same, it may be said that we 'see' God in some extended sense and that, because the inference to his existence is so quick and so certain, we know him 'directly' or 'immediately'.

Though God is not literally perceived, evidence of his existence is everywhere. There is a parallel to be drawn with our knowledge of finite minds: We don't see the minds of other people, since they are not ideas. But the behaviour of human bodies—especially behaviour we can understand by reference to our own—does suggest the existence of a rational agent. Similarly, the order of nature suggests the existence of a divine mind orchestrating its works from behind the scenes. The difference is one of degree: The seemingly rational behaviour of humans is encountered only in their presence, whereas the order of nature surrounds us and is magnitudes more impressive.

---

148. **It seems to be a general** and groundless **pretence of the unthinking herd** of atheists **that they cannot see God.** They will not believe in God until he reveals himself in plain sight: They want to see in order to believe. **Could we but see him with our own eyes, say they, as we see a man,** then **we should believe** at once **that he is, and** once we have a good reason for **believing**—one based on immediate perception—we will then **obey his commands.** But alas,

this demand for visual confirmation of God's existence is born of ignorance. It asks for a sort of seeing that cannot be had, and fails to recognize the sort that can. We *do* see God—just not in the same way that we see a radish or head of lettuce. Indeed, the existence of God is more evident than the existence of other people; **we need only open our eyes to see the sovereign Lord of all things with a more full and clear view,** more plainly and unmistakably, **than we do any one of our fellow-creatures. Not that I imagine we** literally **see God (as some will have it) by a direct and immediate view**: I don't see God as I see a radish on my plate. But why should I? We neither perceive the invisible spirit of God directly, **nor do we see corporeal things** by seeing God's spirit, as Malebranche maintains. According to his theory, we see bodies **not by themselves, but by seeing that which represents them**—intelligible extension—**in the essence of God, which** 'contains the ideas of all the truths we discover' (*Dialogues on Metaphysics and Religion*, Dialogue I, Part X). This strange **doctrine**—that we see things *in* God—**is, I must confess, to me** totally **incomprehensible.** My own theory is much simpler: In a strict and literal sense, we do not see God. **But** in a looser and still familiar sense of 'see', we do. **I shall** try to **explain my** use of 'see' here, and what I **mean** by 'seeing God in nature', by comparing it with the 'seeing' of another person. **A human spirit or person is not,** properly speaking, **perceived by sense, as, not being an idea,** it cannot be seen, heard, smelled, tasted or touched. **When therefore we see the colour, size, figure, and motions of a man**—when we hear his voice, or smell his perfume—**we perceive only certain sensations or ideas excited in our own minds: And these** sensations, **being exhibited to our view in sundry distinct collections** resembling our own bodies, provide powerful evidence for the existence of other people. This was explained in Section 145 above. What we see and hear, then, is not another person, but only **serves to** indicate one. Some of our sensations **mark out unto us the existence of finite and created spirits like our selves,** without presenting them directly to our view. **Hence it is plain,** that **we do not** truly **see a man, if by 'man' is meant that** invisible spirit **which lives, moves, perceives, and thinks as we do.** We do not observe an invisible spirit, of course, **but only** certain ideas, **such** as a soft colour, a tall figure, a smooth texture—**a certain collection of ideas which, as** resembling our own outward appearance, **directs us to think there is a distinct** invisible spirit present. We suppose there must be a **principle of thought and motion** behind the ideas—a person, bearing a **likeness to our selves, accompanying** the collection of ideas **and represented by it.** In this respect only can we be said to 'see' the man. **And after the same manner we 'see' God.** We do not perceive God's invisible spirit directly, but we see effects in the visible world suggesting the existence and workings of a divine agent. **All the** atheists are wrong, then, since God, like other spirits, is seen. But there is a **difference:** The evidence for God **is** greater. It has emerged **that, whereas** in the case of a person, **some one finite and narrow assemblage of ideas** suggests and **denotes a particular human mind,** in the case of God, the evidence is literally everywhere. For **whithersoever we direct our view, we do**—throughout all of nature, **at all times and in all places**—**perceive manifest** impressions and most obvious **tokens of the divinity.** Indeed, **every thing we see, hear, feel, or any wise perceive by sense,** speaks to the **being** and nature of God. The supreme harmony of the natural order is an unmistakable **sign or effect of the** existence and **power of God, as is our perception of those very motions, which are produced by men,** since God's governance makes them possible (see Section 145).

We are inundated by evidence of God, according to Berkeley, to such an extent that a dull person, overwhelmed by its magnitude, may fail to see it for what it is. The existence of atheists is a scandal to human reason.

---

149. It is therefore plain, that understanding nature and knowing God are one and the same. Indeed, **nothing can be more evident to any one that is capable of the least reflexion than the existence of God, or** the dependency of the world on his will. Such knowledge is a sort of vision—like 'seeing' the artist in his work. For God is **a spirit who is intimately present to our minds** at every turn, **producing in them** the sensible objects and events which compose the natural world—in short, creating **all that variety of ideas or sensations, which continually affect us** throughout our lives. He is the ultimate source of everything we know, the eternal being **on whom we have an absolute and entire dependence, in short,** the one **'in whom we live, and move, and have our being'** (Acts 17: 28). **That the discovery of this great truth** should escape the notice of so many minds reflects poorly on our powers of discernment. That the fact of God's being, **which lies so near and obvious to the mind,** and is displayed so beautifully in the order of creation, should be doubted by anyone, that it **should be attained to by the reason of so very few** people, **is a sad instance of the stupidity and inattention of men, who** are easily distracted by the surfaces of things and drawn away from obvious truths. For many otherwise perceptive men, **though they are surrounded with such clear manifestations of the Deity, are yet so little affected by them,** so little capable of making them out, **that they seem as it were blinded with excess of light,** as one who tries to read in the glare of the sun may fail to distinguish characters printed conspicuously on the page.

Someone unhappy with this picture of God as controlling nature directly might worry that the idealist has rendered nature impotent. Berkeley tries to alleviate this worry by considering two things the critic might mean by 'nature': (1) the objects of sense, which conform to natural laws, or (2) something distinct from the objects of sense, distinct from the natural laws and distinct from God as well. As for (1), the objects of sense are ideas, and ideas are wholly passive, as has been shown in previous sections. So the critic is right that idealism puts God in control of nature and renders nature inert; but this is not a mistake. As for (2), it's simply not clear what the critic is getting at. She doesn't seem to mean anything by 'nature'. Of course, Berkeley expects this sort of empty talk from atheists, who are desperate to separate God from the world. But Christians should think differently, for God presides over nature, according to Scripture, and governs all by means of his will.

150. But you might worry that my principles imply the idleness of nature: Spirit does everything, **you will say,** and nature does nothing, on the idealist picture of the world. But **has nature**—have natural objects and processes—**no share in the production of natural things,** you will ask, **and must they be all ascribed to the immediate and sole operation of God? I answer** that your worry is unfounded, for the 'hands-on' conception of God I have been promoting is fully supported by Scripture, and the hypothesis that something other than spirit could make things happen has proven untenable. We've covered this ground already: Ideas are totally inert (see Section 25). So **if by 'nature' is meant only the visible** *series* **of effects, or sensations imprinted on our minds**—the colours and shapes, the sounds and smells, which present themselves to our view **according to certain fixed and general laws**—then I agree that nature causes nothing. If by 'nature' you mean the endless train of sensations of which I am constantly aware, **then it is** quite **plain that nature taken in this sense cannot produce any thing at all. But** God clearly can: He operates in the world by establishing the laws of nature and then furnishing us with sensations. Perhaps you will want to push back at this point and say that 'nature', taken in some other sense, is active. You can certainly say this, but I don't know what you mean: **if by 'nature' is meant some being distinct from God, as well as from the laws of nature and the things perceived by sense,** then I really don't know what you're getting at. If 'nature' is supposed to denote something other than God, the laws he lays down or the ideas he creates, then **I must confess that** the **word** loses whatever sense it had for me. It becomes an artefact and **is** thus **to me an empty sound, without any intelligible meaning annexed to it. 'Nature' in this** extended sense—or in any **acceptation** other than the one specified here—**is a vain** *chimera*—a useless fiction no doubt **introduced by** non-Christians **(those** godless **heathens), who had** no conception of the divine will which creates and maintains the natural order. It is **not just that** they made use of an empty term—or rather, emptied a meaningful term of its content. They also betrayed their ignorance: For only someone with faulty **notions** could think that divine agency alone was not enough to produce all the effects we see. Only someone with no awareness **of the omnipresence and infinite perfection of God** could think that some additional source of activity is required. **But**

that's not how it is for Christians, who have knowledge of God and his revealed word. So **it is** even **more unaccountable**—it's quite inexplicable, really—**that** religious believers should think of nature along these lines. This understanding of nature as *doing* things independently of God is unorthodox, and so it is unacceptable that **it should be received** as true **among Christians professing belief in the Holy Scriptures, which constantly ascribe those effects we see to the immediate hand of God.** That atheists look for causes apart from God, **that heathen philosophers are wont to impute** what happens in the world **to** the activity of material **nature,** is at least understandable. But Christians should know better. For what does Scripture teach? That everything we see is caused immediately by God: **'The Lord, he causes the vapours to ascend** from the ends of the earth; **he makes lightnings with rain; he brings forth the wind out of his treasures'** (Jeremiah 10: 13). **'He turns the shadow of death into the morning, and makes the day dark with night'** (Amos 5: 8). **'He visits the earth, and makes it soft with showers: he blesses the springing thereof, and crowns the year with his goodness; so that the pastures are clothed with flocks, and the valleys are covered over with corn'** (See Psalms 65: 10–14). **But notwithstanding that this is the constant language of Scripture,** some believers are uncomfortable with the idea that God is directly responsible for everything. And **yet** I don't understand why—**we have I know not what aversion from believing that God concerns himself so** closely and **nearly in** all **our** daily **affairs. Faint** outlines of God are all we see, if we are blind, and so gladly **would we suppose him at a great distance off, and substitute some blind unthinking** 'nature' as a **deputy in his stead, though** in truth **(if we may believe Saint Paul) 'he be not far from every one of us'** (Acts 17: 7).

The steady and slow processes observed in nature do not in any obvious way suggest the will of a divine agent as cause. On the contrary, they suggest a non-thinking cause, just as the many evils in the world suggest a non-caring one. Berkeley rejects this line of reasoning: The slowness of natural events is absolutely crucial for making them comprehensible to humans, and the occasional misfortune is the inevitable result of having strict regularity in the laws. The benefits of making nature operate predictably offset the inconvenience of periodic loss.

---

151. In keeping with Holy Scripture, I have argued that in nature we perceive the immediate effects of God's will (Sections 146–150). **It will, I doubt not, be objected** to this idea **that the slow and gradual methods observed in the production of natural things,** the long-drawn-out periods required for biological and geological events to unfold, suggest the workings of blind mechanism rather than divine volition. They **do not seem to have for their cause the immediate hand of an** *almighty Agent*, who, it is supposed, would act more swiftly. **Besides,** apart from the sluggishness and inefficiency of natural processes, indifferent regularity in the laws of nature will occasionally produce ill effects seemingly incompatible with God's goodness. The disfigured creatures whom we shun like **monsters,** the **untimely births** leading to agonizing **deaths, fruits blasted** by winds which shrivel **in the blossom, rains falling in desert places** rather than where they are needed, all the **miseries incident to human life,** all the cruelties heaped upon animals: These **are so many arguments** against a caring lawgiver, each one indicating **that the whole frame of nature is not,** as we suppose, directly set in motion and tended to by God. The abundance of natural evil, in other words, renders doubtful our view that the world is **immediately actuated and superintended by a spirit of infinite wisdom and goodness:** Just the opposite. **But the answer to this objection** and the objection from slowness **is in a good measure plain from Section 62,** where I explained that creating internal complexity in natural machines and establishing regularity in the laws of nature are both necessary for producing effects in a manner comprehensible to human beings. This takes care of both worries, **it being visible, that the aforesaid methods of nature**—their slowness in producing effects and their tendency to cause occasional misfortune—**are absolutely necessary, in order to** ensure the **working** of events **by the most simple and general rules, and after a steady and consistent manner; which** considerations **argue** strongly for **both the** *wisdom* and the *goodness* of God. **Such is the** essence of our creator that he governs unobtrusively: The **artificial contrivance of this mighty machine of nature,** its outwardly deceptive configuration, may fool the weak minded, for the sensible world is so constituted **that, whilst its motions and various phenomena strike on our senses** and are perceived, the true cause that sets it all going—**the hand which actuates the whole**—**is itself unperceivable to men of flesh and blood.** This is confirmed in Scripture: **'Verily (says the prophet) you are a God that hides your self'** (Isaiah 45: 15). **But though God conceals himself from the eyes of the** *sensual* **and** *lazy,* **those men who will not** look beyond appearances or **be at the least expense of thought; yet to an unbiased and attentive mind, nothing can be more** evident, nothing more **plainly legible** in the book of nature, **than the intimate presence of an** *all-wise* **Spirit, who fashions, regulates, and sustains the whole system of being. It is clear from what we have** here and **elsewhere observed that the** operating of the universe **according to general and stated laws, is so necessary for our** practical purposes and for providing us with **guidance in the affairs of life,** for revealing patterns in sensation **and** for **letting us** get a glimpse **into the secret** principles **of nature, that without it** we could know nothing of the world. Were the universe chaotic, we could make no predictions at **all.** Science could **reach** no conclusions **and the compass of thought** would be limited to the current contents of consciousness. In default of stable laws, **all human sagacity and design could serve to no manner of purpose; it were even impossible** in such a situation that **there should be any such faculties or powers** as practical wisdom **in the mind. See Section 31.** It is easy to dwell on the pains and calamities that befall us, the afflictions of our minds and the defects in our frame. Such horrors are caused by the cold constancy of nature, you will say, rather than the benevolent influence of God. But this is to overlook the fact that by means of strict regularity and an elaborate show of parts, nature is made comprehensible to men and joint undertakings become possible. **Which one consideration** effectively solves the problem of explaining the presence of evil in a world created by God: For God wills regularity, which serves our purposes, but not the incidental harms that regularity may occasion. Were God to constantly interrupt the regularity he imposes by performing miracles—safeguarding us from every misfortune or accident—he would undermine the very regularity we need in order to survive. The good arising from having an orderly universe thus **abundantly out-balances** the bad and more than compensates for **whatever particular inconveniences may thence arise.**

A second reason to welcome bad things is that they highlight the good by way of contrast, just as the dark patches in a painting can augment the beauty of light and colour. There is also an argument to be made from wastefulness, the needless destruction of plants and the premature death of animals being taken as evidence of God's incompetence or lack of foresight. But this is to assess God's actions in human terms. Wastefulness amongst humans is indeed reckless, since our resources are limited. But God has inexhaustible resources, so overproduction and massive destruction detract nothing from his wisdom. They rather showcase an excess of power.

152. We should further consider that the very blemishes and defects of nature—the things we find most repellent—**are not**, after all, **without their use.** They serve aesthetic purposes, for instance, **in that they make an agreeable sort of variety** in the world, highlighting **and augmenting the beauty of the rest of the creation** by way of contrast. We may liken such blemishes to the dark patches in a beautiful painting, **as** Augustine (354–430) and Leibniz famously did (see Augustine, *Of True Religion*, Section 76; Leibniz, *On the Ultimate Origination of Things*, p. 153). Inspecting the dark **shades in a picture** up close we might find them ugly, the ugliness casting doubt on the skill of the artist who produced them. But when we station ourselves at a proper distance and view the picture in its entirety, we see that the dark shades **serve to set off the brighter and more enlightened parts**, making the composition as a whole more beautiful than it would otherwise have been. What we took to be accidental splotches on the canvas then appear as central to the artistry and indispensable to the work. Similarly, blemishes in nature set off the beauty of creation as a whole. **We would likewise do well to examine whether** apparent wastefulness in nature is any indication of lavishness or weakness on the part of God. For it may be that **our** habit of **taxing** the creator with these vices, of regarding **the** abundance of natural things as extravagant and **wasteful,** is actually the result of our judging God according to the wrong standards. We may be implicitly comparing God to a finite being—envisioning him as something like an exemplary craftsman—and then applying standards that are more suited to evaluating humans. Here is what I'm getting at: Millions **of seeds and embryos** are created, **and** yet only a small percentage of them become plants and animals. Of those that do, many die very young. The miscarriages far outnumber the successes. Thinking in terms of costs and benefits, then, the vast decimation of seeds and embryos, combined with the **accidental destruction of** countless **plants and animals before they come to full maturity,** might be seen **as** the result of **an** uncommon **imprudence** or recklessness **in the Author of nature.** But it seems that way to us, I submit, only **because** we are conceiving God anthropomorphically. Is the problem **not** rather **the effect of a prejudice contracted by our familiarity with impotent and** miserly humans? Hoarding and **saving** is the business of **mortals!** Men would be foolish, no doubt, to invest their time, labour and resources in projects that are likely to founder. But we must not suppose that what is true of us is true of God. **In** the case of *man,* **indeed,** we judge it proper that he take the utmost care of his hard-earned possessions. He ought to keep **a thrifty** economy and wise **management of those things, which he cannot** produce without time and effort, or which he cannot **procure without much pains and industry.** The frugal man, careful with his outlay, **may be esteemed** for his prudence and praised for his *wisdom.* **But** God is not a man, and he produces all things in an instant, with no effort or materials: He just wills them into being and there they are. And so **we must not imagine that the inexplicably fine machine of** the natural world—not to mention the tiny machines constituting the organs of **an animal or** the structures of a **vegetable—costs the great Creator any more pains or trouble in its production than a** simple **pebble does, nothing being more evident, than that an omnipotent spirit can indifferently produce every thing by a mere** *fiat* **or** immediate **act of his will.** Hence we may not criticize God for eschewing miserliness and restraint. Rather, **it is plain, that the splendid profusion of natural things,** whether they die in embryo or attain to maturity, **should not be interpreted** as **weakness or** wasteful **prodigality in the** divine **agent who produces them, but** should **rather be looked on as an argument** for—as possibly the strongest evidence of—the extent and **riches of his** supreme **power.**

A particular pain or misfortune appears evil only when considered in isolation. From a universal point of view, the pain or misfortune will appear necessary and even desirable. Indeed, the laws of nature that sometimes seem to conspire against us—'If only I hadn't tripped on that stone!', 'If only the fire didn't burn me!'—are a necessary condition of our happiness, since they allow us to make predictions about what will cause us pain and what will bring us pleasure, and then freely choose to avoid the former and pursue the latter.

153. **As for** the shadows and blemishes themselves, **the mixture of pain or uneasiness which is** everywhere apparent **in the world,** they have a tendency to promote irreligious attitudes amongst the ignorant. Atheists, **pursuant to** their impious schemes, call them 'imperfections'. But though the 'imperfections' are caused indirectly by **the general laws of nature** laid down by God, **and** often directly by **the** free **actions of the finite imperfect spirits** he creates, they do not support the atheistic conclusion: **This** tempering of good with 'evil', **in the state we are in at present,** this unobtrusive governing of the world by fixed laws allowing for human freedom, **is indispensably necessary to our** overall **well-being,** as I explained in Section 151. We can focus on the shadows if we like. **But** then **our prospects are too narrow,** our view too personal: **We take, for instance, the idea of some one particular pain** we have suffered **into our thoughts, and account it** *evil* because it is unpleasant to us; **whereas if we enlarge our view,** it will not seem **so.** We must consider the world from above, **as it were,** in order **to comprehend the** whole. Once we understand the **various ends, connexions, and dependencies of things** on the system, once we understand the laws of nature and can predict **on what occasions and in what** degrees or **proportions we are** going to be **affected with pain and pleasure,** once we appreciate **the nature of human freedom, and** grasp **the** purpose and **design with which we are put into the world, we shall be forced to acknowledge that those particular things** that hurt us, those hardships and misfortunes **which considered in themselves appear to be** *evil,* **have the nature of** *good* **when** interpreted in the light of creation as a whole. Particular ills **considered** in isolation rather than **as linked with the whole system of beings** may indeed strike us as evil. But they are no more evil than shadows in a painting. Neither the world nor the painting would be beautiful without them.

We are rolling in evidence for the existence of God, according to Berkeley, and only negligence or irrationality could lead anyone to deny his existence or to question his goodness. There's little hope of swaying atheists and those with

weak conviction; they are too dazzled by the business and pleasures of life to appreciate the evidence. But that's not going to rattle a Christian, who sees God in everything.

154. From what has been said about the need for regularity in nature, and the importance of assessing evil from a global perspective, we may satisfy ourselves that the quibbles of atheists are unwarranted. For **it will be manifest to anyone considering** the topic dispassionately, and to any **person** not intoxicated with sensual pleasures, or engrossed in petty undertakings, **that** the evidence for God is overwhelming. I suggest **it is merely for want of attention and** care, for lack of **comprehensiveness** in outlook, for stubbornness and narrowness **of mind, that there are any favourers of *atheism* or the *Manichean heresy* to be found.** The Manicheans, whom I mention only in passing, posited two divine powers—one good, one evil—because they could think of no way to reconcile the evil we see in the world with a limitless force for good. The explanation they sought (and despaired of finding) has been provided in Sections 151 to 153 above. **Little and unreflecting souls** with no breadth of vision may see no further than what is in front of them. They **may indeed** mock and **burlesque the works of Providence,** heaping scorn on that which should be praised. In this they are either stupid or lazy—blind to **the beauty and order** of nature, **whereof they have not** the intellectual **capacity** to understand, **or,** if they do, **will not** make the effort, or **be at the pains, to comprehend,** however slight those pains would be. **But those who** consider the world as a system—if they **are masters of any justness and extent of thought**—will perceive the order and beauty as clearly as they perceive the individual parts. Those who are willing, **and are** also able, to view creation from above, **with all** its evils and misfortunes put in proper perspective, will not mistake an occasional shadow for a flaw in the design. Indeed, a man used **to reflect**ing on the interconnections of things, **can never sufficiently admire the divine traces of wisdom and goodness** in the governance of the world **that shine** so brightly **throughout the economy of nature. But** there will always be those who object and contradict. The stupid, distracted or prejudiced soul will deny the most obvious truths imaginable. I ask you: **what truth is there which shines so strongly on the mind, that by an aversion** to careful contemplation, a disdain **of** logical **thought,** or **a wilful shutting of the eyes, we may not escape seeing it?** We should not expect everyone to be reasonable. **Is it therefore** at all surprising or **to be wondered at, if the generality of men, who are ever** preoccupied, firmly **intent on business or pleasure, and little used to fixing or opening the eye of their mind** to the consideration of philosophical matters, **should not have all that conviction** demanded by our arguments **and by the flood of evidence** pouring in on all sides? A man is free to doubt **of the being of God.** That is his affair. Should we waver or worry if some lout lacks a belief, **which might be expected in** more **reasonable creatures?** Not in the least.

Reflection on the evidence leads to belief in God. Belief in God leads to virtue. So Berkeley urges reflection.

---

155. It should come as no surprise that those obsessed with pleasure or wrapped up in their own mundane affairs should be blind to God's existence, for men of this description seldom stop and reflect. **We should rather wonder that men** such as these **can be found** at all, men **so** frivolous and foolish as never to reflect, so **stupid** and dull **as to neglect** the evidence right in front of them, **than** wonder **that, neglecting** to ponder and weigh it, **they should be unconvinced of such an evident and momentous truth** as God's existence. It is their failure to deliberate that is really shameful and surprising: Were they to but consider the facts carefully, they would surely believe. **And yet it is to be feared that too many** men **of** greater than average intelligence are becoming atheists by default. Not only the lower **parts** of society, but even educated men with strong minds **and** plenty of **leisure,** those lazy aristocrats **who live in Christian countries** at the expense of others, **are merely through** idle and appalling carelessness— through **a supine and dreadful negligence** of the evidence—turning away from God. Negligence alone has **sunk them into an** unthinking **sort of *atheism*.** It can't be anything else: **Since it is downright impossible that an** observant and reflective **soul**—one whose mind is **pierced and** prevailed upon by the evidence and so **enlightened with a thorough sense of the omnipresence, holiness, and justice of that almighty spirit—should** fail to believe in God and **persist in a remorseless violation of his laws.** In short, reflection leads to belief and belief is conducive to upholding religious practices. **We ought therefore earnestly to meditate and dwell on those important points** I made above concerning the divine origin of our sensations (Sections 29 and 30, 146–149), in order **that** by doing **so we may attain** a strong and well-founded **conviction** that **without** God there would be no nature. Such conviction, founded on insight, will answer **all** doubts or **scruples** that atheists may bring. We may thus assert confidently, **'that the eyes of the Lord are in every place beholding the evil and the good'** (Proverbs 15: 3); **'that he is with us and keepeth us in all places whither we go, and giveth us bread to eat, and raiment to put on';** that he is always **present and conscious in our innermost thoughts; and that we have a most absolute and immediate dependence on him** for our being. **A clear view of which great truths cannot** fail to move us, for a true believer may **choose**

none **but** the path of righteousness. The 'vision' of God will **fill our hearts with an awful circumspection and** concern for the good, inducing in us a **holy fear** of his wrath**, which is the strongest incentive to *virtue*, and the best** way to **guard** ourselves **against** falling into the practice of *vice.*

The engines of inquiry should be powered by morality and religion. They are the aim and the object of conscientious investigation. Berkeley has tried to promote both by refuting the allied doctrines of materialism, scepticism and atheism. Failing in this means failing altogether. Philosophy must enrich our lives to have value.

---

156. For after all, what deserves the first place in our studies, and should always be the primary focus, **is the consideration of God, and our** moral ***duty*;** awareness of the divine, and the betterment of our lives and actions, are the principal themes **which** I have wanted **to promote.** And**, as it was the main drift and design of my labours** to shed light on these themes and to remove obstacles standing in their way—to relieve error and difficulty in the sciences, to defeat scepticism, atheism and irreligion—**so I shall** measure its success in proportion to them. I will judge my efforts a failure if the book does not bring my readers to a deeper religious understanding, or cause them to refer their speculations to practice—I will **esteem them altogether useless and ineffectual, if by what I have said I cannot inspire my readers with a pious sense of the presence of God** and impress upon them the need for studying those things as are likely to improve the situation of man. I come now to the close of these *Principles*; **and, having shown the falseness or vanity of those barren** materialist **speculations, which make the chief employment of learned men** and keep them holed up in their libraries, I hope that **the** discovery will **better dispose them to** action. And having exposed the fallacy of atheism, I hope that my conclusions will move them to adopt an attitude of **reverence and** to warmly **embrace the** morally indispensable teachings of religion and the **salutary truths of the Gospel, which to know and to practise is the highest perfection of human nature.**

List of Primary Sources Referred to in the Text

Aquinas, Thomas. *Summa Theologica*. In: A. C. Pegis (ed.), *Basic Writings of Saint Thomas Aquinas: Volume I*. New York: Random House (1945).

Aristotle. *De Anima*. In: J. Barnes (ed.), *The Complete Works of Aristotle: Volume One*. Princeton: Princeton University Press (1995).

Aristotle. *Metaphysics*. In: J. Barnes (ed.), *The Complete Works of Aristotle: Volume Two*. Princeton: Princeton University Press (1995).

Arnauld, Antoine and Pierre Nicole. *Logic or the Art of Thinking*. J. V. Buroker (ed.). Cambridge: Cambridge University Press (1996).

Augustine. *Of True Religion*. In: J. H. S. Burleigh (ed.), *Augustine: Earlier Writings*. Louisville: Westminster John Knox Press (2006).

Bayle, Pierre. *Historical and Critical Dictionary: Selections*. R. Popkin (ed.). Indianapolis: Hackett Publishing Company (1991).

Descartes, René. *Discourse on Method*. In: J. Cottingham, R. Stoothoff and D. Murdoch (eds), *The Philosophical Writings of Descartes: Volume I*. Cambridge: Cambridge University Press (1996).

Descartes, René. *Meditations on First Philosophy*. In: J. Cottingham, R. Stoothoff and D. Murdoch (eds), *The Philosophical Writings of Descartes: Volume II*. Cambridge: Cambridge University Press (1996).

Descartes, René. *Principles of Philosophy*. In: J. Cottingham, R. Stoothoff and D. Murdoch (eds), *The Philosophical Writings of Descartes: Volume I*. Cambridge: Cambridge University Press (1996).

Hobbes, Thomas. *Leviathan*. E. Curley (ed.). Indianapolis: Hackett Publishing Company (1994).

Hooke, Robert. *Micrographia*. London: Jo. Martyn and Ja. Allestry, Printers to the Royal Society (1665).

Johnson, Samuel. *The Berkeley–Johnson Correspondence*. In: J. Dancy (ed.), *George Berkeley: A Treatise Concerning the Principles of Human Knowledge*. Oxford: Oxford University Press (1998).

Leibniz, Gottfried Wilhelm. *A New System of Nature*. In: R. Ariew and D. Garber (eds), *G. W. Leibniz: Philosophical Essays*. Indianapolis: Hackett Publishing Company (1989).

Leibniz, Gottfried Wilhelm. *On the Ultimate Origination of Things*. In: R. Ariew and D. Garber (eds), *G. W. Leibniz: Philosophical Essays*. Indianapolis: Hackett Publishing Company (1989).

Locke, John. *An Essay Concerning Human Understanding*. P. H. Nidditch (ed.). Oxford: Oxford University Press (1979).

Lucretius. *De rerum natura*. In: A. A. Long and D. N. Sedley (eds), *The Hellenistic Philosophers, Volume I*. Cambridge: Cambridge University Press (2006).

Malebranche, Nicolas. *Dialogues on Metaphysics and Religion*. N. Jolley (ed.) and D. Scott (trans.). Cambridge: Cambridge University Press (1997).

Newton, Isaac. *Principia*. In: A. Janiak (ed.), *Newton: Philosophical Writings*. Cambridge: Cambridge University Press (2004).

Raphson, Joseph. *De Spatio Reali*. London: John Taylor (1697).

Sextus Empiricus. *The Ten Modes*. In: P. Hallie (ed.) and S. Etheridge (trans.), *Sextus Empiricus: Selections from the Major Writings on Scepticism, Man, and God*. Indianapolis: Hackett Publishing Company (1985).

Index

matter: belief in 100–4; contradictory 45, 51, 60, 65–8, 101, 103–4, 124, 128, 130–2, 145; explains nothing 62–3, 95–7, 99–100, 115–16; meaning of term 51, 58, 78, 101–2, 116–18, 126–7, 129–30, 132, 144; negative definition of 116–18, 129–30; occasion of ideas 52, 84, 99–100, 116–22, 124–6, 128–9, 132–3; passive 51, 99, 108, 109–10, 114, 117–20, 122, 124–5, 127, 128–9, 144, 155–6; science and 95–7, 105–6, 116, 135, 154; as substratu`m 48–9, 58–60, 122–3, 126–7, 132; unintelligibility of 44, 47, 58–9, 67–8, 100–1, 104, 115–16, 128–9, 129–39; unknown 80, 117–18, 124–7, 129, 133, 138, 157; *see also* scepticism; materialism; substratum

medieval philosophers 27, 31, 34, 90, 99, 130, 137, 155; *see also* Al-Ghazali, Abu Hamid; Aquinas, Thomas; Augustine; Nicolas of Cusa

Medusa 43

melancholy 32, 102, 153

memory 21–2, 41, 179

metaphor 118, 121, 207

metaphysics 3, 6–7, 27, 132, 141, 149, 152, 195, 196, 205, 206–7; *see also* people and professions: metaphysician

method: Berkeley's 34–40

microscope 92, 108

microstructure xxviii, 104, 109–10, 111, 113, 116; *see also* internal parts

mile 85, 188–9, 190

mind: vs ideas 42, 197–206; immortality of *see* immortality; interaction and 61–2; notion of 70–1, 204–6; powers of 69–72, 79, 97–8, 150–1, 199–202, 206–8; weakness of 2–6, 20, 75; *see also* knowledge: of other minds

minimum sensibile 194

miracle 104, 111, 112, 133–5, 217

miscarriage 218

modern philosophers 53–4, 56–7, 96, 99, 103, 149; *see also* Arnauld, Antoine; Bayle, Pierre; Descartes, René; Hobbes, Thomas; Johnson, Samuel; Leibniz, Gottfried Wilhelm; Locke, John; Malebranche, Nicolas; Nicole, Pierre; Nieuwentijd, Bernard

morals 64, 147, 152–3, 195, 203, 206–7, 207–8, 222

monster 216

Moses 133–4

motion 8–13, 17, 41, 48, 50–3, 55–7, 59–60, 65, 68–9, 71, 75, 82, 88, 95, 102, 104, 105–12, 114–15, 117–18, 122–3, 126, 128–9, 138, 143, 146, 149, 151–3, 155–6, 158, 165–74, 183, 197, 204, 207–8, 210–13, 216; absolute vs relative *see* absolute vs relative: motion; relative circular motion

music 113, 121

names *see* nouns: proper

natural law 73–5, 96, 110–11, 159, 161–4, 204, 211, 213–14, 216, 219

natural philosophy *see* science

natural signs *see* signs: natural

nature: defects in *see* problem of evil; order of 73–8, 79, 84, 96, 104, 108, 110–16, 120–2, 134, 144–5, 158–61, 165, 209, 211, 213–17, 220; *see also* environment; natural law

Newton, Isaac 95–6, 110, 163, 165–71, 173, 175

Nicholas of Cusa 177

Nicole, Pierre 8, 14

Nieuwentijdt, Bernard 192

nominalistic science 179

notion: of mind *see* mind: notion of; of relations 204–6

nouns: common 28–30, 32; proper 29, 32–4; *see also* words

number 31, 50, 54–5, 69, 115, 123, 176–8, 180–3; unity 55, 178; *see also* infinitesimal parts; mathematics

numeral 164, 178, 180–2; *see also* number

objections against idealism *see* idealism: objections against

occasionalism 99–100, 116–21, 124–6

omniscience 160, 209 *see also* God: attributes of

other minds *see* knowledge: of other minds

pain 1, 5, 14, 21–2, 28, 32, 74, 84–5, 87, 96, 108, 113–16, 119, 123, 191, 193, 210, 217–19, 220

particles 52, 68–9, 92–3, 110, 115–16, 120, 146, 154–7, 159, 162, 197

parts of body *see* body parts

passions *see* emotions

Paul, Saint 215

Pegasus *see* animals: Pegasus

people and professions: Arabians 180;
artist 213, 217; baker 81; barrister 78;
blacksmith 78, 110, 149; blind man
87, 127; bookbinder 111; carpenter
110; celebrity 198; clergyman 175;
farmer 78, 80–1, 149, 153; gentile
185; geometer 182–3, 185–7, 189,
192–3; *see also* people and professions:
mathematician; Indians 180; maid 44,
115; mathematician 37, 176–7, 179,
182–3, 186, 191–4; *see also* people and
professions: geometer; metaphysician
149; *see also* metaphysics; philosopher;
miner 5; musician 121; nurse 38;
oppressor 33; outlaw 33; peasant 153;
philosopher *see* philosopher; priest
78, 175; scholar 194; schoolboy 185;
scientist 110–11, 116, 154–63; servant
44, 149; soldier 73; tailor 111; teacher
19; theologian 27, 148; uncle 199;
victim 33; villain 153; watchmaker
108, 111–12
perception 3, 8, 11, 14, 32, 25–6, 41, 43–
7, 49, 51–2, 55–7, 60–1, 66–8, 71–2,
80–1, 85–7, 89, 91, 94, 103, 105–7,
112, 114, 119, 121, 126–8, 130–1,
133, 135, 137–9, 145, 149–53, 166,
173, 183, 197–8, 202–3, 211, 213;
see also ideas; perceptual relativity;
senses
perceptual relativity 55–8, 123
philosopher 1, 4–5, 7–9, 11, 13–15,
18, 23–4, 27, 29, 31–2, 34, 36–7, 39,
44–6, 50–1, 53–9, 62, 69, 78–80, 82,
89–90, 92, 95–6, 99–104, 111, 113,
116–17, 130, 132, 135–7, 139, 144–5,
145–6, 148, 150–1, 153, 155, 158–62,
169, 171, 174–5, 177, 181–3, 190,
196–7, 204, 206–8, 215; *see also* Greek
philosopher; medieval philosopher;
modern philosopher; people and
professions: metaphysician
physics 56, 105, 134, 153–4; *see also*
science
place 11, 17, 52, 100, 117–18, 129, 143–4,
149, 167–8, 170–1, 180, 212, 216, 221
power *see* mind: powers of
practical applications 2–3, 111, 146, 153,
165, 177–82, 193–4, 195, 216; *see also*
mathematics: practical application of
prediction 74, 97, 104, 106, 110–11, 113,
116, 159–64, 215–6, 219
prejudice xxviii, 2, 15, 102, 124, 125,
127, 160, 185, 193–4, 196–7, 218, 220

primary qualities *see* qualities: primary vs
secondary
problem of evil 215–20
proofs *see* demonstrations
proper nouns *see* nouns: proper
providence 4, 75, 109, 111, 125, 146, 220
purpose: in nature *see* cause: final; of
Principles xxvii, 222

qualities: abstract ideas of *see* abstract
ideas: of determinate qualities; abstract
ideas: of general qualities
qualities: primary vs secondary 50–3,
123, 126
quiddity 130

Raphson, Joseph 175
reality *see* appearance vs reality,
existence
reflection 12–13, 20, 30, 32, 34, 36, 38,
41, 46–8, 52, 54–5, 65, 67–9, 71, 78,
82, 89, 97, 101, 124, 130, 140–1, 152,
173, 194, 202, 206–7, 220–1; *see also*
introspection
regularity *see* nature: order of
relations 140–1, 205–6; *see also* absolute
vs relative
relative circular motion 168, 171–2
religion xxvii, 64, 122, 131–6, 144–8,
175, 195–6, 199, 204, 215, 219, 221–2
representation 10, 13, 18, 24–5, 36,
41, 50, 63, 69–71, 76, 138, 181–2,
187–90, 198–201, 206, 212
rerum natura 77, 138, 207
resemblance 11, 17–18, 25, 49–51, 53–4,
56, 60–2, 69, 70–1, 87–8, 103–4, 137,
142, 160, 166, 199–201, 203, 206,
209, 212; *see also* Likeness Principle
resistance 42, 172–4
round square 199

sadness *see* melancholy
scepticism xxvii–xxviii, 1–3, 5, 60, 64,
83–4, 136–41, 144, 146, 148, 153–4,
191, 195–7, 199–201, 222
schoolmen *see* medieval philosophers
scientists vs non-scientists 98, 158
science xxviii, 6–7, 23, 27, 28, 34–5,
38–9, 81, 95–8, 102, 105–6, 110–12,
115–16, 135–6, 149, 153–66, 195,
197, 206, 216; *see also* astronomy;
biology; mathematics; matter: science
and; physics
Scripture 131–5, 210, 214–16, 221